The Old Regular Baptists
of Central Appalachia

The Old Regular Baptists of Central Appalachia

Brothers and Sisters in Hope

Howard Dorgan

The University of Tennessee Press
KNOXVILLE

Copyright © 1989 by The University
of Tennessee Press / Knoxville.
All rights reserved.
Manufactured in the United States of America.
Cloth: 1st printing, 1989.
Paper: 1st printing, 2001.

The paper used in this book meets the minimum
requirements of ANSI/NISO Z39.48-1992 (R 1997)
(Permanence of Paper). The binding materials have
been chosen for strength and durability.

Library of Congress Cataloging in Publication Data

Dorgan, Howard
    The Old Regular Baptists of Central Appalachia : brothers
and sisters in hope / Howard Dorgan.
        p.   cm.
    Bibliography: p.
    Includes index.
    ISBN 0-87049-616-6 (cl.: alk. paper)
    ISBN 1-57233-160-7 (pbk.: alk. paper)
    1. Old Regular Baptists—Appalachian Region.
    2. Appalachian Region—Church history.   I. Title.
BX6389.D67   1989
286'.5 — DC20

To Darvin and Ganell

Contents

Illustrations

Introduction: "You Want to Visit an Old Regular Church?"

In April 1982 I was involved in field research for *Giving Glory to God in Appalachia: Worship Practices of Six Baptist Subdenominations,* and I had planned to spend the summer focusing on Baptist "Homecoming traditions in the northwest mountains of North Carolina.[1] Preparatory for this effort, I approached Appalachian State University's news bureau to suggest an article on my project, hoping by this effort to obtain additional invitations to homecoming events within the region.

The news release was written, and it ran in a number of area newspapers and specialty publications, including *High Country Magazine,* a newsprint journal serving the southern Appalachian tourist trade.[2] A copy of this article subsequently made its way to Florida, where it was read by a woman who promptly called her brother in Sandy Ridge, Virginia.

"There's a man in Watauga County, North Carolina, who is studying traditional Appalachian Baptist practices," the caller reportedly said. "You might want to phone and see if he is interested in the Old Regulars."

The following week I received a call from Darvin Marshall, who, after introducing himself, asked if I would like to visit an Old Regular Baptist church.

Prior to Darvin's call my only introduction to the Old Regulars had been through a film, *In the Good Old Fashioned Way,* through one essay each by Ron Short and John Wallhausser ("We Believed in the Family and in the Old Regular Baptist Church" and "I Can Almost See Heaven From Here"), and through a small collection of other published sources.[3]

My own field work before 1982 had been with Missionary, Union, Primitive, Regular, and Free Will Baptists in the northwest corner of North Carolina and parts of southwest Virginia. But now this serendipitous series of events was about to involve me in six years of concentrated field study of this interesting subdemonination of Appalachian Baptists.

The Marshalls

Darvin Marshall and his wife, Ganell, live on Sandy Ridge, an unincorporated community in Wise County, Virginia, approximately seven miles north of Coeburn. Darvin spent his last working years managing the computer operations of a bank in Coeburn, a job from which he took early retirement because of a major heart attack. Ganell has always been a housewife, but now she also works the craft fair business, selling corn-shuck dolls she makes in the basement of her home. She learned this art from her mother-in-law, "Mother Marshall," and now several dolls from the hands of each of these two women are housed in a Smithsonian collection.

Both Darvin and Ganell possess a deep appreciation for their cultural heritage, and they have adopted Appalachian studies somewhat as a hobby. In the process they also have adopted my research.

Their home, on Virginia's Route 654, is some two hundred yards from Sandy Ridge Old Regular Baptist Church, the fellowship with which Darvin's late father was affiliated and which he served a number of years as clerk. In 1982 Darvin and Ganell frequently attended the monthly meetings of this congregation, although neither was then, or is now, a member of this or any other Old Regular church. Nevertheless, over the years Darvin has developed a deep fondness for this small worship facility and a profound love and respect for the "old-time way" traditions of Old Regularism. He had arrived at a strongly held conclusion that the customs, beliefs and values of this faith should be documented, having inherited many such attitudes from his father, who once helped a scholar interested in Old Regular lined singing.[4] After his retirement Darvin intensified his interest in this "documentation" idea, and so he called me that April morning in 1982: "You want to visit an Old Regular church?" My answer was unhesitatingly affirmative.

Darvin immediately sent me a copy of the published minutes of the 1981 annual session of the Union Association of Old Regular Baptists of Jesus Christ, and at the same time provided directions to "the Ridge" and Sandy Ridge Church; but as it turned out the first Old Regular fellowship I visited was Bethany in Kingsport, Tennessee, the only Old Regular church in that state. Using information supplied in those 1981 minutes, I contacted Elder Foster Noel Mullins, at that time assistant moderator of the Bethany congregation, and arranged that first visit.

Later I traveled to Sandy Ridge; witnessed a service at that church; met elder Raymond Smith, who was to become strongly supportive of my Old Regular research; stayed for a fellowship meal in what was once an old two-room schoolhouse (now the Sandy Ridge Community Center); and established my acquaintance with Darvin Marshall and his family. Since that time, Darvin, Ganell, and I have traveled over a substantial part of central Appalachia, visiting Old Regular churches and association meetings, with Darvin serving as my guide and contact, and with Ganell providing assistance in understanding Old Regular women and the Old Regular home and family. What developed was a true partnership for research.

Locating the Churches:
"You Can't Miss It."

The advantages of working with someone like the Marshalls in the study of Old Regulars are numerous, not the least being the fact that it is a lot easier to locate these churches

Darvin Marshall (left) *and Elder Raymond Smith after a service at Mary Lou Church, Buchanan County, Virginia.*

with someone familiar with the region as your guide. Not only are the buildings often tucked away from main roads, but they are also remarkably inconspicuous, as we will see in chapter 1. There usually is a sign, but only a modest one, and a first-time visitor to an Old Regular church frequently has to park his or her car on the side of the road and walk right up in front of the meetinghouse before being certain of the building's identity.

Together Darvin and I have identified sixteen associations of Old Regular fellowships; and on his own Darvin has mapped the general boundaries of several of these groups, making progress in locating the individual churches within each cluster. His work has proved invaluable, particularly when the Marshalls have been able to guide me through a maze of narrow mountain roads directly to a church. Early in my field work I learned that it was no easy matter to find an Old Regular meetinghouse simply by following directions provided by the fellowship's moderator, assistant moderator, or clerk. Most scholars who have worked with indigenous Appalachians realize that these people tend to give directions not by road numbers and highway signs, but by natural geographical features of the land — ridges, hollows, creeks, rivers, bottoms, forks, etc. I have often been amused at the close of Old Regular services when visiting elders give their "appointments," announcements during which the meeting Sundays of home churches are provided, along with directions to the respective houses of worship. What one usually hears are recitations of strings of geographical features, each appended to an identifying appellative (Caney Ridge, Turkey Creek, Cedar Bottom, Rocky Fork, Bent Branch), interspersed with community names that never seem to be on maps (Maxie, Virginia; Wolfpit, Kentucky; Panther, West Virginia), and closed by the apparently obligatory "You can't miss it." Needless to say, I occasionally found that without Darvin and Ganell I was very capable of missing "it."

Locating a church, however, has been just the initial step in this entire field work process. I have had to meet the people, become accepted as a nonthreatening and friendly agent, and learn how to talk to the various elements in the fellowships. Again, the Marshalls have often made the difference between success and failure, giving my work an aura of acceptability, and providing information critical to determining viable strategies of approach. Wherever we have gone Darvin has worked the crowd before and after the meeting, speaking enthusiastically to church leaders about my study, selling the idea that Old Regularism must be documented. In addition, he has collected information applicable to other visitations — types of services scheduled, location of the churches, names of contact persons, and the like.

Ganell's role in all of this has centered on providing a better understanding of Old Regular women and the Old Regular family. After one of my early presentations on gender

*Ganell Marshall (*standing alone at left center*) after a service at Samaria Church, Wolfpit, Kentucky.*

roles in Old Regularism, Patricia Beaver, a colleague at Appalachian State University, warned that I might never capture the true essence of Old Regular women without a female assistant who could better relate to the feminine side of the subdenomination.[5] To a large degree Ganell has become that assistant, helping me to better appreciate the feminine point of view within Old Regularism, and curbing my tendency to generalize about Old Regular women.

Both Darvin and Ganell have read the notes I have written after each visitation and the several essays I have authored about Old Regulars. Their careful scrutinizations of these materials have provided a valuable check against inaccuracies and misinterpretations. I should add that in this process they have not tried to move me toward unrealistically positive attitudes and a romanticized approach, just as they have not exposed me only to the more modern associations and fellowships.

Travels with the Marshalls

During the summers of 1986, 1987, and 1988 in particular I spent many hours traveling Virginia and Kentucky mountain roads with the Marshalls, and these trips proved beneficial in ways other than just the locating of Old Regular churches. Discussions that transpired increased my understanding of what I had just seen or was about to see and led into detailed examinations of doctrines, worship practices, and a host of Old Regular attitudes and values. In addition, the Marshalls and I talked of mining in central Appalachia; about the politics of coal; of earlier days of company camps and company stores; of the ethnography of the people, education in the mountains, and the general images and stereotypes of Appalachians; and about the nomenclature of ridges, creeks, rivers, and bottoms. All of this enriched my understanding of the country in which Old Regularism was born and flourished.

Both Darvin and Ganell soon made clear their strong opinions on past depictions of Appalachian mores, culture, and life styles, decrying the many portrayals of central Appalachia that had become mixtures of all the negative images of Li'l Abner, Snuffy Smith, Hatfields and McCoys, and *Deliverance*, with Appalachian religious traditions in particular getting a bad image from the snake-handling-is-the-mode myth and the *Dark of the Moon* suggestions of a native religion mixed with superstitions and witch stories. As suggested above, the Marshalls don't want romanticism, but they do hope for balance.

Methodological Concerns

Recording of services became a significant aspect of the field work for *Giving Glory to God in Appalachia: Worship Practices of Six Baptist Subdenominations*; but aside from some initial taping of the preaching and singing at Sandy Ridge Old Regular, I have not employed a tape recorder or video camera in my research for this work. The reason is that Old Regulars are especially sensitive about allowing the use of audiorecording, videorecording, film, or still photography to preserve their worship services. They have been victimized too many times by the "one visit only" documenters (from academia or the mass media) who "breeze in without a may I or pretty please," make their recordings or shoot their film, and then leave without any explanations or assurances concerning use of the materials. Old Regulars don't want to be viewed as oddities to be preserved and marketed as curiosities. "I'm not a two-headed calf," said one elder, "and I don't want to be treated like one."[6]

Some churches would have permitted discreet recordings, but even in those fellowships I could not have been certain that *everyone* would remain comfortable and unoffended. I saw a possibility of losing more than was gained through during-the-service use of recorders or cameras. Thus I have generally opted for their absence.

For the most part, my use of still photography has been confined to exterior shots of the churches, after-service fellowship meals, and interior gatherings before and after worship. I have, however, felt freer during association business meetings and worship sessions, and with outdoor memorial services, making photographic records of several of these events. The times when I have been most hesitant to use a camera have been those emotional moments during preaching, singing, or footwashings when impassioned displays of religious fervor were being exhibited throughout a church — crying, shouting, dynamic physical behavior, and the like.

Operating in this manner—without extensive use of a recorder or a camera—I have tried to make more careful written observations of my visitations than I ordinarily might
have made. Thus I recorded a number of pages of notes immediately after each church visit, notes which in turn were
checked by the Marshalls for general accuracy. Copies of
these three hundred or so typed pages of my visitation jour-
nals have been turned over to the Appalachian collections at
both Appalachian State University and Berea College for
whatever use other students of Old Regularism might want
to make of them. My collection of Old Regular association
minutes has been housed in the Appalachian Collection at
Appalachian State.

Acknowledgments

The first acknowledgment of debt I must make is to
Darvin and Ganell Marshall. I might have been able to establish contact with Old Regulars without the assistance of
these two; but I would have been forced to move more slowly,
and I am certain that I would not have felt as confident of
my analyses had I not had these research partners to read my
notes and respond to my probing discourse. In a very real
sense, Darvin and Ganell have become participating partners in this scholarship and must share in any triumphs arising from it.

There are always dangers in such team efforts: scholarly
objectivity could become subverted by friendships, conclu-
sions that might offend could be avoided, exposure to the phenomenon being studied could become selective, and general
emotional contact with subject matter could become intensified. I will not claim total avoidance of all these dangers.

The many contacts I have made with Old Regular leaders
have increased this problem of objectivity simply because
this group has proved so cooperative, even more so, in fact,
than I initially expected. It is almost unfair to single out for

recognition any limited collection of these individuals, since there are literally scores of elders, deacons, brothers, and sisters who have helped me in this study; but some names must be mentioned, starting with three past or present association moderators: Elders John Layne, Edwin May, and Wardie Craft each assisted me in some significant way.

Until the 1987 annual session, when ill health forced him to step down, Elder Layne was the moderator of the Union Association of Old Regulars. He spent nineteen years in that position, watching the organization grow from sixty-four churches in 1968 to seventy-two churches in 1987. Largely because my Old Regular work began with Union fellowships, I ended up visiting more churches in this association than in any of the other individual clusters. Through Elder Layne's leadership an environment was created that made my visitations welcome. I appreciated that open door policy. John Layne died February 11, 1988, and thus was not able to see the completion of this work.

At the time of this writing Elder Edwin May is the moderator of the Sardis Association of Old Regulars. In February 1985 he invited me to his home in Abingdon, Virginia, for what turned out to be a daylong discussion touching on almost every aspect of Old Regular beliefs and practices. May has since followed my field research with supportive interest.

I have also visited the home of Elder Wardie Craft, moderator of the Thornton Union Association. During two such visits Elder Craft and his wife, Sister Hazel, have not only tolerated my hours of questioning, but have also supplied me with a variety of Old Regular documents, including a large collection of association minutes, a number of photographs, and an account of the short-lived Old Regular Baptist Orphanage Home, to be discussed later.

Other association moderators I need to mention are Elder Hurshell Hurley (Old Friendship), Elder Grover Adkins (New Salem), Elder Elwood Cornett (Indian Bottom), and Elder Elmer Church (Original Mountain Liberty), all of whom allowed me to witness annual association meetings.

Two people who deserve very special credit for making my work much easier than it might have been are Brother Dexter Dixon and Elder Walter Akers. Currently, Dixon is clerk of the New Salem Association, and Akers is an elder from the Little Salem Church of that group of fellowships. In 1983 these two men published, in bound mimeographed form, the minutes of this progenitor of all Old Regular associations, New Salem. In performing this service, Dixon and Akers preserved a very valuable part of Old Regular history.

Numerous individual Old Regular leaders must be mentioned. Elder Bill Campbell from the Bull Creek fellowship, Union Association, became one of my earliest and strongest supporters, providing me with an endless amount of information on doctrine and practices, and closely critiquing an earlier version of this manuscript. Elder Dallas Ramsey, Ash Camp fellowship, Union Association, not only welcomed me to his church on a number of occasions, but allowed me to microfilm a large collection of Union Association minutes that he had pulled together from various sources. Elder Atlas D. Hall, assistant clerk of the Original Mountain Liberty Association, supplied me with some minutes, helped me in locating the two Mountain associations, read an earlier version of this work, and provided over thirty pages of critical observations on my discussions of the various associations. Elder Jimmy W. Hall, Hemp Hill Church, Union Association, sent me a number of Old Regular documents, gave me the strongest support possible in his fellowship, and encouraged me with some of the kindest words I received from any Old Regular leader. Elder Fred Stiltner, Bull Creek fellowship, sat through at least three dinners-on-the-ground with me, patiently fielding my questions. Elder Raymond Smith, Lonesome Dove, Union Association, endured several of my interviews, invited me to visit two memorial services at his home in Canada, Kentucky, and even allowed me to stay in his home one evening. Deacon Ted DePriest, Elder James O'Quinn, and Deacon Richard Edwards, Tivis Chapel, Union Association, were especially cordial and helpful when I visited their church to witness DePriest's ordination as a deacon. Finally, Elder Toby Bailey of Birchleaf, Virginia, invited me into his home for a Sunday meal, joining Elder Campbell in explaining to me their understandings of Old Regular atonement doctrine.

Many other Old Regular elders have been particularly cooperative in one fashion or another, all of whom I could not name; nevertheless, here are a few — from several associations — who stand out in my mind: Ivan Amburgey, George Baker, Eulys Bentley, Fon Bowling, Spencer Burks, Arnold Clevinger, Bob Fields, Leroy Hall, Josh Justus, Jr., Clifford Maynard, Paul McClanahan, A. O. McKnight, Foster Mullins, Frank O'Quinn, Baxter Osborne, Jimmy Dale Sanders, Lloyd Sesco, Conard Stallard, Claren Williams, and Wesley Yonts.

In addition, I must thank the memberships of the following Old Regular churches I visited, several of which welcomed me more than once: Ash Camp (Ashcamp, Kentucky), Bent Branch (Meta, Kentucky), Bethany (Kingsport, Tennessee), Bethel (Dunham, Kentucky), Bethlehem (Grundy, Virginia), Bull Creek (Maxie, Virginia), Fairview (Pound, Virginia), Hemp Hill (Hemp Hill, Kentucky), Holston (Abingdon, Virginia), Hurricane (Wise, Virginia), Lebanon (Clintwood, Virginia), Little Freedom (Vansant, Virginia), Little Home (Red Fox, Kentucky), Little Martha (Leemaster, Virginia), Little Sarah (Haysi, Virginia), Lonesome Dove (Canada, Kentucky), Mary Lou (Paynesville, West Virginia), North Springs (Hurley, Virginia), Old Beaver (Minnie, Kentucky), Ramsey Ridge (Ramsey Ridge, Virginia), Samaria (Wolfpit, Kentucky), Sandy Ridge (Sandy Ridge, Virginia), Stone Coal (Garrett, Kentucky), Thornton (Mayking, Kentucky), and Tivis Chapel (Haysi, Virginia). Although I was not able to attend one of their services, I also visited the New Hope Church in Winnabow, North Carolina, the only Old Regular fellowship in that state. That visit did, however, result in an extensive inteview of Sister Rena Caudill, the contents of which I will relate later in this work.[7]

For two summers (1986 and 1987) my travels to these churches and to various association meetings were financed in part by Appalachian Studies Fellowship Grants awarded by the Appalachian Center of Berea College, Berea, Kentucky. I am greatly indebted to Loyal Jones and his fellowship grants committee for this assistance.

Financial support was also received from the Appalachian State University Research Committee and the Cratis Williams Graduate School. In addition, the Appalachian State University Center for Appalachian Studies, the late Carl Ross, director, provided valuable assistance by microfilming a large collection of Old Regular association minutes.

Finally, I want to recognize the supportive efforts of Acquisitions Editor Cynthia Maude–Gembler, the other members of the University of Tennessee Press staff who worked with me on this project, and Deborah V. McCauley, who provided a detailed review of the submitted manuscript.

Unless otherwise credited, all photography is by the author.

The Old Regular Baptists
of Central Appalachia

1. An Overview of Old Regularism

The real heart of Old Regular territory covers a relatively small area, concentrated as it is in central Appalachia along both sides of the southwestern Virginia and eastern Kentucky border. This is high country, drained on the Virginia side by headwater streams of the Powell and Clinch rivers, and on the Kentucky side by forks and tributaries of the Cumberland, Kentucky, Licking, and Big Sandy. Fingers of this core region reach up into southwestern West Virginia and southern Ohio and also down slightly into northeastern Tennessee, but the true heartland of the Old Regular Baptist Church of Jesus Christ is some eighteen to twenty counties of eastern Kentucky and southwestern Virginia.

This Baptist subdenomination has spread elsewhere as migrations from the mother region have taken isolated fellowships into Indiana, Michigan, Illinois, North Carolina, Florida, Arizona, and even — until recently — Washington state.[1] Nevertheless, Old Regularism seems inextricably tied to central Appalachia — coal-mining country that is mountainous, rugged; marked by both immense natural beauty and by unsightly man-made scars; and still somewhat insular and unexplored by the larger outside world. It is a land that the nation periodically rediscovers — when labor disturbances rack the coal-mining industry, when a "War on Poverty" declares the region part of "the other America," when environmentalists decry the earth-stripping horrors of modern mining methods, and when students of Appalachia explore (as I am doing now) some of the interesting patterns of its cultural fabric.

Still this is a land that has remained relatively unvisited

by the average American and thus is generally unknown to him or her. No federal interstate crosses the mountainous terrain, and the region's core is penetrated only shallowly by two highways bearing heavy tourist traffic — the Daniel Boone and Mountain Parkways, both coming in from the west. So most Americans in transit — on their way to here or there for business or pleasure — move above, below, or around Old Regular country, setting their courses to Knoxville on Interstates 81 to 40, to Lexington on Interstate 75, and to Charleston, West Virginia, on Interstates 64 and 77, and leaving the lopsided square of country in between comparatively unexamined.

With the exception of the Breaks Interstate Park, the Daniel Boone and Jefferson National Forests, and several large lakes, there are no major attractions that have been promoted to create a thriving tourist industry in this region. In addition, there is no retreat-to-the-mountains, second-home real estate market comparable to that which has developed in the Blue Ridge and Great Smokies ranges from northwest North Carolina to northern Georgia. Coal mining, with its black-dusting appearance of unhealthiness, its mountain-tearing ugliness, its history of violent labor-management struggles, its unsavory past in political manipulations, and its current treacheries for private land ownership, appears to have driven away many less toublesome public and private interests, leaving the region only to commercial and industrial developments compatible with the extraction of coal.

There are some stereotypic generalizations about this region that should be avoided. It is no longer a land of Hatfields and McCoys or of characters like Snuffy Smith and Li'l Abner — if it ever were. Nor does every third person you meet wear bib overalls, smoke a corncob pipe, and speak in Elizabethan English. It is not exclusively an isolated wasteland of rickety cabins, rifle-toting mountaineers, sleeping hounds, and rusting old cars; although there are towns and communities still possessing the old mining camp image, and there are pockets of real economic deprivation, environmental ruin, and cultural decay. Furthermore, it is not a region univer-

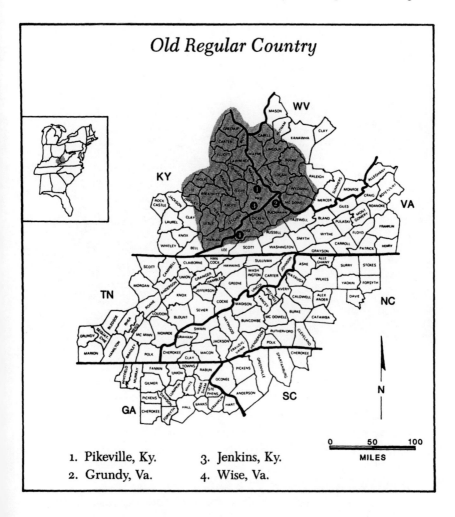

Old Regular Country

1. Pikeville, Ky.
2. Grundy, Va.
3. Jenkins, Ky.
4. Wise, Va.

0   50   100
MILES

sally blighted by illiteracy, genetically induced retardations, and illnesses long since alleviated in less "backward" environs; although again there are restricted regions in which some of these harms no doubt persist. And, regardless of what was said above, it is not today a land of unrelenting mining waste and denatured hills. Even though there are multitudinous signs of industrial, civic, and individual irre-

Mining operations, Vansant, Virginia.

sponsibility toward the environment, this region still possesses a wide range of natural beauties, particularly in the spring, summer, and fall when Mother Nature camouflages, in colors of lush green or autumn reds and golds, all but the crudest of man's unkindly cuts. As a land of strongly dichotomous contracts between the beauties of nature and the waste-laying destructiveness of man, central Appalachia seems a fitting place for both the joyful and wailful sounds of Old Regularism.

Old Regularism: A Preliminary Glance

"Old Regular Baptists are a peculiar people"—so the elders of this subdenomination are fond of declaring. But when these preachers use this phrase they are not thinking of any strangeness and eccentricity present in their flocks. Instead they are making reference to phraseology employed in the King James version of Paul's letter to Titus and in Peter's first epistle:

> For the grace of God that bringeth salvation hath appeared to all men,
> Teaching us that, denying ungodliness and worldly lusts, we should live soberly, righteously, and godly, in this present world;
> Looking for that blessed hope, and the glorious appearing of the great God and our Saviour Jesus Christ;
> Who gave himself for us, that he might redeem us from iniquity, and purify unto himself a peculiar people, zealous of good works. (Titus 2: 11–14)
> But ye are a chosen generation, a royal priesthood, an holy nation, a peculiar people; that ye should shew forth the praises of him who hath called you out of darkness and into his marvelous light. (I Pet. 2:9)

Thus Old Regulars view themselves as a special people, not in the sense of having been "particularly elected" as the Primitives believe, but in the sense of being "redeemed" and "zealous of good works," of "denying ungodliness and worldly lusts," as having been "called . . . out of darkness," and as living "soberly, righteously, and godly."

A significant part of all this specialness, however, is embodied in Old Regulars' tenacity in preserving "old-time" ways of worship and in their strict adherence to a collection of traditional codes of general behavior. When dealing with such issues as the proper length of hair, the proprieties of dress, the mixing of genders during worship, the decorum of church business (including rules for female involvement), the acceptability of divorce, the settling of fellowship disputes, and the operations of family life, Old Regulars doggedly preserve the "old-time way," following a mixture of Pauline mandates, other biblical directives, and customs pulled directly from the eighteenth and nineteenth centuries. Indeed, these codes are honored with such persistence that Old Regular fellowships frequently find themselves at odds with much of twentieth-century America. Consider, as examples, the following scripture-instituted rules, all followed *to some degree* by Old Regular Baptists.

Women are denied a formal voice in church governance (I Cor. 14:34). Men are commanded to cut their hair, and women are admonished not to do so (I Cor. 11:14–15). Women must not dress in men's clothing—slacks, jeans, pantsuits (Deut. 22:5).[2] Men are to command their own homes (Eph. 5:22–23), particularly those to be ordained as deacons (I Tim. 3:12). Both men and women should remain married to their original spouses as long as these spouses live (I Cor. 7:10); but if couples do divorce, neither should remarry (I Cor.7:11), except in the case of the injured party when the divorce is obtained on grounds of adultery. Disputes between members of a fellowship should be settled within the church family, rather than in civil courts (I Cor. 6:1–6). Finally, if any member has a charge against another member, he or she must go through the steps prescribed in Matt. 18:15–17: (1) approach the offending party with the charge; (2) if satisfaction is not received, then go to the offending party with "one or two" other fellowship members; and (3) if satisfaction is still not received, take the charge before the church.

Furthermore, a number of traditional customs of worship have been preserved, some by such determination that the particular liturgical practice has become one of the absolutes in defining Old Regularism.[3] Such is the case, for example, with lined singing, a hymnody method in which a song leader (one of the elders) chants the hymn one couplet at a time, with each chanting then being followed by the congregation's rendition of that couplet. This is a singing method that apparently dates back to the practices of the Westminster Assembly of Baptists in England in the 1600s and which became highly serviceable in eighteenth- and nineteenth-century frontier America, when congregations often could not read and had no songbooks when they could.[4]

Old Regulars are so fond of their lined singing—a slow, wailful hymnody that seems to ignore customary melodies—that they constantly scold those of their number who attempt to introduce into services any element of the contemporary Southern gospel or folk sound, and fellowships that have adopted "notebook singing" have immediately faced the threat of expulsion from their respective associations.[5] Furthermore, worship through singing "the old songs of Zion" stands on equal footing with worship through preaching, prayer, and communion.

The preservation of footwashing, however, is mandated by an Old Regular obligation that is more doctrine-tied than is lined singing. Considered along with baptism by immersion as an "ordinance of Jesus Christ (John 13:14)," the annual communion-footwashing service is a ritual in which every church member should participate, unless prohibited by health or other critical circumstances. So the ceremonial washing of feet, preceded by the once-a-year taking of communion, is another fundamental factor defining Old Regularism.[6]

Then there are other distinguishing features: the various types of special services, all of which will be discussed later in this work; the particular nature of church governance, including the operations both of the local churches and the associations; the many traditions that intensify the interpersonal involvements of Old Regular worship — the constant handshaking, embracing, and additional forms of tactile contact; the numerous examples of an unstructured informality in procedure — the casual treatment of time and form, the spur-of-the-moment selection of everything from hymns to preachers, the wholly improvisational sermonizing, and the general acceptance of all monetary expressions of religious fervor; the rigid adherence to a modified Calvinism — a "God calls; man does not" theology that causes nonmember churchgoers to wait patiently, sometimes for years, for that clear sign of an individual "election by grace"; the deep distrust of any form of a man-nurtured religiosity — generating, among other things, a prohibition of Sunday schools and a reluctance to embrace any form of youth outreach; and the dogged insularity that forbids most forms of interdenominational involvements, even with other Appalachian Baptist groups.

Finally, there is the deeply embedded sense of specialness, a concept of covenantal relationship with God that allows and encourages almost a total lack of curiosity about the larger world of religious doctrines and institutions, knowing only a few groups with whom they specifically disagree — Primitives, Free Will Baptists, some Regular Baptists, United Baptists, and Missionary Baptists.

The Associations

Within this limited region of Appalachia there are sixteen (perhaps seventeen) associations of Old Regular Baptists in operation at the time of this writing. The largest of these confederations of fellowships is the Union Association of Old Regular Baptists of Jesus Christ, with (by 1987 statistics) a total of 3,225 members in seventy-three churches, distributed primarily in Kentucky and Virginia. The Union Association, however, has affiliate fellowships as far north and south of the regional core as Ypsilanti, Michigan, and Crystal Springs, Florida, manifestations of Appalachia's outward migrations.[7]

These seventy-three Union fellowships are relatively small, as the figures above might suggest, showing an average membership of only forty-four; but when the Union's annual "association time" arrives, with its large assemblage at the fairgounds in Wise, Virginia, daily crowd sizes occasionally exceed that 3,225 total membership, since large numbers of visitors from corresponding associations (New Salem, Sardis, Indian Bottom, Philadelphia, Northern New Salem, and Old Friendship) will also be in attendance. These yearly events are to be discussed in chapter 4, where attention will be given to the operation of associations.

The second largest of the associations is the New Salem group — 2,951 individual members, fifty-eight churches (1986 statistics), concentrated primarily in Kentucky, with isolated fellowships in Illinois, Indiana, Ohio, West Virginia, and even Arizona.[8] This oldest of the Old Regular associations is

Union Association tent at the fairgrounds, Wise, Virginia.

mother, grandmother, or great-grandmother of all of the various clusters of this Baptist subdenomination, with the possible exception of the two Mountain associations.

Because of this progenitor relationship with other Old Regular associations, New Salem's annual sessions tend to be the best attended of all such events, attracting between three and four thousand delegates, regular members, and guests to the late September gatherings at their permanent association building in Minnie, Floyd County, Kentucky.

Thornton Union, an association that currently is not in correspondence with either Union or New Salem, is third in size. This group's 1,563 members are distributed among twenty-seven churches (1986 statistics) in Kentucky, Virginia, Indiana, Ohio, and Florida, with the first two of these states again being the primary zones of activity.[9] Their annual sessions are held in Mayking, Letcher County, Kentucky, in Thornton Church and the adjacent "Delegate House." Atten-

Thornton Union Delegate House, Mayking, Kentucky.

dance usually ranges around 1,000, including delegates, regular church members, and visitors.

Indian Bottom Association, with twenty-six fellowships in Kentucky, Indiana, and Ohio, may be fourth in total size, having just under 1,400 members (1985 statistics).[10] This group was once larger in number of affiliated churches, but it split in 1960 into two associations, Indian Bottom and Old Indian Bottom, the latter group now having 365 members in fifteen fellowships (1986 statistics).[11] The larger of these two groups convenes on Friday before the first Saturday in each September at its permanent association building in Sassafras, Knott County, Kentucky, attracting to its three-day annual session between 1,000 and 1,200 members and guests. The smaller Indian Bottom Association rotates its yearly meetings between its member churches and may draw between 200 and 250 delegates and spectators. Among Old Regulars this smaller Indian Bottom cluster of churches is often called the "Frank Fugate side," named after the elder who became the moderator of these fellowships after the split. In turn, and for the same reason, the larger Indian Bottom division has been called the "J. W. Pratt side." Today the most common way of referring to these two groups appears to be to use "Old Indian Bottom" for the smaller cluster and just plain "Indian Bottom" for the larger cluster. These are the terms I will utilize throughout this work. In chapter 6 I will examine the factors that precipitated the Indian Bottom split.

I stated above that Indian Bottom "may be" the fourth largest of the associations, and I used that qualifying statement simply because I don't know the current membership of Friendship Association. In 1976 this latter group had nineteen churches, reporting a total membership of 1,487.[12] Friendship's enrollment apparently held in the low 1,400 range through 1979, but I have no information on the cluster after that date, except that these fellowships have adopted worship practices which the more traditional Old Regular groups consider heretical.[13]

Sardis Association, with a membership of just under 1,300 in twenty-nine churches (1985 statistics) in Kentucky, West Virginia, and Florida, is next in size, and like the Old Indian Bottom Association still rotates its annual meetings among its member fellowships.[14] Sardis, however, corresponds with five other associations, including both Union and New Salem, and thus attracts members from these groups to its yearly conventions, generating in the process attendance figures of around 1,000.

The remaining Old Regular groups (Old Friendship, Philadelphia, Northern New Salem, Mud River, Bethel, Kyova, two Mountain associations, and Mountain Liberty) are all much smaller, both in numbers of churches and in membership totals. For example, statistics provided in 1986 minutes showed Old Friendship to have 667 members in ten churches, Bethel to have 274 members in eight churches, Philadelphia to have 178 members in seven churches, and Mud River to have only 61 members in three churches.[15] Northern New Salem's 1987 minutes reported 944 members in twenty-six fellowships, and 1987 Mountain Liberty minutes reported 166 members in five churches.[16]

Mountain Liberty just reorganized (August 29, 1987) after having been in disorder for ten years, and they now have assumed the official title Original Mountain Liberty Association. When first founded in 1973, this association contained four churches and a total membership of 143.[17] After only four years, however, the alliance fell apart, with three of the original churches then affiliating with Thornton Union.

I have reasonably current statistics for only one of the Mountain associations (975 members in twelve churches in 1984), and I possess no contemporary figures for Kyova.[18] Indeed, the current status of this association, like Friendship, is open to debate, since other Old Regulars consider Kyova to have adopted pratices not compatible with the true nature of Old Regularism.[19] A seventeenth Old Regular association, Cumberland, once had three fellowships in Wise County, Virginia, but I have been told—without direct contact to verify the story—that as of this writing they have fallen into disorder and no longer meet as an association.[20]

The best estimate of the total membership for all of the Old Regular associations appears to be about 15,000, with another 15,000 to 20,000 serving as nonmember regular church attendants. This is not a sizable figure, considering the total geographical area covered, but the number is sufficient to suggest a meaningful impact upon central Appalachia.

The Individual Churches

Old Regular Baptist churches are frequently rather difficult to locate, in part because they tend to be tucked away
on mountain-meandering secondary roads that crawl up hollows and coves and along ridges, but also because they are
so architecturally unobtrusive and bear few proclamations
of their identification. Unlike the typical Southern, Free Will,
or Missionary Baptist church that cries out its presence in a
number of different ways, Old Regular structures seldom exhibit those symbols so traditional to Christian houses of worship — large crosses, steeples, stained glass windows, and eye-
catching marquees that announce service times, ministers,
sermon topics, and other advertising details. In addition, there
seldom is a sign down by a main road proclaiming the church's
existence and welcoming visitors to its services. Instead, the
worship structure is usually marked only by one small sign,
often facing away from the road, as if striving for anonym-
ity and seclusion, bearing solely the fellowship's name, the
monthly meeting times, and the year of establishment.

This Old Regular church will be relatively simple and un-
adorned: a small rectangular building of wood, concrete block,
or brick; possessing a low roof of asphalt shingles or tin sheet-
ing, with no elaborate gables. Traditionally, windows are bar-
ren of any purely decorative features — no arching cathedral-
like design in the frames and no artistry in the glass work.
However, windows might be covered by heavy, very functional shutters, since churches often sit empty and unguarded
for most of the month.

The image I want to project, however, is not one of stark,
unrelenting severity in design and mood. In fact, there is often a charm about the simple functionalism of these structures, a New England–like plainness in the image, augmented
by the rustic mountain settings within which they are usually placed. However, Old Regular fellowships make few attempts at providing either the exteriors or interiors of their

churches with purely ornate features, just as their services themselves are stripped to the bare essentials of worship— fellowship, singing, praying, preaching, and piety.

Old Regular church interiors fall into a fairly set form. The space is divided roughly into two equal parts—the out-front division of pews used primarily by the nonmember regular churchgoers and by nonmember visitors, and the raised "stand" area reserved for the actual members of the fellowship, visiting Old Regular laypersons, home and visiting elders, and other Old Regulars of import (visiting deacons and the like).

This stand area is again divided, with right and left sections that traditionally face in toward the stand (pulpit) and a behind-the-stand section that of course faces out toward the nonmember pews. Old Regular fellowships have no choirs or special singing groups, so all three of these raised seating sections are occupied by regular worshipers and preaching elders. The general pattern is for female church members to sit in one of these side sections and for the male church members to sit in the opposite side section. Although there are numerous churches that reverse this rule, the women usually will be on the left side for a spectator who is facing the stand from the church's front entrance.

Seating in the center raised section will be determined somewhat by the capacity of this area; but often this will be an all-male space, with the forward pew always being used by the fellowship's moderator and local and visiting elders. Male seating will also frequently extend to the front pew on the female side, thus closing in the stand with an inverted horseshoe-shaped phalanx of male support for all of the preachers of the morning. Later we will see how this male support system functions during services.

As my descriptions have already suggested, in the Old Regular lexicon "stand" serves both for the pulpit at which the preachers operate and for the larger raised area I have been describing. The actual stand (pulpit) is usually constructed so that it provides three top surfaces, the center section which

Sign on Bethel Church, Dunham, Kentucky.

will hold a large King James Bible, and two slightly lowered wing sections. On one of these wing sections there will often be a portable water cooler and the requisite dispenser for paper, plastic, or styrofoam cups. During a typical service — particularly in summer months — this cooler will see considerable service, as elders wet their mouths before, during, or after preaching, and as worshipers from anywhere in the congregation seek to refresh themselves. In earlier years a bucket and common dipper took the place of this cooler.

Another object frequently found on one of these wings is a jar of rock candy. Some Old Regular peachers find this

Hurricane Church, Wise, Virginia.

candy helpful both as a source of energy and as a throat lozenge. In addition, children occasionally approach the stand to help themselves from this jar, even while the service is occurring. The behavior of children in Old Regular churches will receive some special attention later in this work.

Two other types of objects are usually found on the wing sections of these stands — an assortment of song books and the published minutes of the most recent association meeting. These minutes contain information frequently used in the fellowship's Saturday business meetings (rules of decorum, constitution, etc.), and they also contain the "calls" (elders requested to attend) for memorial and union meetings. The song books include only the lyrics of hymns (no notes), and these published collections will have originated from a number of different sources, since there is no recognized Old Regular hymnal.[21] Several churches, for example, have published their own anthologies of sacred songs, often containing both original pieces written by members of a fellowship and older established hymns, some of which appear to have been modified for local use.[22] Individual elders also carry with them their own favorite song books.

The interior walls of Old Regular churches generally remain undecorated, except for that wall behind the stand area. Here photographs of past and present church leaders often are hung, creating a gallery of patriarchs. For older fellowships this display may become quite extensive, resulting in almost every available space being covered, thus causing the exhibit to wrap around onto the upper ends of the side walls. Occasionally these photographs will provide a complete record of the moderators of the respective church, plus key association leaders of the past. Pictures of early Old Regular patriarchs, such as the bearded image of Elder David Church (founder of several churches in the Union Association), have found their way into a number of individual church collections, including fellowships from several different associations.

Historical accounts of Old Regular churches and associations tend to center upon men who have served as significant leaders of the subdenomination; and before-church and after-church discussions between members and visitors like myself tend to be held in front of these patriarch galleries, fingers pointed here and there toward figures of past and present renown. Visitors will often see artistic renditions of the last supper or other biblical scenes displayed among these photographs, but it has always seemed obvious to me that the actual men and women (wives of elders) of the denomination's past take prime focus in the attention of these people.

One feature of many of these churches is the interior kitchen and serving-eating area, usually an added-on structure running the length of one side of the building or stuck on the back of the church. If a fellowship has not built this type of interior structure, then they probably will have a covered exterior serving area for dinners-on-the ground, typically a twenty-five-to-fifty-foot-long open shed, set on a concrete slab or over bare earth, designed to accommodate several tables or plywood sheets placed on sawhorses. The reason for these arrangements is that large fellowship meals become a part of many, if not most, Old Regular gatherings, but particularly those of a special nature, such as communion-footwashings, union meetings, and memorial meetings.

Individual Old Regular fellowships meet only one weekend a month, with the business meeting and an abbreviated worship service on Saturday and a full worship service on Sunday. At these monthly meetings there usually will be as many visitors as there are actual members, since Old Regulars are heavily encouraged to attend the meetings of other fellowships on the Saturdays and Sundays when their own church is not in session. In addition, there will also be the visiting elders, either those specially called for the particular service or those who are just doing their duty of traveling to keep themselves available for any preaching needs that might develop.

The point here is that visitors are a significant element at these gatherings, and Old Regulars believe visitors ought to be fed and perhaps even put up for the night, an attitude born of frontier days, when such individuals probably would have traveled a day or more on horseback or by wagon to reach the church. From this reality Old Regular housewives were trained to be on the lookout for those brothers and sisters who might need shelter or food, and one practice which developed was for women to call out at the close of a service, "Anyone needing feeding, come home with me."

This custom of calling out invitations to the family table still prevails in many Old Regular settings, but the large post-service fellowship meals generally have taken the place of such practices. The longer and more widely attended services (again the communion-footwashing, union, and memorial meetings) are almost always followed by meals at the church or at a private home nearby; and some congregations

Gallery of Patriarchs, Old Beaver Church, Minnie, Kentucky.

stage these food affairs after every monthly Sunday service or at least during the spring, summer, and fall seasons.

Such meals are handled like traditional dinner-on-the-ground events, with women of the church bringing one or more generous meat, vegetable, salad, or dessert dishes, all to be arranged on a common table. The largest of such spreads will cover an extensive serving area and feed hundreds, perhaps closing out a worship service that has lasted until 2:00 in the afternoon or later. Interior dining facilities will usually include a small kitchen, a long counter for the dishes of food, and a few tables and benches; but after special meet-

Dinner-on-the-ground is served, Bull Creek Church, Maxie, Virginia.

ings the feasting will extend into the church sanctuary and out onto the surrounding grounds, covering the entire scene with small clusters of fellowshipping members and visitors.

The aesthetics of the totally outside dinners-on-the-ground seem purer, less contaminated by the modernity of stainless steel, formica, and linoleum; but there is always the problem of weather, with spring or summer showers frequently driving the feasters back inside the church. Little Martha Old Regular Baptist Church of Leemaster, Virginia, has no interior dining area, and the fellowship usually stages its post-service meals in an open area at one side of the church. On two occasions, however, I attended services at this church that closed with a meal moved indoors. In such events this congregation rearranges back pews so that the plywood sheets can be placed across backs of benches, thus providing a serving area. Old Regulars are not bothered by food being served or eaten inside the worship area of the church. A church facility is loved, but it is seldom restricted in its use by any foolish, impractical decorum.

Preliminary Observations About the People

To a significant degree the Old Regular Baptist subdenomination is weighted, in its age demographics, toward the elderly. Indeed, in many fellowships one receives the distinct impression of a growing-old faith, of congregations substantially devoid of the young people necessary for long-term sustenance.

Three reasons for this imbalance in ages stand out, the first being that Old Regular fellowships institute few, if any, programs specifically for the young. Sunday schools, for example, so much a part of the more mainline Baptist groups, don't become a feature of Old Regular worship. Indeed, in Old Regular theology, as we will see more clearly later, there are doctrinal barriers to all practices that attempt to nurture or evangelize individuals into faith.[23] According to the tenets of this subdenomination, salvation is the product of an individual man's or woman's responding to his or her individual God-issued call, and is not something inspired, manipulated, or instituted by the instruction or evangelism of other men or women. God calls; man does not. Therefore, there is too much danger that Sunday schools would usurp the role of the Deity in the redemption process.

Second, in addition to this aversion to Sunday schools, Old Regular adults seem reluctant to compel their young people to attend worship services, largely for the same reasons provided above. One prevailing rationale of the faith appears to be that an individual forced to sit through religious services is less likely to be receptive to a divine call than one who seeks out that experience on his or her own volition. So Old Regular strategy in handling the young seems identical to that followed in working with adult nonmembers: Don't push; don't entice; don't implore; but simply testify and exemplify, waiting patiently for the Deity to work his will on those yet to experience their calls.[24]

This no-pushing strategy is evident even in the way these congregations handle their preschool and early-elementary-aged youngsters, a group present in these services in far greater numbers than is the case for adolescents and young adults. In most Old Regular fellowships children from the toddler stage to about the third or fourth grade are allowed to run relatively free inside and outside the church when the service is in session. With little or no restraint from parents or other adults, the young people of this highly active age group may sit or lie quietly in their pews, run outside to play around the church, make trips to the stand for water or rock candy, move from out-front pews to stand area pews in treks from "Mom" to "Grandma," sit on the floor of this raised area while "Grandpa" preaches, or practice any of a number of childlike behaviors.

In a very real sense children are allowed to comport themselves quite naturally, and their antics become part of the charm of an Old Regular service. Furthermore, these relaxed practices frequently result in behavior far less distracting than the squirmings and audible protestations of the children who in more mainline churches are held close to parents under tight discipline. Keep in mind, also, that a typical Old Regular service will be very dynamic in nature, with the impassioned responses of adult worshipers tending to overmaster even the most boisterous behavior of children.

There have been moments during the Old Regular services I have visited when a particular child's conduct assumed a high degree of poignancy. There was the scene near the close of a meeting at Hemp Hill Old Regular Baptist Church, Hemp Hill, Kentucky, when a girl of about four had found a seat on the floor at the end of a pew on the women's side of the stand. The preaching was finished, and a final hymn was being sung as an emotional, shouting, embracing, weeping scene was being played out in this area of the church, a scene in which the child's mother figured prominently as one of

Two young boys playing outside Tivis Chapel, Haysi, Virginia.

the shouters. I recall watching the little girl as she in turn watched her mother, and the expression I saw was not one of anguish experienced in response to her mother's crying shouts. Instead, it was an expression of concentrated and thoughtful analysis, the look of a child who was carefully and lovingly measuring the behavior of a parent, determining, I suppose, her own perception of this scene of impassioned spirituality.[25]

Another reason for the "growing-old" look that seems to prevail in most Old Regular congregations is the strong Anabaptist strain that runs through the faith, a doctrinal bent that causes the subdenomination to reject infant baptism totally and to hold baptism of preadolescents and even adolescents in profound distrust. While Missionary, Free Will, and other Baptist groups might lead their subteen youth to the water, Old Regulars feel more comfortable with immersions occurring later in life. In fact, the average age for Old

Regular baptisms may be as late as thirty-five or forty, with a sizable number of faithful churchgoers making it into their sixties or seventies before being plunged ceremoniously into the frigidness of a mountain stream. Elder Bill Campbell argues that "maturity" is a major factor in all this, since this time of "spiritual maturity" determines when an individual hears his or her call, an awareness of sin that in turn initiates a "travel" toward redemption.[26]

Campbell also reasons that there is a final cause for this growing-old look within Old Regularism: "Possibly because our strict adherence to traditions and customs that we feel were instituted by the apostles is not particularly appealing to modern ways of life; i.e., long hair for women, modest dress, abstaining from some social functions."[27]

In addition to this age factor, there are some dominant socioeconomic and cultural characteristics that should be mentioned. First, it must be remembered that "Old Regular country" is predominantly a coal-mining region, with a large portion of the male members of the subdenomination working or having worked in surface or deep-shaft mining. The most frequently noticed consequence of all this is the number of mining-related disabilities, particularly black lung respiratory problems and mining accident injuries. This is not to suggest that every male in these churches is either wheezing or on crutches, but there is sufficient visibility of the problem to impress any frequent visitor with the reality of this Old Regular phenomenon.

Two specific examples of mining disabilities I have witnessed come to mind: one the injuries of the late Elder Billie Mullins of the Lebanon Old Regular Baptist Church near Clintwood, Virginia, whom I observed maneuvering around the Lebanon stand on one leg, the other having been severed near his left hip; and the second disability belonging to an elder whom I observed at the Bent Branch Church in Meta, Kentucky, a man who was surviving only by use of a portable oxygen tank and breathing mask.

The image of one-legged Elder Billie Mullins was etched

indelibly in my memory when I viewed his painstaking and laborious efforts to make it through a footwashing service, manipulating not only his own out-of-balance body but also all of the paraphernalia of the ceremony — basin, pitcher, towel, water. Mullins obviously had trained other members of the Lebanon congregation not to help him, and the intense concentration he devoted to every precariously balanced movement lent poignancy to a service already heavily imbued with emotional fervor.[28]

According to Darvin Marshall, Mullins' accident involved a mine cave-in that not only crushed the elder's missing leg but opened up his lower abdomen as well, forcing him to lie pinned for a period of time with a portion of his entrails exposed.[29] The incident has been spoken of within the Lebanon fellowship as evidence of the "sacred role" the injured elder would play. Mullins died in 1987, and his obituary appears in the Union Association minutes of that year.[30]

I have no comparable information about the elder at the Bent Branch Church in Meta, Kentucky, but I recall how agonizing it became to hear this brother lead a prayer, struggling with each word to breathe. Meta is on Highway 119 northeast of Pikeville, approximately twenty miles from Williamson, West Virginia, and I remember that afternoon listening to a Williamson radio station that proclaimed itself the voice of "coal country." The elder's destroyed lungs reminded me of a price often paid in the past to work in "coal country."[31]

Another socioeconomic factor needing to be discussed is the educational level of Old Regulars, for most older members of the faith have experienced marked deficiencies in this area, at least in formal schooling. In addition, none of the ministers — of whom I have become aware — have received any seminary training. He whom God calls to preach, the faith argues, God also equips to preach. No man-instituted schooling is necessary to prepare an individual to do what God has inspired him to do.

There is a younger stratum of Old Regular members, how-

ever, who occasionally show higher degrees of both education and general sophistication, gained in some cases from
college and university programs. Indeed, there are numerous elementary and secondary teachers and administrators
within Old Regular ranks and what appears to be a number
of accomplished small business operators and managers, many
of whom have assumed leadership positions in the various associations and within their respective communities. Thus there
is a body of politically astute Old Regulars who have climbed
to positions of power in municipal or county governments.
There are, however, few members of the faith who practice
professional occupations, such as law, medicine, higher education, engineering, etc. Undoubtedly numerous such individuals have risen from the ranks of Old Regularism, but
upon doing so they may have withdrawn from the operations
of the church. I have seen little or no evidence of a trend to
remain within the faith once the fortunes of upward mobil-
ity have placed an individual within such professional ranks.
However, these circumstances may be changing, as Old Regulars develop a greater sense of pride in their cultural distinctiveness. I have in mind a son of Elder Bill Campbell. At the
time of this writing the young man is an honors student in
high school with aspirations of studying engineering at Virginia Tech. Discussions with this young man have established
that at the moment he never intends to leave Old Regularism, no matter how far in life he goes.[32]

In general wealth or economic sufficiency, there appears to
be a wide set of conditions among Old Regulars, ranging all
the way from a pronounced poverty to recognizable affluence.
Although the prototype is lower middle class and blue collar,
a visitor to these churches will see individuals and families
whose clothes, cars, and general demeanor suggest images
of considerable economic comfort. Old Regularism does not
necessarily correlate with indigence and social deprivation.

I am choosing my words carefully when discussing the cultural and socioeconomic characteristics of Old Regularism
because I don't want to create pictures that lean toward either

an unredeemable bleakness or a romanticized rosiness. Suffice it to say that numerous people have chosen to remain with this faith even after they have experienced some degree of economic, educational, and social advancement; and there appears to be a sizable group of individuals — perhaps an increasing number in recent years — who have felt called to the faith and its confining customs in part because they believe the strict codes work, having experienced life styles not nearly so comforting for them.[33] In attitudinal kinship with such groups as the Amish and Mennonites, Old Regulars don't always place great faith in modernity. The old ways, they say, can be very satisfying.

Perhaps one way to capture Old Regular people would be to allow one member of the faith to speak for herself. During the 1987 annual session of the New Salem Association, held in Minnie, Floyd County, Kentucky, Sister Beulah Jones Patrick gave me a poem she wanted me to publish. At that moment I didn't know how to honor her request, but now the writing appears to have relevance to my immediate task of characterizing Old Regularism. So here is Sister Beulah's poem:

Old Regular Baptist

We may Ask you to go to church;
We will not beg you in.
We believe you will follow
When Jesus forgives you for your sins.

We have no guitars in our church,
No piano or tambourine.
All we have are saints of God,
And our music is when they sing.

Our songs may be a little slow,
And some of us may cry.
We may stop and hug your neck and
Shake your hand as we pass by.

We may not be very educated.
Some of us may not read.

But our preachers can paint a picture
That a child can plainly see.

You won't see much make–up on
Our sister's face,
For she has a new look now:
She's cleaned . . . by His saving
grace.

If you wonder who I am,
Why this way I do feel,
I'm an Old Regular Baptist,
Who's been raised in these old hills.

Beulah Jones Patrick
Bypro, Kentucky[34]

Emergence of Old Regularism

When Baptists first found their way into Kentucky at
the close of America's colonial period, they brought with them
a name division that had developed during the Great Awakening, "Regular Baptists" and "Separate Baptists."[35] This Great
Awakening, an extended revival that swept up and down
America's eastern seaboard (from Georgia to New England)
in the years immediately prior to the American Revolution,
split Presbyterians, Congregationalists, and Baptists into two
camps each, those supporting the impassioned movement
and those rejecting it. In the case of the Baptists, "Separates"
were those "enthusiasts" who fell in behind the revival, a
heavily emotional, field-preaching-oriented, predominantly
noneducated-ministry-led religious, social, and political phenomenon. "Regulars," on the other hand, were those holding
to the more established Baptist tradition, institutionalized as
that tradition had become through growth of a few large
fellowships (such as the Boston and Philadelphia congregations), by emergence of associations (the Philadelphia Association, 1707), and by creedal unification under the Philadelphia Confession (1742).[36]

Baptist ministers who moved into the western frontier,

A United Baptist Church at Caney, Kentucky.

therefore, called themselves Regulars or Separates and established fellowships bearing these names.[37] However, at the turn of the century, as the "Second Great Awakening" swept the settled areas of Kentucky and southwestern Virginia, there was a rapid increase in Baptists and a general movement toward denominational unification.[38]

Following a trend that in 1787 began in Virginia, Kentucky Separate and Regular Baptists gradually progressed toward appelative and doctrinal harmony under the name "United Baptists."[39] The most significant of such moves, relative to the subject of this volume, was accomplished in 1801 and involved the Elkhorn Association (Regulars) and the South Kentucky Association (Separates). The "Terms of General Union," drawn as a prerequisite to this pact, represented a compromise between the more detailed and explicit doctrines of the

Regulars (tied as they had been to the Philadelphia Confession) and the creedal sparsity of the Separates (who had held solely to the Bible, distrusting all man-formulated doctrinal codes). The result was a set of theological and governmental canons that set aside as unresolved the issue of greatest division, the question of universal versus limited atonement. On this point some Separates, free from strong creedal confinements, had moved from their more staunchly Calvinistic position to an Arminian general atonement doctrine.[40]

To avoid conflict over this particular disparity in dogma, the Elkhorn and South Kentucky associations adopted article nine below, leaving unresolved a dispute that would plague these "United" Baptists as they slowly evolved toward what was to become Old Regularism:

Terms of Union between the Elkhorn and
South Kentucky, or Separate Associations

We, the committees of Elkhorn And South Kentucky Associations, do agree to unite on the following plan:

1st. That the Scriptures of the Old and New Testament are the infallible word of God, and the only rule of faith and practice.

2d. That there is one only true God, and in the Godhead or divine essence, there are Father, Son and Holy Ghost.

3d. That by nature we are fallen and depraved creatures.

4th. That salvation, regeneration, sanctification and justification are by the life, death, resurrection and ascension of Jesus Christ.

5th. That the saints will finally persevere through grace to glory.

6th. That believers' baptism by immersion is necessary to receiving the Lord's supper.

7th. That the salvation of the righteous and punishment of the wicked will be eternal.

8th. That it is our duty to be tender and affectionate with each other, and study the happiness of the children of God in general; to be engaged singly to promote the honor of God.

9th. And that the preaching Christ tasted death for every man, shall be no bar to communion.

10th. And that each may keep up their associational and church government as to them may seem best.

11th. That a free correspondence and communion be kept up between the churches thus united.[41]

The same year this "uniting" was accomplished, there was an amicable division of the South Kentucky Association, creating the North District Association and the South District Association. Then, twelve years later (1813), the North District "gave off" the Burning Spring Association, a Baptist alliance which is now Primitive, but which at its inception was United.[42]

It was 1825 before the first association now existing as Old Regular was formed. That year the Burning Spring Association "armed" the New Salem Association, eight Baptist fellowships in Pike, Floyd, Perry, and Harlan counties, Kentucky, that were to become the mother churches of Old Regularism. It was agreed, recorded the 1824 Burning Spring *Minutes*, "that a line be drawn as follows for a division of this Association, beginning at the mouth of Rockhouse Fork of the Kentucky River, thence to Prestonburg, thence to the mouth of Bull Creek on the Tug Fork of Sandy, and also dismiss all the churches above this line to become a new Association."[43]

Of the original fellowships in the New Salem (United) Baptist Association, only New Salem of Harold, Kentucky, and Stone Coal of Garrett, Kentucky, remain among the fifty-eight churches affiliated with the present New Salem Old Regular Association, the remaining six having, in the 163-year interim, fallen to the Primitive Baptist ranks or into other Old Regular clusters.

During those early years New Salem remained in correspondence with Burning Spring (later to become a Primitive association), and established additional correspondence with Washington District (also to become Primitive), Paint Union (destined to remain United), and Red Bird (apparently no longer extant).[44] But for twenty-nine years New Salem appeared satisfied with the name "United Baptists," holding to that term until 1854, when these churches returned "Regular" to their formal title — the New Salem Association of Regular United Baptists.[45] A year later the association empha-

Stone Coal Church today, Garrett, Kentucky.

sized this change by formally requesting that annual letters from their member fellowships bear the name "Regular United Baptists."[46]

Neither the New Salem minutes of 1853, 1854, or 1855 provide any explanation for this renaming, and the only circumstances recorded in these documents that conceivably could have influenced this change were (1) that the association ordered (in 1853) their constitution be printed and annexed to the minutes and (2) that two new fellowships, both from Russell County, Virginia, were added to the association's roster in 1854.[47] The writing of a constitution could have formalized a name that had already crept into common usage, or the addition of two fellowships from Virginia might have precipitated a reexamination of doctrine, which in turn generated the name change. In these years, perhaps still under the influence of the Separates with whom the Regulars had united, the New Salem Association did not publish articles of faith in their minutes, thus failing to provide a picture of the year by year evolvement of doctrine.

Another justification for the name change, however, seems plausible. Throughout the 1820s and the 1830s the unity that Spencer said came to Kentucky Baptists in 1801 was ravaged first by the antimission movement and then by the restoration movement, represented by Campbellism, both opposed not only to missionary organizations, but also to all benevolent or secret societies and Sabbath schools. Then there were oppositions to the doctrine of general atonement voiced by the more Calvinist elements of the antimission movement and attacks upon the Philadelphia Confession leveled by those Campbellites who saw every extragospel creed or practice as questionable. During this period a number of individual churches and associations divided to opposite sides of these issues, and a period of general instability reigned within the Kentucky Baptist community.[48]

There is no record of any antimission or Campbellite precipitated debates in the New Salem minutes of 1853 to 1855, but in 1856 a resolution was passed calling for the rejection of all "Missionary baptisms" and making the rule retroactive to 1846.[49] This action suggests a strong influence from the antimission movement and seems to show the New Salem fellowships moving back to the Calvinistic base of the Philadelphia Confession. Much later, 1876, the annual session voted through a resolution declaring "non-fellowship with all modern institutions such as Missionary Baptists, Bible and Tract societies, Sunday School Union, or Masonry, and all societies set on foot by men or devils outside the Word of God," thus demonstrating support for causes that have been supported by both the antimissionary and Campbellite movements.[50]

During the debates that resulted from these resolutions the New Salem fellowships may not have been seeking to support antimissionism and Campbellism so much as they were attempting to find their way back to the creedal foundation

Regulars had received from the Philadelphia Confessions, a stablizing influence the Separates had not shared. Thus, such an inclination could have motivated New Salem's 1854 action to reassert their connection with Regularism. "Old Regularism," however, was still not a part of their appellative picture.

The Rufus Perrigan work, *History of Regular Baptist and Their Ancestors and Accessors*, an eclectic compilation of sketchy, often anecdotal, and frequently undocumented accounts of the origins of Old Regularism, credits 1870 as being the year in which the New Salem Association became "Old Regular."[51] The actual New Salem minutes of that year, however, don't support that claim. Indeed, 1870 may have been a year in which the proponents of Calvinism gained a temporary but significant control over this mother association of Old Regularism, for the delegates to that year's annual meeting adopted the following resolution: "Ordered that all the churches that belong to the New Salem Association use the title, 'Regular Primitive Baptist' in all letters written from or to any other association hereafter." Furthermore, the minutes of that session were titled "Minutes of the New Salem Association of the Primitive Baptist or Primitive Regular Baptist."[52]

This name change, though lasting only one year, is important, because "Primitive Regular" or "Regular Primitive" became titles applied to a number of Baptist associations that during the last thirty years of the nineteenth century slipped firmly into the more traditionally Calvinist "Particular Baptist" camp (shortly to be defined), notably the Mates Creek Regular Primitive Baptist Association, which armed off New Salem Association in 1849. Mates Creek, after a split that formed Sardis Association (now Old Regular), adopted the limited atonement–particular election doctrine represented by their current fifth article of faith.[53] That article reads, "We believe the atonement made by Christ was full and complete and *exclusively for the elect*, or heirs of promise."[54]

Although the New Salem annual session delegates of 1871 reversed the name change mentioned above, placing the asso-

A Regular Primitive Church in Canada, Kentucky.

ciation back under the "Regular Baptist" banner, it appears that 1870 not only was not the official birth of "Old Regularism"— at least as the term is understood today — but was a year in which the New Salem fellowships slipped dangerously close to a fixed affiliation with the Primitive Baptist subdenomination.[55]

This mother association now continued to call herself "Regular Baptist" until 1892, when the title "Old Regular Baptist" was first employed in minutes of the yearly meetings.[56] Even today the "Old" part of this title is not always used in this subdenomination, as illustrated by the Bent Branch Regular Baptist Church, Meta, Kentucky, a fellowship affiliated with Sardis Association. Instead, members of the faith speak of themselves as "Regulars" or "Old Regulars," the "Old" simply having grown to signify a particular level of traditionalism that separates them from the "Regulars" of North Carolina and Virginia whom they know to be different, a difference that will be examined shortly.

The 1892 emergence of the term "Old Regular," however, appears to have been tied to a theological distinction developing at that time between Regulars and Primitives. This distinction centered upon the atonement doctrines of the two groups.

Development of the Old Regular Doctrine of Atonement

Old Regular atonement doctrine, "election by grace," falls between the "particular election" of Primitive Baptists and the "universal" or "general" atonement theology of the more Arminian Free Will and Missionary Baptists. Particular election is held to mean that there is a "particular" body of individuals, known by God from the beginning of time, who were predestined to be the beneficiaries of Christ's atonement — "the elect." Universal atonement, on the other hand, suggests a propitiation for the sins of all men: one needs only to believe, demonstrate faith, and accept the unmerited grace.

Throughout the second half of the nineteenth century, New Salem fellowships apparently held much closer to a doctrine of limited atonement than to one of general atonement. Influenced no doubt by the surge of Calvinism that coincided with the early years of the association's existence and by the very precise language of the Philadelphia Confession's treatment of this doctrine, New Salem's annual sessions consistently accepted one article of faith that was very open to a "particular election" interpretation.[57] It read, "We believe in election *according to the foreknowledge of God*, the father, through sanctification of the Spirit unto obedience and the sprinkling of the blood of Jesus Christ."[58] This is precisely the language that was employed in the articles of faith of New Salem's mother association, Burning Spring; but Burning Spring, it will be remembered, eventually went Primitive.[59]

In 1891, however, the year before the New Salem Association first formally called itself "Old Regular," the session's delegates voted through a resolution that moved away from one particular direction characteristic of some Primitive Baptist doctrine, found especially in Old Regular country: "Resolved, that we, the New Salem Association, cannot endorse the sentiment teaching absolute predestination of all things, held and preached by some of our brethren, which declares God to be the author of sin, or that He influences men thereto."[60] This resolution is significant because it shows New Salem rejecting the theological path many Primitive congregations were following, the movement from particular election to a doctrine of absolute predestination.

Fearful, however, that this antipredestination position might be interpreted to mean the association was sliding toward some Arminian position of free will, the 1892 delegates modified the doctrine so that it would be clear that "Old Regulars"—as that year they called themselves—stood between two extremes: "Resolved, that we drop the nineteenth item of our last year's minutes and advise our churches to cleanse, or abstain from the doctrine that teaches that God is the author of sin, or that He influences men thereto, and the doctrine of Arminianism that claims the work of the creature [man] to be essential to eternal salvation."[61] Neither redemption nor damnation, therefore, were predestined ends; nevertheless, this didn't leave man in total control of his own salvation, able on his own and at any time to work his way into redemption or will his way there. According to this emerging Old Regular doctrine, man could not, as the Free Will Baptists were claiming, simply exercise autonomous power to choose salvation by opting to believe.[62] There are things that the unredeemed can and must do, argues Elder Bill Campbell, but the initial call and ultimate salvation come from God. According to Elder Campbell, when unredeemed man hears his call—a kind of awakening to a consciousness of sin—he must quickly respond and then begin a "travel" toward true repentance and salvation. "Works are required before salvation is applied," says Campbell. "Not works of nature such as doing good to others or paying tithes, but works described in John 6: 28–29. Taking heed to the call to repentence and belief in God are in themselves works."[63]

Old Regulars have not always been in agreement — and perhaps they are not so even today — relative to exactly when "salvation" comes, whether it is acquired immediately upon receiving the "call" (the "Light of Christ" doctrine) or whether it becomes a fact only after the sinner has taken certain responsive actions (the "Travel from Nature to Grace" doctrine). Elder Campbell expounds the latter position, and this apparently is the doctrine held by a majority of the mainline Old Regulars, (preachers in such associations as New Salem, Union, Sardis, Old Friendship, Philadelphia, Indian Bottom, and Northern New Salem). Nevertheless this division in doctrine has caused considerable argument over the years and has been the basis for one split, the Bold Camp controversy, to be examined in chapter 6.

By 1905, however, the officially proclaimed Old Regular doctrine of atonement — the same one as exists today in most of the published articles of faith — had found full expression in a combination of four theological pronouncements.

> We believe in the doctrine of election by grace, for by grace ye are saved through faith.
> We believe in the doctrine of original sin, and of man's inability to recover himself from the fallen state he is in by nature; therefore the Savior is needed for our redemption.
> We believe that sinners are called to repentance and belief in the gospel and regeneration of the same, and sealed with the Holy Spirit of promise, and none such shall fall away and be lost.
> None of the above Articles shall be so considered as to hold with particular election and reprobation so as to make God partial, directly or indirectly; nor to injure any of the children of men. . . . [64]

It is my understanding that in mainline Old Regular thought these four articles may be translated into the following statements. Unredeemed man is in a state of original sin from which he cannot escape solely by an act of his own volition: he must heed his call from God, a summons to redemption which comes to *all* men. This call "to repentance and belief" constitutes an "election by grace," since a sinful man cannot possibly merit, initiate, or institute his own salvation. Once aware of his sinfulness, however, man must "work" his way to salvation through the aforementioned repentance and belief. Christ's atonement, therefore, was for those who hear and respond to their personal calls, and no man is automatically excluded from this process by some preordained election. Once truly redeemed, however, man cannot "fall away" from this salvation. Thus what gives the appearance of backsliding is merely evidence of having never been "saved" in the first instance.

This atonement doctrine appears to represent a sharp movement away from the far more particular-election language of the Philadelphia Confession: " . . . some men and angels are predestined, or fore-ordained to eternal life. . . . "[65] Nevertheless, there seems to be no mistaking the meaning of the final article: "None of the above . . . shall be so considered as to hold with particular election . . . so as to make God partial. . . . " And this statement is included in the articles of faith of eight of the Old Regular associations I have identified.[66]

Indeed, in 1912 the New Salem fellowships indirectly took note of their disagreement with the Philadelphia Confession and officially proclaimed their doctrine to be in line with a more general atonement theology. I say "indirectly" because while the following resolution mentions the London Confession, this document was the model for the Philadelphia Confession, particularly in reference to the election principle.

> We, as advisory council, say to all our churches, we do not hold to nor endorse all the Articles of Faith put forth and known as the London Confession of Faith, nor do we understand that it was ever accepted as the true doctrine and faith of the great Baptist family of Europe and America. It was not put forth by the Regular Baptists but by the Particular Baptists of Great Britton or England.

We never have agreed in full with the Particular Baptists
of England on the one hand and the General Baptists on the
other and have never at any time been in fellowship or identified with either of them. But have always been Regular
Baptists and opposed to the fatalism of the Particular Baptists and the Arminianism of the General Baptists. And are
now and always have been standing on the confession of
Faith put forth by Christ and the Apostles (the Old and New
Testament scriptures) and are the same church and hold to
the same Faith that Christ and the Apostles set up and put
forth in the beginning of the Gospel dispensation.[67]

Although this statement was not entirely correct in its depic-
tion of Regular Baptist doctrinal origins, it did clearly separate
Old Regulars from the Primitives on one end of the atonement
theology spectrum and from the Free Will and Missionary Baptists on the other. After this pronouncement there would be no
doubt in the minds of Old Regulars that they were different
from these other two Baptist subdenominations.

Old Regulars vs. Regulars

This discussion of Old Regular atonement doctrine, however, has not explained the differences that have emerged between Old Regular Baptists and other Baptist associations in
Appalachia and elsewhere that just call themselves "Regular"; and here I am not referring to the Bent Branch example
I mentioned earlier. Instead I am thinking of a cluster of Baptist fellowships in northwest North Carolina, southwest Virginia, and isolated spots in Pennsylvania and Maryland. The
two associations which I will use as my examples are the
Original Mountain Union Association of Regular Baptists
and the Little River Regular Baptist Association. Mountain
Union contains eleven churches drawing memberships from
Ashe and Alleghany counties, North Carolina; Smyth and
Grayson counties, Virginia; and from Pennsylvania and Maryland. The Little River Association contains only six fellow-

ships, one in Darlington, Maryland, and the remainder in Alleghany County, North Carolina.[68]

In their articles of faith, these two associations are almost exactly like the Old Regulars. Compare, for instance, the articles given here with those of the New Salem Association that have already been examined:

> We believe in the doctrine of election by grace.
> We believe in the doctrine of original sin and in man's impotency to recover himself from the fallen state he is in by nature, by his own free will and ability.
> We believe that sinners are called, converted, regenerated, [and] sanctified by the Holy Spirit and all who are thus regenerated and born again by the Spirit of God shall never fall finally away.[69]

These statements are from the Little River Regular Baptist Association's Articles of Faith, and the comparable ones held by the Original Mountain Union Association are essentially the same in wording.[70] They vary from the New Salem articles only in that they don't contain that final clause against particular election, but neither do a number of the creedal documents of the other Old Regular groups. How then are Regulars and Old Regulars sharply different from each other?

There may be no major doctrinal variances between Old Regulars and their cousins the Regulars, but there are wide disparities between the two in subdoctrinal areas and in worship practices. The Sunday school question makes a good beginning example.

Old Regulars (including all of the associations listed earlier) have never altered their nineteenth century position on Sunday schools.[71] As suggested earlier, like the Primitives, Old Regulars view such institutions as being extragospel and dangerous intrusions upon God's prerogative to call. The Mountain Union and Little River Regular associations, however, encourage the establishment of "Sabbath Schools":

> We believe that a Sabbath School is the foundation for a revival meeting that will lead to the upbuilding of the Association, and . . . having Sunday Schools in our different

churches is one way of letting our light shine to the children, and will lead them to the altar of repentance.[72]

We believe that Sabbath Schools are a great help to our children; for the Bible says in Proverbs 23:6, "Train up a child in the way he should go and when he is old, he will not depart from it."[73]

Another factor clearly characterizing Old Regular fellowships is that adamancy in preserving their lined-singing and no-musical-instruments policies. Past actions of the New Salem Association have clearly demonstrated a willingness to exclude fellowships practicing "note-book singing," and none of the Old Regular associations I have mentioned allow any musical instruments in their services.[74] In contrast, churches in the two Regular associations being discussed apparently use the lined method only at special moments (immediately prior to communion, for example), occasionally employ hymnals, and even at times permit some use of musical instruments (generally for midweek or Sunday night "sings").[75]

A third distinguishing characteristic of Old Regular churches is centered in their reluctance (even refusal) to interact with other Baptist subdenominations. While Regular elders of Ashe and Alleghany counties, North Carolina, frequently share pulpits with preachers of other Baptist affiliations, particularly for funerals, most Old Regular associations have adopted strict policies of nonfellowship with any church other than those belonging to Old Regular associations with which the respective group corresponds.[76] At the time of this writing, New Salem corresponds with Union, Sardis, Mud River, Old Friendship, Northern New Salem, Philadelphia, and the larger of the Indian Bottom associations (the J. W. Pratt side in the original split). On the other hand, New Salem no longer corresponds with Old Indian Bottom or Thornton Union, having severed those relationships in 1961 and 1969 respectively.[77] This of course means that if a New Salem elder were to "share the stand" with either a Thornton Union elder or an Old Indian Bottom elder, the New Salem preacher would most likely be removed from that association's roster of ordained ministers. The Thornton Union fellowships, however, have demonstrated a more liberal position on this issue, even to the point of establishing correspondence with — and thus sharing pulpits with — the Mt. Zion United Baptist Association.[78] And certain churches in the newly reorganized Original Mountain Liberty Association fellowship share with congregations of the Eastern District Primitive Baptist Association.[79] Still these last two examples are not typical for Old Regular fellowships, for whom the norm is a more closed policy of fraternization.

A final distinguishing characteristic of Old Regularism that must be mentioned is that great variety of traditional codes governing member life styles, worship practices, and church governance — codes that have remained largely unchanged since the emergence of Old Regularism in the 1800s. Perhaps the best way to illustrate this characteristic is to quote a number of representative resolutions passed by various associations over the last 145 years, resolutions still, for the most part, in force in all of the more traditional Old Regular fellowships:

1843 — *New Salem Association*

Query from Stone Coal Church: Is it right to receive a woman who has been married and parted from her husband and has obtained a divorce afterwards and married another man after getting divorced?
Answer: We advise the church not to receive any such person.
Query from Elkhorn Church: Is it right to receive a man that has twice married and both the women living?
Answer: We advise the church to have no fellowship with any person in violation of the laws of both God and man.[80]

1890 — *New Salem Association*

Resolved, we amend the 11th Article of Faith to read as follows, to wit: We believe that the Lord's supper and feet washing is an ordinance of the Lord's and is to be observed by his followers until His second coming.[81]

1927 — *Union Association*

We advise all the churches in the Union Association to exclude all [female] members that have bobbed hair who will not agree to let their hair grow, and we further advise not to receive any member with bobbed hair unless such member agrees to let her hair grow.[82]

1940 — *New Salem Association*

Query from Little Dove Church: Would it be out of order for our Brethren to preach with preachers of other sects which are not in our faith and order, when called in funerals?

Answer: We, as an Advisory Council, hereby say to all our Brethren to not preach with those of any other sect or order different from ours and those who are not in full fellowship with us and of our same faith and order, in any way, in funerals nor on any other occasion, for it is our opinion to do so, would be involving ourselves in their disorder and bidding them God speed and being partakers of their evil deeds.[83]

1948 — *Union Association*

In answer to the query from Home Creek, We, as Advisory Council say, "That no Sister has any right to officiate in any official capacity of the church."[84]

1964 — *Sardis Association*

By motion and second, it is ordered that we advise our Ministers of our Association not to marry people into adultery, where either man or woman has a living wife or husband [in other words divorced but living].[85]

1986 — *Sardis Association*

Query: Does the Sardis Association believe in Sisters wearing pants, slacks or shorts?

Answer: We believe the Sardis Association should advise the Churches to advise their members — Brethren and Sisters — to dress soberly and modestly and to conduct themselves in a manner that becometh a Child of God. We believe that each Child of God will adorn themselves in a manner that they can easily be identified from the World. We feel the Bible, the infallible Word of God, sets forth and the Spirit will teach us how we should dress and conduct ourselves [reprinting from 1975 minutes].[86]

Old Regular policy relative to this question of female attire has experienced some change over the years, softening toward a more liberal position. As evidenced by the Sardis response above, associations have been forced to adopt policy language that is somewhat equivocal, and in one fairly recent situation (Union Association annual session, 1979) a stiff dress code was voted down, allowing the individual churches to set their own standards.[87]

Nevertheless, as has already been suggested, Old Regulars generally hold tightly to their old ways, viewing almost all changes in doctrine, worship practice, or codes of behavior as unwarranted. This stubborn adherence to the modes of the past has preserved their distinctiveness and indeed made them "a peculiar people."

2. "Brethren, We Have Met to Worship"[1]

Each Old Regular Baptist fellowship meets only one weekend a month, with an abbreviated worship service and a business session taking place on Saturday (usually in the morning) and a full worship service transpiring on Sunday. The precise weekend to be used — first, second, third, or fourth of the month — is established in the annual association meetings and usually doesn't change from year to year, unless a time conflict develops between two fellowships in close proximity to each other.

Most Old Regular associations hold to the tradition of using Saturday, rather than Sunday, as the day by which to make these counts. Thus in the Union Association the Ash Camp congregation, for example, meets the third Saturday and following Sunday of each month. This method of numbering the weekends means that if the first day of a month were to be a Sunday, then it would be considered as the fourth or fifth Sunday of the previous month. Because fifth Sundays are irregular events, they become days on which no services are held anywhere in the association, unless there is to be a special gathering, perhaps as a memorial meeting or some other worship or business activity.

In frontier days the once-a-month meetings were about as much churchgoing as a Cumberland mountain man and his family could manage, since problems associated with travel via horse-drawn or oxen-drawn wagons, over rugged terrain, turned pilgrimages to and from these events into three- or four-day efforts. One consequence of all this was that members of different Old Regular fellowships seldom saw each other except at union meetings (to be discussed later) or during the annual sessions of the association. Today all of that is changed, and the more faithful Old Regulars go to meetings of churches within their own or corresponding associations whenever their particular fellowships don't gather. As we will see, this practice makes visitors a very important dynamic in Old Regular services. A typical fellowship will have fewer than one hundred actual members, with several congregations numbering less than twenty.[2] But special services (communion-footwashings, memorial meetings, and union meetings) may attract crowds of two hundred to four hundred worshipers, particularly during spring or summer months. Meetinghouses must be large enough to accommodate crowds several times the size of the formal membership, and often when a church plans expansions or improvements appeals are made to nearby fellowships for financial help, since individuals from these fellowships frequently visit this church. In the world of Old Regularism one is a member of a particular church, but there are factors that often spread one's loyalties and involvements to perhaps a half-dozen or more fellowships and meetinghouses.

On meeting mornings visitors and members may start arriving at the church as early as 8:00, even though there will be another hour and a half before anything approaching a formal service begins. Many worshipers seem to enjoy these prompt arrivals simply because they give time for fellowshipping before the singing starts. Thus is produced a period of warm interchanges between church members who perhaps have not seen each other for a month and between church members and visitors who may not have seen each other for a year or more.

This eight o'clock hour, however, is far from being a time at which the entire congregation gathers. In fact, people will continue to enter the church until well into the formal service (10:00, 10:15, even 10:30 or later), with almost every new arrival making a slow circle of the full sanctuary for fellowship handshaking or embracing.

This is one of the warmest of Old Regular rituals, the initial entrances during which members and visitors make their rounds, greeting male and female friends and strangers alike, shaking hands, hugging, perhaps in silence, perhaps with verbal expressions of cordiality and fervor, perhaps even in tears as emotions are immediately triggered by the atmospherics of these highly impassioned gatherings. Elderly worshipers especially are prone to revel in these ceremonies, viewing each meeting as possibly the last at which they will see some of their friends. Singing may have started; preaching may have even begun; still the new arrivals wander through all sections of the church (including the stand area), making the warm verbal and tactile contacts so vital to the spirit of an Old Regular service. So rich with emotions are some of these opening scenes that I have seen Old Regular matrons begin crying and shouting very shortly after their initial entrances.

But the formal procedures of the service seem to get started rather slowly, never exhibiting a sense of rush. When I first started visiting Old Regular churches, I was somewhat shocked by the apparent lack of any structured format for worship, and particularly by what seemed to be no precise beginning moment. The service just appeared to slide slowly into order. It was as if these warm-hearted, loving, expectant people simply gathered for something to happen, not knowing exactly what this happening would be. Then this something would gradually take place, but by no preset pattern that I could see.

I eventually discovered that there was a form, subtle though it was, and that part of the Old Regular method — and charm — was the minimization of structure in worship, as if to suggest that anything planned by man is not directed by God, much the same rationale that later we will see applied to preaching. But this unplanned-happening analogy definitely does apply to these opening moments of an Old Regular Sunday service. There are the slow and nonregimented arrivals, the casual entrances and rounds of handshaking, the general fellowshipping that has no precise cutoff point, and then eventually the singing—to the uninitiated seeming to break out spontaneously, having no appearance of being directed.

By around 9:30 a sufficient number of worshipers will have arrived to warrant beginning this singing; so, without any announcement and without anyone assuming a directorial position at the stand, the lining of a hymn will begin, or one elder may just start singing by himself. However, so low-key will be this initial effort at structuring a service that a person sitting in the visitors' section of the church may not be able to discern who is doing this lining or singing. The sound will have arisen from an area immediately behind the stand, but because the liner will be sitting, view of him may be blocked. The voice will belong to one of the elders who are officiating that morning, perhaps the fellowship's moderator, but not necessarily so. My point here is that no one will have stood and announced the beginning of the service, and no one will have assumed focus as the director of events. Singing will simply start, and each individual worshiper will follow this lead only as he or she feels so inclined. Indeed, at this point in the service perhaps only a third of the congregation will be ready to sing, the rest of the gathering still being occupied with entrance fellowshipping.

Such an undertoned beginning often results in several hymns being sung before a majority of the congregation becomes settled into this part of the worship. Keep in mind that individuals may still be moving about the sanctuary, completing their entrance rounds of embracing and handshaking, and a general casualness in form will still be prevalent among all the worshipers.

Thirty or forty minutes of singing will transpire before the service moves into another phase. During this time elders behind the stand will take turns with the lining. All this singing occurs under the loose direction of the fellowship's moderator, one elder who has been elected by this fellowship to lead the church during both worship services and business meetings.

As the dynamics of this part of the morning's worship become more centrally focused, the singing may shift into a highly spirited and even emotional tone, setting off congregational shouting and praising, especially among the women. I witnessed such an occurrence during a visit with the Bull Creek Church in Maxie, Virginia. The meetinghouse was packed, probably with as many as four hundred people, drawn by the expectations that often permeate an Old Regular memorial meeting. A strong tone of congregational exuberance had been established early in the singing, with the ultimate result that when one elder began lining "The Old Ship of Zion," a favorite with many Old Regular fellowships, two women immediately began to shout, a high pitched, elongated holler that reverberated throughout the church and engendered reciprocal responses from several other female worshipers.[3] The shouting began during the fellowship's rendition of the first verse and continued through all of the song, peaking during the fourth stanza. By then many worshipers had left their pews and were wandering about the sanctuary, tearfully embracing all their brothers and sisters. It was the type of crowd reaction one often sees near the close of an Old Regular service, but which is somewhat infrequent this early in a morning's events. The old hymn in question goes as follows:

> I was standing on the banks of the river,
> Looking out over life's troubled sea.
> I saw an old ship that was sailing.
> Is that the Old Ship of Zion I see?
>
> Its hull was all bent and battered,
> By the storms of life I could see.
> The waves were rough but that old ship kept sailing.
> It's the Old Ship of Zion I see.
>
> At the stern of the ship is the Captain.
> I can hear as He calls out my name;
> Get on board, the old ship is a leaving,
> It will never pass this way again.

As I step on board, I'll be leaving
All my sorrows and heartaches behind.
I'll be safe with Jesus, the Captain,
Sailing out on the Ship of Zion.[4]

The Preaching Service

Unlike what would be expected in most mainline religious services, a Sunday morning in an Old Regular church will expose a listener to the exhortations of three or more preachers. Traditionally a meeting will involve a minimum of three sermons, but it is not unusual for a morning of worship to involve four or five speakers. In addition, if the meeting includes a communion-footwashing service — an add-on affair conducted after the regular meeting is concluded — there may be as many as seven sermons before the day is over.

As has already been indicated, in the Old Regular faith ministers are identified as "elders," and none of them are seminary trained. As is the case with other subdenominations of Baptists, ordination is handled at the local church level, with these fellowships requiring little of their ordination candidates other than a demonstrated "call," a righteous life style, a caring temperament, a demonstrable skill in preaching, and an adherence to the "bishop" requirements delineated in I Timothy 3:2–7:

> [He] must be blameless, the husband of one wife, vigilant, sober, of good behaviour, given to hospitality, apt to teach;
> Not given to wine, no striker, not greedy of filthy lucre; but patient, not a brawler, not covetous;
> One that ruleth well his own house, having his children in subjection with all gravity;
> (For if a man know not how to rule his own house, how shall he take care of the church of God?)
> Not a novice, lest being lifted up with pride he fall into the condemnation of the devil.
> Moreover he must have a good report of them which are without; lest he fall into reproach and the snare of the devil.

All of these factors, however, are considered to be embodied in that concept of "call," since it is generally agreed that "he whom God calls, He also equips," meaning conversely that if the life style, temperament, and skill are not there, then the call is specious.

The I Timothy rule that presents Old Regularism with perhaps the most trouble is the one concerning being "the husband of one wife." This is generally interpreted to mean that divorced and remarried men ("double married") may not become elders, even when the divorce in question was obtained on the grounds of adultery. Usually such a man will be required to wait until his first wife dies — if she goes prior to him — before he can be ordained.

To reduce the likelihood of an error or false claim (concerning a call) culminating in an unwise ordination, local churches "license" brothers who believe themselves to have been divinely summoned to preach, allowing them to test their calls by preaching not only to home fellowships but also to any church in the association. Thornton Union identifies these men in their association as "libertized ministers," meaning that they are at the liberty to preach when invited to do so by a local church.[5] Sardis Association calls them "liberated brethren."[6] In some cases they are apparently referred to as "licensed preachers"; however, they should not be compared to "licensed preachers" in the Methodist faith, for they have gone through no course of study and have been examined by no ecclesiastical body other than the membership of their local fellowship. The emphasis is upon that divine "call to preach."

There is no set length of time that a candidate for ordination will stay in this "licensed" stage. Elder Atlas Hall tells of an Old Regular brother who preached for fifty years and was never ordained.[7] Such matters are controlled by the respective local churches, or rather by the male members of these churches, who will want to be certain of a call's legitimacy. Thus the fellowship will probably wait at least a year, carefully watching the development of a candidate's preaching skills. If this licensed preacher fails to make sufficient progress as an exhorter, in both style and sermon substance, then the fellowship is likely to interpret his ineptness as a sign that the "call" was not a true one.[8]

When I visited the Lebanon Church on July 27, 1986, I heard the pulpit efforts of Danny O'Quinn, a twenty-six-year-old licensed preacher from the Caney Fork fellowship of Coeburn, Virginia. During the break between the main service and the communion-footwashing service, I interviewed O'Quinn concerning the role he had been playing since his licensing eight months earlier. He reported that most of the fellowships wanted to hear the "new brothers" and that these men get called by the local moderators more than is average for established elders.

I recorded in my notes on O'Quinn's sermon that he had already learned the traditional Old Regular oral style and was quickly mastering the impromptu delivery to be described shortly. Only occasionally did he lose his concentration and thus his fluency, and there appeared to be every indication that he would eventually satisfy his fellowship about his preaching skills. Such was indeed the case, and in 1987 the Caney Fork church ordained Elder Danny O'Quinn.[9]

Once ordained, Danny O'Quinn and his fellow Old Regular elders receive no money for their preaching and other forms of service, not even through the "love offerings" so common within other small denominations of Baptists. Therefore they will work at their regular employments, perhaps in the many coal mines of the area, and they will spend a significant number of weekends each year traveling to Saturday and/or Sunday meetings of churches other than their own, making themselves available for preaching during regular services, or responding to "calls" for union and memorial meetings, services for which fellowships request specific exhorters, usually their favorite elders from other churches. Since some Old Regular fellowships have been established in the upper midwest and as far south as Florida, these calls to preach at special services occasionally involve lengthy interstate travel.

Summer months will be especially busy for many of these elders, since the services to which preachers are called are clustered during this period. For example, the Union Association minutes show the young elder Danny O'Quinn to have been called for thirteen union or memorial meetings to be held between June and October 1988.[10] In addition, during the same period O'Quinn may be called by fellowships in associations corresponding with Union. More established and better-known elders could find themselves summoned by twenty or thirty churches for spring and summer special services. Elder Frank O'Quinn, assistant moderator of Union Association at the time of this writing, has been requested for twenty-six 1988 union and memorial meetings, not counting those calls to fellowships in corresponding associations.[11] He may not be able to honor all of these requests, since for three Saturday or Sunday meeting times there are two calls each; however, in some instances an elder is able to meet both such calls by first preaching at a Saturday service and then traveling to a different church on Sunday. A popular and conscientious Old Regular elder will find himself running all over southwestern Virginia and eastern Kentucky during any given summer, with perhaps a trip or two into the upper Midwest or down into Florida — all at his own expense.

Old Regular ministers never prepare sermons, at least not in any traditional way. Instead they "take the stand" and deliver wholly improvised messages, believing that written or outlined sermons allow only men to speak, but that improvisation subjects speakers to the divine inspirations of the moment and allows God to speak. Thus if an elder performs poorly on any particular morning he will say that God was not with him or did not bless him. On the other hand, if he performs especially well, he will simply credit the Deity with having used him as an instrument.[12]

In addition to the improvised nature of these sermons, there is the equally difficult rhythmical delivery pattern that has become the hallmark of Appalachian preaching — a chanted, sung, or wailed vocal style, dominated by a pronounced ca-

Preaching at the Smith Family memorial, Canada, Kentucky.

dence and accompanied by an equally dynamic set of physical behaviors. Variations of the style to which I am referring
can be found in the pulpit performances of preachers in a
number of different Baptist subdenominations in Appalachia
(Primitive, United, Free Will, Union, Missionary, Regular,
Old Regular, and perhaps others), and the delivery mode
serves one important purpose in addition to the aesthetics involved: it permits these speakers to manage the exuberance
and speed of their sermons by providing a systematic breathing pattern, a functional way to regulate air intakes while
exhorting at delivery rates that may approach or exceed two
hundred words per minute. The fast-paced flow is broken into a series of linear segments that are chanted, sung, or wailed,
with each new line peceded by a quick inhalation.[13]
   Although there is an endless variety of individualized ver-
sions of this rhythmical style among Old Regular preachers,

the truly distinctive contribution that this subdenomination makes to this Appalachian sermonic mode is an elongated, upward-sliding wail that rises on a phrase like "Oh, God," peaks in power and emotion, and then cascades downward through a series of briefer and weaker miniwails, each lower in volume and pitch than the previous, until the speaker settles on a base line for several rhythmical moments before starting the pattern all over.

Accompanied by equally dynamic physical movements that may thrust the elder's body upward, forward, and then downward into a floor-touching genuflection or bow, followed or preceded by bounding leaps or strides, these wails become the absolute epitome of the exhorter's emotional exuberance. They are the ultimate expressions toward which the speaker's passions are always building, and they frequently engender reciprocal audience responses that are equally dynamic, particularly from Old Regular women — the high-pitched, arm-waving shouts and verbal exclamations, in rhythmical synchrony with, or as a counter measure to, the exhorter's eloquence.

One of my favorite Old Regular preachers, respecting his physical delivery, is Elder Jimmy W. Hall of Jenkins, Kentucky, at the time of this writing the moderator of the Hemp Hill fellowship in Hemp Hill, Kentucky. Hall is a relatively young elder, probably in his early to mid-forties; and, as was mentioned in my introduction, he has been one of the most ardent supporters of my Old Regular research. His enthusiasm for Old Regularism in general is always obvious, and he brings to his preaching an abundance of energy and an honest passion for his message.

When Hall reaches the peaks of his exuberance he falls into the traditional rhythmical pattern but adopts a more strongly punched cadence, closing many of his linear units of rhetoric with three quick, spasmodic gasps for air before rising into that elongated wail mentioned above. Immediately following many of these soaring lines, Hall will execute a rapid series of short jumps as he moves across the stand, shouting and slapping his hands against the front of his thighs as he does so. The effect is quite dramatic and does not in any sense become farcical. In fact, on two occasions I heard Elder Jimmy Hall preach he became the decided favorite with the congregations, enlisting audience responses just as dynamic as his exhortations.[14]

Old Regular preachers don't begin their sermons by immediately falling into these fast-paced, energetic, soaring styles. In fact, the first few moments of one of these sermons are apt to be marked by struggle, awkwardness, and general indecisiveness and absence of direction. The elder may even apologize one or more times for his lack of anything to say, ask his audience to pray for him, observe that he is doubtful that he will be able to "pull any message down from heaven," and suggest that any of the other elders present could do a better job than he.

During these beginning moments he may pace back and forth behind the stand, occasionally fumble with the Bible as if looking for some verse that will give him a hint of what to say, and decry the folly of his efforts to speak for God, being the imperfect man that he is. Meanwhile, brothers in close proximity to him may shout encouragements: "Go on, Brother. You'll find it. God will lead you."

Then shortly this elder will quicken his pace, drop his vocal style into a choppy and punchy cadence, adjust his breathing to the emerging rhythm, begin to elongate certain phrases, and perhaps move to his first wail. By that time he may have moved his right hand up to a spot just behind or below his right ear, have raised his left arm above his head, have closed his eyes, and have begun to rock forward slightly — all this preparatory for that forward-thrusting genuflect that is apt to accompany his first soaring cry. From this point on he may assume a transcendent demeanor, eyes still closed or partially so, appearing almost hypnotized by his own sounds. He may occasionally make contact with the other elders around him, perhaps calling them by their names, frequently shaking their hands; but to a large degree he becomes captivated by his own spell, engaged in a form of visual and audio dynamics that allows him to be largely oblivious to external distractions. Later he may report that he has little memory of exactly what he said, and as explanation of this loss of awareness he will credit God as having used him.[15]

For every Old Regular service there is a moderator in charge. As I mentioned earlier, this man is elected by the fellowship to play the role of presiding elder, both for regular worship services and for business meetings. Other officers of the fellowship will include the assistant moderator, the clerk, and the assistant clerk.

It is not required that the moderator actually have his membership with the church over which he presides. In fact, because of the one–meeting–weekend–a–month situation, an elder could serve as moderator of his home fellowship, while also moderating three other churches in the association. Such a responsibility, however, would become excessively burdensome, considering all the travel it could necessitate. Still there are elders who moderate two or three churches. The 1985 minutes of Sardis Association showed Elder Lloyd Sesco of Meta, Kentucky, to be moderating three fellowships and both Elder Wallace Muncy of Nolan, West Virginia, and Elder Willis Lowe of Turkey Creek, Kentucky, to be moderating two fellowships.[16]

According to Elder Atlas Hall, traditional interfellowship decorum requires that a formal request be sent to a church when one of its elders is being sought for the moderator position of some other church. Hall also observes that in such cases there is an understanding that "the home fellowship reserves the right to recall him [the elder] at their pleasure or for cause."[17]

One task to be performed by the moderator on meeting Sundays is to determine which available elders will do the preaching, a choice that usually is not made until the moderator takes the stand at the close of the singing. Even if the moderator were inclined to make this decision ahead of time, he would have difficulty doing so since he would not know which elders would be present. With the exception of two special annual services (union and memorial meetings) for which, as noted earlier, specific individuals are called to preach, the moderator must depend upon the home–based elders and those from other fellowships who just decide to visit. A fellowship may have ordained a half dozen or more men from their own number, so there usually is no shortage of preachers, at least not in the larger congregations. Occasionally in one of the smaller churches, and particularly in the smaller associations, a fellowship might find themselves in a situation in which the expected number of preachers cannot be mustered. I have been witness to such a situation, however, only on one occasion, when I visited the North Springs Church in Old Friendship Association.[18]

Some churches become known for their particularly spirited services, thus attracting to their services not only sizable numbers of visiting laypersons but also quite a few visiting elders, all of whom will find a place on the stand during the opening singing. Therefore, when the moderator looks around he may discover as many as a dozen preachers from which to choose; and on such occasions this act of selecting is fraught with interpersonal, social, and political sensitivities, so much so that the moderator may apologize profusely for not being able "to preach more of the brothers," and the chosen brothers will apologize for having been selected.

As mentioned earlier, the traditional number of morning sermons is three, but if the moderator feels he has an especially talented group of men from which to select, as suggested above, he may decide to use four or even five of them. Therefore, in addition to choosing the exhorters for the morning, the moderator must decide how to sequence them. It has been my observation that this second decision is a critical one, not only in the politics of the moment but in the overall dynamics of the service, since certain preaching talents appear to fit best at specific points in a morning's service.

The first preacher delivers the "introductory sermon," which appears to have two main objectives: to establish a properly focused congregation and to create the initial instance of high emotionalism. As has already been reported, throughout the song service individuals have been entering the church and then proceeding to move about the church shaking hands with all the other worshipers. The result will have been the creation of a warm but disordered environment, and thus this introductory speaker must gain attention, unify, and establish focus.

All of the speakers will employ that slow, low-keyed start I have already described, but there is some need for the introductory preacher to move into his fast-paced, rhythmical style more quickly than is typical, simply because his sermon will be the shortest of the morning, ten to twenty minutes; and in that time he must turn his audience into a unified body, concentrating their energies and their emotions.

One practice that helps in this task is the "sing down" and the sound dynamics thus produced. In the past this "sing down" was a technique employed to force a preacher to close a sermon that had grown too long, and the procedure is still occasionally followed.[19] Given the impromptu nature of Old Regular preaching, it is not uncommon for an elder to become so absorbed with his own sermon (he would call this "inspiration" or possession by "the Spirit") that he will lose track of time. Elder Raymond Smith told me of a morning when he preached for over two hours and thought he had been in the stand only thirty minutes.[20] On these occasions the respective preachers do need help in closing out their messages, and Old Regular preachers view the "sing down" in that light. Without such help, the "inspired" exhorter might go on and on, completely unaware of the passage of time.

This "sing down" practice takes on a somewhat different purpose when applied to the introductory sermon. Once this introductory preacher has reached a peak of exuberance and has had time, perhaps, to get some shouting started, another of the elders will begin lining a hymn, which the audience then follows. Now what will immediately happen is that there will be a competition in sound between the preaching, the singing, and the shouting. The exhorter will increase his volume against the singing; the singing will build against the preaching; and the shouters, further stimulated by the volume and intensity of everything else, will reach for a more forceful level of expression.

Eventually the preacher will begin to give way, easing down his exhortations, but not too quickly. If he moves out of the competition too soon the sound dynamics will not develop, for the other two expressions will have no counter force against which to struggle and grow. Thus one skill of the introductory preacher is to have a sense of timing, knowing when to surge against and when to yield. The younger, inexperienced, and as yet unskilled preacher will more frequently demonstrate his novice status at this point than at any other juncture in his sermon.[21]

By the time the liner progresses to the second or third couplet of his hymn all of the congregation will be standing, continuing to sing or shout, but also shaking hands or embracing, experiencing the first moments of complete crowd contagion. The preacher may have left the stand area, still holding to his exuberance in exhortation, but now moving out into the nonmembers' and visitors' section, occasionally finding one single individual toward whom to direct his sermonic passions.[22]

Some preachers actually call for the "sing down," in the sense that they say to the other elders in the stand area, "Brothers, get a song ready." On several occasions, however, I have had the feeling that this was being done simply because a preacher was having trouble getting a message started and didn't want to be held in the stand too long.

With the ending of this "sing down" hymn all three of the competing sounds subside, but the intensity of these expressions now is transferred to the first prayer of the morning, occasionally led by the same elder who preached the introductory sermon, but contributed to by everyone who wishes to be involved. In *Giving Glory to God in Appalachia* I described the "concert prayer" used by the Mount Paran Missionary Baptist fellowship in Watauga County, North Carolina, a joint congregational effort in which everyone prays his or her own prayer, but aloud and in an orchestrated synchrony with the whole.[23] The Old Regular version of this "concert prayer" is somewhat different, with the leader's voice dominating and the congregational voices acting as a support sound. This prayer follows the basic cadence and wailing pattern of a sermon, but the people's supplications usually stay low and muffled until the leader's voice begins to fall after one of those elongated wails. At this point the congregational voice rises as a counter measure, only to cascade downward as the elder's voice makes another upward surge. The voices of other elders in the stand tend to lead the congregational offering and some of the women contribute a sound that is not so much a prayer as it is an accompanying low cry. When executed well, this prayer becomes one of the most interesting of Old Regular expressions.

After all the drama that usually follows the introductory sermon, the second preacher has to start anew if he is to build any significant congregational passion; but often he will not even attempt such a feat, choosing instead to deliver a sermon that is more subdued in tone, as if acknowledging that the people's emotions need a momentary rest. It thus becomes the task of a third exhorter — or the third and fourth speakers in coordinated stages — to move the congregation toward that final emotional level that ideally climaxes the morning's worship, generating a closing round of shouting, singing, hand shaking, and embracing.

If a moderator really knows his preachers he will make choices that in essence orchestrate this entire pattern of events, placing the individual elder at a stage in the sequence at which he can best perform.[24] Then if the various parts of this plan work at their best, a closing mood will be created which allows the moderator to stand quietly at the pulpit — surrounded by diverse expressions of religious drama — and "open the doors of the church." But usually he will make no ringing appeal; generally he will not urge the unbaptized to come forward; and never will the emotions of the moment be intensified by endless verses of "Just As I Am" or "Almost Persuaded." Instead this typical Old Regular moderator will make his brief announcement and then just stand behind or beside the pulpit until all of the various emotional expressions have subsided, his low-key approach to evangelism in keeping with the subdenomination's strong belief that individuals should come to "redemption" without being improperly urged: "God calls; man does not." My readers, however, should keep in mind Elder Bill Campbell's views on this issue of "urging," that it is perfectly legitimate for an Old Regular elder to plea for nonmembers of the church to respond to their calls. Campbell, therefore, sees it as fitting and proper to do just this, as long as the preacher is not enticing someone into the fellowship who has not been truly redeemed.[25]

A Service at Bull Creek

As an example of much of what has been discussed above I now turn to a service I witnessed at Bull Creek Old Regular Baptist Church on June 14, 1987. Bull Creek has been one of my favorite Old Regular fellowships, and as a result this church has received three of my nosey visits. In *Giving Glory to God in Appalachia* I described the congregation's 1984 memorial meeting.[26] Indeed, the service I am about to treat was also a memorial meeting, but this time I will concentrate on the preaching and the congregational responses.

To locate Bull Creek Old Regular Baptist Church the traveler should take Highway 460 northwest out of Grundy, Virginia, and go approximately five miles before turning to the left onto Route 609. This narrow, two-lane road twists up a mountain valley along Bull Creek and in about another three miles leads past the church, a rust-red brick structure sitting on the right and identified by a small sign near the rear of the structure.

Bull Creek Church was organized in 1891 and at that time belonged to the Washington District Association, now Primitive Baptist.[27] In 1895 Bull Creek broke away from Washing-

Elder Bill Campbell converses with an Old Regular sister, Bull Creek Church. (Photo by Joel Poteat)

ton District over the doctrine of predestination, and in 1897 the fellowship joined the Union Association at a time when Old Regulars were defining their theology as distinct from more Calvinistic doctrines.[28]

One of the patriarchs of this fellowship during these formative years was Elder David Crockett Church, later moderator of the Union Association from 1939 to 1946. Church is important to the history of Old Regularism in Buchanan County, Virginia, and Pike County, Kentucky, having provided leadership in the "arming" of several fellowships in this region, and his bearded image hangs among the photographs of past leaders in a large number of Old Regular churches in several associations.[29]

The present unofficial patriarch of Bull Creek is Elder Fred M. Stiltner — eighty-one years old at the time of this

Author talking with Elder Fred Stiltner at Bull Creek. (Photo by Joel Poteat)

writing, still preaching, and very mentally alert. Stiltner loves to talk about Old Regularism, and two of his favorite topics are the reasons Bull Creek and other Old Regular fellowships broke from Primitive doctrine and his charge that Old Regulars spend far too much time fighting among themselves over insignificant matters.[30]

Elder Bill Campbell, whom I have already mentioned in several contexts, is the current moderator of Bull Creek, and has created an environment in that church that is very open to my visitations. Campbell is also, in my judgment, one of the most effective Old Regular preachers I have observed, employing a delivery style that is both dynamic and communicative.

At the beginning of the June 14, 1987, preaching service at Bull Creek, Elder Campbell announced that, in accordance with tradition in that fellowship, the women of the church had selected the called ministers for the year's memorial meeting. Every summer, before the Union Association's annual session, the female members of the fellowship determine the list of elders to be requested for Bull Creek's June memorial meeting, names that are then placed in the association's minutes as the official "call" for the event. For this 1987 service the women had chosen Elders Frank O'Quinn, Arnold Clevinger, Casby Conaway, Freeland Yates, Paul McClanahan, and Frank Newsome.[31] Conaway and Yates had appeared for the Saturday morning service, and Clevinger, O'Quinn, McClanahan, and Newsome were in attendance for the Sunday service. Campbell announced that all four of these elders would preach, with Clevinger introducing the service, followed by O'Quinn, McClanahan, and Newsome, in that order.

Before yielding the stand to Elder Clevinger for the introductory sermon, Campbell determined who would perform the ritual of reading the names of the church's deceased, a standard feature of an Old Regular annual inside-the-church memorial meeting. (I say "inside-the-church" in this instance because there are two other standard forms of memorial meetings which we will examine in the next chapter of this work.)

The young assistant clerk of Bull Creek was chosen to read the names, and he was immediately handed two lists, one of all deceased individuals (from the very beginning of the church) who had been formal members of the fellowship, and the second a list of people who had regularly attended Bull Creek's services without ever joining. Old Regulars don't declare either baptism or formal church membership to be essential to salvation, and they accept the possibility that an individual's call to redemption could be made and accepted in a private environment. Therefore, at memorial meetings some fellowships read the names of these nonmembers with the assumption that they, too, could have been "elected by grace."[32]

At the 1984 Bull Creek memorial meeting which I reported in *Giving Glory to God in Appalachia* Elder Campbell handled the reading of the names, and in the process he turned this part of the service into a very dynamic event, engendering impassioned audience responses when names of the more recently deceased were called. On this June 14, 1987, occasion, however, no such drama developed, and the calling of the names progressed under a somber but subdued congregational mood and demeanor, eliciting only a few muffled sobs. Outburts of joy and exuberant religiosity would come from this congregation that day, but later in the service.

When Campbell turned the stand over to the morning's preachers, the pattern that developed—with one exception that I will note—was very much in accord with the one I have already described. Elder Clevinger introduced the service and generated the initial round of impassioned fellowshipping, followed by the prayer and Elder O'Quinn's contribution to the preaching. However, Frank O'Quinn, one of the Union Association's most popular preachers, didn't play the prototypic second preacher role; but he delivered a highly spirited message, eliciting individual expressions of exhilaration, yet no general outburst of emotion. Essentially the same situation developed for Elder Paul McClanahan: there were spotty outbreaks of shouting from the women's side of the stand, but nothing of a general nature developed.

Then Elder Frank Newsome took the stand, and, as many Old Regular preachers are prone to do, he began what was to have been his part of the service by singing an old hymn. Newsome had not finished the first stanza of his song, however, before it all happened—one of those congregation-wide explosions of religious fervor that I have witnessed at the close of a number of Old Regular services.[33]

The outbreak of passion began with three ladies who all seemed to start shouting and praising at once, exciting the entire women's section of the stand area to similar responses—standing, waving arms, clapping hands, tearfully embracing, shouting, crying out personal testimonies, and just generally expressing their great joy.

At this point Elder McClanahan was suddenly back on his

feet, and as Newsome continued to sing McClanahan started shouting himself, jumping up and down as he did so. Now the explosion of emotions swept like a fireball down the right side of the church and brought that entire section of worshipers to their feet — clapping, shouting, crying, singing — crowd contagion in its most climactic form — surging, pulsating, pounding, defying all individual inclinations to remain passive.

Bill Campbell had now commanded the left side of the stand and was waving the remainder of the audience to their feet. In addition, he began his own preaching, in competition with the contributions of Newsome, McClanahan, and a portion of the congregation. It was obvious now that this would be the closing, that Newsome would not get a chance to preach, that this general outbreak of joyous celebration would eventually end the service.

But before the closing much more would occur. Several sisters had now begun to move among the congregation, on the stand and off, proclaiming their own joyous convictions, embracing others as they went, occasionally stopping to perform little jumps of religious ecstasy, always clapping their hands or waving their arms, hands thrust toward the ceiling, palms up, fingers spread, eyes cast high, but often with lids closed, faces flooded with expressions of rapture.

Campbell communicated above the myriad of dynamic happenings that he was "opening the church doors." No one rushed forward, but there were other movements everywhere: people milling about to shake hands or embrace; two or three women continuing their travels from one fellow worshiper to another, testifying and praising; Elder McClanahan literally stepping across the backs of pews in his efforts to reach pockets of exalting worhipers; one woman fanning another who had slumped back into her pew, still shouting, still waving her hands above her head; an elderly gentleman crying and softly voicing some exaltations, but as if speaking to his own private self; a younger woman simply covering her face and sobbing; a teenaged boy looking uncomfortably out a window, but apparently on the verge of tears himself.

The church had been packed with approximately 400 members and visitors — mostly visitors, since Bull Creek shows a membership of only 120 — and throughout all of this it had been very difficult to move about, unless you were sitting on the aisle.[34] And even those areas tended to become impassable due to the wanderings of the shouting, praising, and testifying women. This general congestion is what motivated McClanahan to stride across the backs of pews. In the general intensity of the moment he wanted to make contact with fellow exalters, and he did what was necessary to achieve that goal.

A person unaccustomed to the intense emotionalism of Old Regular services might have felt uncomfortable with this combination of closeness and ardent pathos. Even considering all of the footwashings I have attended — in Old Regular churches and elsewhere — this twenty or thirty minutes of high passion probably became the most exuberant expression of religious fervor I have ever witnessed. The event left me somewhat drained just from having observed the scene as an outsider, and I have no doubt that the real participants experienced a deep catharsis.

After all this action had subsided somewhat, Campbell again reminded the congregation that the church doors were open. Still no one came forward. That perhaps was not unusual. Alive as the Bull Creek fellowship has been, there still were only two baptisms performed by this church during the 1986–87 statistical year, and the previous year had brought only five.[35] Nevertheless, seven baptisms in two years is above the Union Association average, suggesting that reponses to the opened-church-door announcements are somewhat rare. During six years of visiting Old Regular churches I witnessed only three such responses, one at Stone Coal Church in Garrett, Kentucky, and two at Samaria Church in Wolfpit, Kentucky.[36]

This dearth in baptisms may be caused in part by the Old Regulars' traditionalism in life styles and worship practices, by their insistence upon a personal call and "travel from nature to grace," and by their cautiousness in evangelizing. Re-

Samaria Church members in prayer before a baptism in Russell Fork of the Big Sandy.

member the "God calls; man does not" principle. Indeed, some elders refuse to say anything during the "opened door" part of the service, fearing to interject themselves into a process they view as God controlled. So when a meeting is under the direction of one of these particular elders the emotional intensity of a service may rise as high as it did that morning at Bull Creek, but without the moderator taking advantage of that mood and urging the unredeemed to come forward. There will be no endless pleading, no special techniques employed to rouse the "sinners" from their pews, no hellfire-and-damnation threats, no "with all eyes closed" whispered or tearful supplications. "That," says Elder Raymond Smith, "is what the Free Willers do."[37]

On the other hand there are Old Regular elders who do believe in at least a prudent form of evangelism. Elder Bill Campbell falls into this camp, along with quite a number of the other Old Regular preachers I have heard. "We would never plead for unredeemed to come forward," says Campbell, "since our invitation to the opened church door is only

Baptism of Brenda Joyce Adkins, Russell Fork of the Big Sandy.

to those who feel they have repented and are then among the redeemed. . . . We believe only these are worthy of baptism." However, some evangelism, says Campbell, is not only proper but desirable: "We plead and urge and even beg sinners to take heed to the call and repent."[38] So that morning at Bull Creek Elder Campbell did do some urging during the "open door" call, though to no avail on that particular occasion.

Following the closing of the church doors, generally there are only three additional things that happen: (1) an extremely low-key collection of contributions for the support of the church, (2) the hearing of "appointments" from visiting elders, and (3) the final benediction.

Concerning the first of these acts, it must be noted that Old Regulars make no pleas for money. Collection plates are not passed, and there is no pressure placed upon individuals or families to make specific contributions. Tithing is simply not a practice in which Old Regulars believe. In fact, the only times I have heard money mentioned at the close of these services have been under circumstances in which fellowships were repairing church facilities or extending them in some way. What usually happens is that a clerk or assistant clerk will unobtrusively move to the stand and collect donations brought forward, all without any formal solicitation. Indeed, you have to go out of your way to make a contribution, in the sense that you must leave your pew, move to the stand, and place your money there to be collected.

The announcing of "appointments" is a procedure under which every visiting elder is allowed to call out the meeting times of his home fellowship and to give directions to his church. These directions often culminate in the "you can't miss it" statements I mentioned in chapter 1. Visiting deacons also occasionally make these announcements.

Benedictions are short, nonelaborate, and fairly traditional, involving a moderator-pronounced congregational blessing, usually with most of the other elders lifting their right arms and joining the pronouncement in some individualized way. The closing is always immediately followed by a general round of fellowshipping — handshaking and embracing, often accompanied by final outpourings of emotion.

Before closing this chapter I need to say something more specific about the messages in Old Regular preaching, and the "God calls; man does not" principle provides a bridge to such a purpose. In a number of instances I have employed the words "exhort," "exhortation," and "exhorter" in reference to the elders and their preaching, but in one sense these terms may be inappropriate. To exhort means to urge strongly, and I have already stated that some Old Regular preachers don't engage in such a strong form of evangelism. Can these particular sermons be considered "exhortative" if they do not "urge" listeners to conviction? I argue that they can, but in a subtle and indirect way.

It has been my observation that many Old Regular elders tend to preach "the joys of redemption." In such sermons emphasis is placed upon the present-life love, happiness, and peace that Old Regulars argue come from "an answered call," or it is placed upon the beauties and beatitudes of an eternal afterlife with God. There is plenty of emotionality in this genre of sermons, but the hard-hitting, hellfire-and-damnation appeals to fear that focus on the negatives of life seem to be largely avoided. In their place are the constant allusions to "love and peace," which mesh effectively with those warm, tactile fellowshipping practices I have previously described and with the Old Regulars' absolute insistence that no church business be conducted until it has been established that the members are in interpersonal harmony, a custom to be examined in chapter 4.

Perhaps because there have been so many bitter splits in this and other Baptist subdenominations, particularly in the Appalachians, there is within Old Regularism a constant emphasis upon "love" within the church community. "Beloved, our whole spiritual life is the product of love," declared Elder Jimmy Dye in his 1986 circular letter to the New Salem Association, "and not only our whole spirit lives, but love is the foundation of all our true churches and associations."[39]

Therefore, love, peace, joy, fellowship, all built upon the righteous life style that constitutes "a peculiar people, zealous of good works," are themes frequently found in Old Regular preaching. Consequently, the particular form of exhortation I have in mind is indirect, saying something like, "Here is the happiness we feel. It springs in part from the fact that we are a unified fellowship of believers. You may watch us, and if you trust our expressions of joy and our rationale for that joy, then you might keep your heart and mind open to the call we believe we have received and accepted."

It would be misleading, however, to suggest that Old Regular preaching never slips into the negative, that traditional hellfire-and-damnation rhetoric finds no place in these sermons. "Many of the preachers have gifts which differ a great deal," says Elder Campbell. "Some preach by showing the benefits of repentance, thus the beauties of heaven, the joys of righteousness, the absence of death and pain . . . ; while others preach by showing the consequences of failing to repent, i.e., hell fire, lack of peace and joy."[40] My observations, however, suggest that there is less of this latter message within Old Regular preaching than there is within the exhortative rhetoric of some other Baptists sects, such as the Missionary and Free Will Baptists.

Another Old Regular theme deserving mention is the subdenomination's emphasis upon personal humility. Accentuation of this value can certainly be seen in the openings of Old Regular sermons when elders disparage their own unworthiness to occupy the stand — unworthiness in both preaching skills and spiritual inspiration. But the principle is also present in the tendency of all Old Regulars to be very cautious about assumptions concerning their own righteousness or even their own salvation. Always there is a slight uncertainty in an Old Regular's claim to redemption. Over and over again he or she will employ the phrase "brothers and sisters in hope," suggesting by this language that there can be no absolute assurance about the question of who has been "elected by grace."[41] This in turn causes the Old Regular elder to be cautious in making judgments about the state of grace of other people, as is suggested by Bull Creek's tradition of reading the list of deceased individuals who regularly attended but were never baptized, individuals whom Elder Atlas Hall identifies, not disparagingly, as "dry land Baptists."[42]

In a note concerning this "theology of hope," Elder Hall explained that the doctrine "can be illustrated by the following Scriptures":

> Therefore my heart is glad, and my glory rejoiceth; *my flesh* also shall rest in *hope*. (Ps. 16:9)

The wicked is driven away in his wickedness; but the righteous hath *hope in his death.* (Prov. 14:32)

For we are *saved by hope.* . . . (Rom. 8:24)

That being justified by his grace, we should be made heirs according to the *hope of eternal life.*(Titus 3:7) [Emphasis provided by Elder Hall][43]

So for Old Regulars hope becomes both a theological creed and a circumscription for all claims of rightness and righteousness, undergirding a principle of humility that gets translated into a whole set of behavioral codes applicable both to elders around the stand and to ordinary church members in all interpersonal exchanges. In essence the principle has become embodied in the art of deferring; and self-disparagement, followed invariably by praise for another, has developed as the basic rule for mos correct business or worship exchanges. Unfortunately it is a rule that has its own subtle applications to gamesmanship in the politics of local church or association governance, but in its best application this art of deference engenders a spirit of civility that is quite honest, quite pleasant, and quite productive. It becomes a kind of Old Regular style that overlies all the operations of this body of believers, and it at least controls divisiveness in form when it proves harder to control it in substance.

A final message or theme that I find emphasized in Old Regular preaching is the general admonition about preserving "old-time ways." As I have already indicated, these "peculiar people" tend to define themselves through a large body of highly traditional behavioral codes and worship practices which they have preserved from much earlier periods. One favorite Old Regular hymn stresses the idea that these believers will make their way to eternity via "the good old fashioned way":

> When the storms of life are ended
> And the clouds have passed away,
> I shall find the gates of Heaven
> In the good old fashioned way.[44]

These old fashioned ways, however, frequently become the bases for church-splitting or association-splitting disputes, perhaps even more so than doctrinal disagreements. With perhaps one significant exception (to be examined in chapter 6), the major doctrinal divisions were debated — and resolved one way or another — during those years around the turn of the century and before. Disputes over length of hair, quarrels about dress codes, arguments about involvement of women in worship, disagreements on handling of divorces, schisms over sharing the stand with other Baptist groups, and a host of other such controversies continue to shatter the "love and peace" ideal mentioned above. These are the elements of discord Elder Fred Stiltner decries, charging that a greater degree of diversity should be accepted in many of these matters.[45] For this particular Old Regular elder "love and peace" may be the higher value when measured against traditionalism.

3. "I Am Glad That I Can Follow in the Good Old Fashioned Way"[1]

Focus in the last chapter fell on operations of a regular monthly service, but this chapter looks at some special Old Regular worship sessions: memorials, communion-footwashings, union meetings, and a fifth-Sunday healing service. Readers familiar with *Giving Glory to God in Appalachia* have already been introduced to glimpses of three of these events, and I won't repeat that earlier material except when necessary to an understanding of scenes recorded here.[2] My goal is to provide additional information about these services, supported with fresh examples, and to record more of the general atmosphere surrounding the events.

Memorial Meetings

Old Regular Baptists place strong emphasis on the memorialization of deceased brethren, building into traditional activities a number of practices designed to preserve memories and to communicate regard and reverence. There are the obituaries, written by loved ones and published in annual association minutes; there are the yearly memorial meetings inside the church, highlighted by readings of the names of all deceased members (and sometimes nonmembers); there are the family memorials, held at private homes and attended by a great variety of friends and relatives; and there are the outdoor memorials staged in the hundreds of small Old Regular cemeteries of the region.[3] In the following discussion emphasis is placed on the last two of these activities, the family memorial and the cemetery memorial, beginning with the latter.

At most Old Regular cemeteries there will be a once–a–year memorial meeting that serves much the same purpose of the "Decoration Day" services familiar to many other denominations. Held during spring, summer, or early fall months, these events first result in a general cleaning and repair of the grave plots and surrounding areas, accompanied by placement of fresh flowers or new artificial floral displays, the latter being much in vogue today. Then there will be a service conducted in the cemetery as a memorialization of all who are buried there.

In the case of Old Regular cemetery memorials this event will be held in and around an arborlike, roughly constructed, open shed, built much in the shape of the stand area of one of this subdenomination's churches, with bench-type seats surrounding at least three sides of the floor space in which the preaching takes place. The facility is a slightly more modern adaptation of the old brush-arbor structure and ranges all the way from the most primitive of constructions to a tightly roofed and neatly painted unit that possesses fold-down sidings to increase protection from rain.

The heart of any Old Regular memorial meeting is again the preaching, a series of three to five sermons put together in exactly the same pattern followed in any regular service. In fact, the sermons don't necessarily take on any memorialization-of-the-dead theme, adopting instead messages traditional to all ordinary Old Regular preaching. What you generally have is simply a regular monthly service that has been moved to a cemetery, creating in the process an honoring of these deceased brethren. But names of those buried in this spot will not be read, and very little, if anything, will actually be said in the sermons about these individuals. It seems sufficient to be in the presence of their graves.

Preachers are "called" for memorial meetings, meaning that notices are published in the association's minutes requesting specific elders to appear. In the case of family memorials these calls are determined by various individuals in the respective families, and the process usually results in the favorite preacher of each of these persons being summoned. Meeting these calls is a fairly important obligation of these elders, and some of the more popular preachers, as mentioned in chapter 1, find themselves going somewhere almost every Saturday and Sunday that their own fellowships are not meeting.

On July 6, 1986, I attended a memorial meeting at the Mary Lou Cemetery in Buchanan County, Virginia. This plot of ground lies off State Line Ridge Road just north of Stacy, Virginia, approximately a quarter mile from the Mary Lou Old Regular Baptist Church, an affiliate of the Old Friendship Association. To reach this area from Grundy, Virginia, take Highway 83 northeast toward Bradshaw, West Virginia. Stay on 83 for about fifteen miles, until you come to State Line Ridge Road (also known as Panther Road). The intersection will be on your left just before you cross into West Virginia. Follow State Line Ridge Road northwest for perhaps another two miles and you will come to the "Jones Store," on your right. Mary Lou Church sits on a rise in the ridge approximately a hundred yards beyond this point. The Mary Lou Cemetery occupies another rise on the left before you reach the store and church.

This area of State Line Ridge Road is one of the most scenic Old Regular church locations I have visited. From the front steps of Mary Lou Church one can look northeast over much of McDowell County, West Virginia, and southwest over a sizable segment of Buchanan County, Virginia. There are no noticeable mining operations in the immediate vicinity, and the nautral beauty of this ridge communicates a vivid message of what all the Old Regular country must have looked like prior to industrialization of the region.

As indicated earlier, Mary Lou Church is a member of the Old Friendship Association, an alliance of ten small fellowships which draw members from such communities as Stacy, Hurley, and Wolford, Virginia, and Jolo, Paynesville, Panther, and Mohawk, West Virginia. The 1986 minutes of this association indicated the total membership from these ten fellowships to be 667, with one of the churches (Mountain Home) having only eighteen members.[4]

Old Friendship is a small, poor, but proud association that tends to be one of the most traditional of the Old Regular clusters. In correspondence with Union, New Salem, Sardis, Philadelphia, and Northern New Salem, Old Friendship fellowships consistently throw their support behind efforts to stem the encroachments of modernism.[5]

Once a much larger association of twenty-seven churches in Buchanan and Tazewell counties, Virginia, and McDowell and Wyoming counties, West Virginia, the original Friendship group of fellowships split into two highly divergent clusters (Old Friendship and Friendship), leaving behind a legacy of bitter disputes over a multitude of the old-time ways for which the Old Friendship contingent has continued to struggle, both within its own cluster of fellowships and in its correspondence with other Old Regular groups.[6] One result of all this traditionalism is that Old Friendship may be the most insular of the associations with which I have had contact.[7]

Mary Lou Cemetery is rather small, not more than two dozen or so graves, most identified by professionally produced granite gravestones; but several are marked by hand-hewed and engraved native rock, and at least two are headed only by heavy slabs of aging wood. The small rise which serves as the location for these graves is accessible by a narrow, steep, and rutted dirt driveway that climbs about fifty yards from the main ridge road. On the morning of July 6, 1986, this lane showed signs of having been recently cleared of obtruding limbs, bushes, and tall grass, providing space for one line of parked vehicles and three or four feet of walking path.

Around the graves and stand-arbor at the top of the rise there were additional indications that in the past week someone had devoted an appreciable amount of labor to preparing the site for this occasion. Encroaching underbrush, newly sprouted trees, tall grass, and weeds had been cut back, an annual activity necessary to preventing the small clearing from being reclaimed by nature. In addition, fallen limbs, old floral displays, and miscellaneous debris had been removed from around the graves and piled neatly at one edge of the cemetery. Finally, each resting place had been freshly groomed, with all of the ground immediately around a plot having been finely cultivated with a hoe and then the dirt raked into a smooth mound along the full length of the grave. Fresh flowers or those newly acquired plastic bouquets adorned most of these plots, with one single blossom — sharply isolated from the rest — stuck near the breast area of the newly cultivated mound.

At the back edge of this cemetery, but immediately adjacent to the burial plots, rests the unpainted (except for the support posts) stand-arbor, a twenty-five to thirty-foot-square open-sided shed, equipped with a flooring of two-inch-thick rough-cut timber and with crude backless benches made from the same wood stock. This lumber had not been smoothly sanded, and I noticed that a number of worshipers brought newspapers or cardboard strips upon which to sit to prevent their clothes from being snagged. The roof of the structure is supported by 4" x 4" posts and is constructed of irregular widths of wood planking. At the rear of the shelter the foundation posts lift the structure about three feet off the steep slope, and during much of the morning service a small boy entertained himself by climbing back and forth from the ground to the railing. This railing circles all of the shed's inner area, except for about a six-foot opening at the front.

Facing this shelter are four rows of plank benches set on stout posts buried in the ground. During memorial meetings people sit on these outside benches and face those occupying the seats within the shelter. The end result is a seating configuration remarkably similar to that present during an inside-the-church service.

Under the shelter the benches are permanently fixed to the floor and have been arranged so that there is a center aisle. Most of the women sat to the right of this aisle, as one faced the outside benches and the burial area; most men sat to the left. For the preaching area the elders used an open spot down front on the men's side, turning inward to address people under the shelter and outward to address people on the exterior benches or in clusters scattered around the cemetery.

During summer months all of this complex is heavily shaded by a thick canopy of vegetation, giving the scene an image of lushness, coolness, seclusion, and quiet reverence. It is difficult to find natural beauty surpassing that of an Appalachian summer — spectacular vistas crowned by a dark richness of foliage.

I had journeyed with the Marshalls from their home on Sandy Ridge to this spot on State Line Ridge Road, and when we stepped from our car we immediately heard Old Regular singing coming from the wooded knob above us. The slow, elongated, somewhat wailful sound floated out along the ridge and down into the valleys, and I recall wondering how far the soaring strains would travel, remembering a tale an old-timer once related to me about "singing them in," an early technique employed to pull mountain folks from their homes during times of revivals.[8] This was no revival — something in which Old Regulars don't believe, since such an activity would violate their antievangelism position — but I still thought there might be someone on this ridge who would be attracted by this sound and end up at the Mary Lou Cemetery.

We had parked among a long string of cars and pickups that lined the ridge road for a hundred yards or so, and we joined a small group of people who were moving up the narrow driveway toward the graves. I recall noting at that moment the general mood of the people around us, expecting, I think, to find that spirit rather somber, in view of the fact that this was to be a memorial to the dead. That anticipated darkness in tone, however, was not present within the conversations I was overhearing, and I did not later encounter it within either the sermons of the morning or the interactions of the people. Indeed, the mood throughout seemed uplifted and cheerful.

When the Marshalls and I arrived at the cemetery some thirty or so people had already gathered under the shelter; these were the individuals who were singing, while another thirty or thirty-five persons milled around the graves, reacquainting themselves with the spot and the various resting places. By the time the service was really under way, these numbers had probably doubled.

One perception I received that morning was that there were two distinctly different events taking place at the Mary Lou Cemetery, one religious and one social. Under the shed were clustered the older members of the congregation, and these individuals, in conjunction with the fifteen or twenty persons on or immediately around the outside benches, constituted the worshiping segment of the gathering, carrying on a very intense service of singing, praying, and shouting. At various spots around the outer perimeter of the cemetery, on the other hand, were smaller clusters of people who just quietly socialized, including a group of young people in their teen and subteen years.

The actual service that morning was very much in line with the traditional format I described in chapter 1: first the singing, followed by four sermons, an "opening of the doors" to the Mary Lou Church, and the round of visiting elders announcing their "appointments." Very little was done or said of a special nature to make this a memorial service, with the exception of one sermon in which the preacher advanced some wishes about his own death and funeral, and one hymn that set forth expectations of an eternal life, "When My Feet Touch the Streets of Gold":

> When this life on earth is ended,
> And our troubles and trials are o'er,
> I am told we will go to a country
> Where no tears ever come any more.
>
> Oh, they tell me that there is a mansion
> And a glorious crown and a robe
> And we all will be happy up yonder
> When our feet touch the streets of gold.[9]

Sung in a cemetery setting, this hymn appeared to have an especially powerful effect upon the older members of the gathering, resulting in some shouting and some hand clapping. I recall thinking at that moment that I would like to be down on the main road just to get a feeling about how these shouting and clapping sounds would travel along the ridge. When I re-create in my mind any of these Old Regular visitation experiences, my recollections tend to focus on sounds and images that have lingered in my memory, the visual and auditory moods of singing, preaching, shouting, and praising. Apparently other people do this also, for one of the most interesting stories I have heard from an Old Regular elder was an account of when, as a small child, he played under the church during services, drawing patterns in the cool earth and listening to the singing, shouting, clapping, and feet stamping coming from "on high," while in the process also watching dust particles float down from the flooring planks above his head. There are sights and sounds of Old Regularism that a reader must hold in his or her imagination in order to receive the full impact of narratives in this work.

This comment is certainly applicable to Old Regular preaching, and a few words need to be said about the exhorting I witnessed in this particular environment, as contrasted with what was described in chapter 1. An observation requiring special attention is that these elders must grow accustomed to preaching in a large variety of settings, including homes (for funerals and family memorial meetings), outdoor surroundings of all sorts, and a wide selection of churches. What seems preeminently critical to an elder's training is that he learn to preach under spatial restrictions similar to those in effect during a service at Mary Lou Cemetery.

As I have already mentioned, the shed at the Mary Lou burial grounds has a railing running around all four sides of the facility and open only in the center of the front side. Attached to this railing and projecting inside the shed is a bench structure that circles the entire interior space. Then set inside this initial perimeter of seats are the two sections of benches I have already mentioned, the one occupied primarily by men and the other occupied primarily by women. In the narrow space between the front bench on the men's side and the railing seating of that area is the small amount of open space that constitutes "the stand."

In this tight rectangle of space, closely flanked in every direction but one by a fellow elder or a deacon, the preaching elder must rise and take his initial stance. His first struggling moments of improvised expression are worked out under this circumstance of a confining envelopment, and he must search for spiritual inspiration with a distracting ring of humanity only inches away. But his experience with the ensemble nature of Old Regular preaching equips him to use this closeness to his advantage, turning first to one brother and then another as he slowly builds the momentum of his delivery, reaching out to grasp the extended hand of one supporter before pivoting to take the hand of someone on the opposite side, speaking directly into the faces of his auditors, leaning forward to embrace a fellow elder, then placing a hand on the shoulder of another for spiritual or physical support. The image here should be one of a tight group performance, in which the speaker and adjacent auditors feed off each other's energy and passion, building together as an expression takes shape and soars.

I once used the phrase "helping him catch the spirit" to describe the relationship existing between the speaker and his phalanx of male supporters, and Darvin Marshall argued that this was not an appropriate description since no Old Regular elder would feel he could help another "catch the spirit," a product they both would charge to be of divine inspiration. I understand Darvin's argument; nevertheless, there is a particular dynamic that develops between the preacher and these other participants, a dynamic that appears to be intensified by closeness. Consequently, even in the more spacious environment of a church setting there is always the leaning in and the other evidences of a projected auditor involvement, verbal as well as nonverbal.

Another point I want to make here is that, after years of teaching university public address courses, I am well aware of the effects such close proximity with an audience may have on a novice speaker. If as a consequence of inexperience or just timidity in personality a speaker is still subject to high degrees of platform anxiety, then this "wedged in" feeling could become absolutely terrifying, with the result that the performer tends to push back desperately for greater space. But like an actor performing "in the round," an Old Regular preacher must learn to work within this confined space and use it to his advantage, sinking deeper into his mood and message, and developing a communication style that is much more intimate than is the average (more person-to-person and tactile).

At the close of the memorial service Elder George Baker, moderator of the Mary Lou fellowship, announced that a meal would be served at the church. This information didn't prevent one woman from fulfilling that duty from the past of calling out, "Anyone needing to eat is welcome at my house." Motivated by a desire for totality in this experience, I was tempted to suggest to Darvin and Ganell Marshall that we go with this woman; but I didn't make the suggestion, and we ended up at the church.

The Mary Lou Church building is a wood frame structure sitting on a relatively high foundation that in the rear rises some ten or twelve feet off the slope of the hill. On the left side of the facility, attached lean-to fashion and running the length of the building, is the fellowship's kitchen and dining area. Inside the sanctuary the worship space is arranged in Old Regular design, with a raised area for the stand and membership seating, and the front section for nonmembers and visitors. The rear wall is covered with the customary display of past church leaders.

These gallaries of patriarchs make a great deal of sense within the patterns of Old Regular thought and behavior. Members of the subdenomination possess a special reverence for time, history, and tradition, believing that Old Regular Baptists have held to biblically mandated beliefs and practices when others have abandoned them. The photographs

of their past leaders not only symbolize respect for a patri-
archal system but communicate the group's sense of a firm
connection with the past. These people don't want to see in
their customs and beliefs a Johnny-come-lately faith or a mixture of modernism and 101 different traditions. A blending
of earlier modes and methods is certainly there, but Old
Regulars are at least a little more comfortable with that reality if they can see the roots of their grafted tree extending
well into the soil of the eighteenth and nineteenth centuries.
Aging photographs of past leaders help in that visualization.

Mary Lou's fellowship meal that early afternoon was characterized by all the proverbial dinner-on-the-ground traditions, with the exception that it was served indoors. Women
of the church had supplied a large variety of meat, vegetable, salad, and dessert dishes, all to be arranged on a long
counter in the kitchen area. As the meat fare, fried chicken
and country-cured ham prevail at these events; but there are
barbecued pork dishes, stacks of sausage biscuits, and plat-
ters of country-fried steak, along with the obligatory pots of
chicken and dumplings. Snap beans and yellow corn pre-
dominate among the vegetable choices, with hominy and
various cooked greens also being popular. Trays of sliced cu-
cumbers and vine-ripened tomatoes, long Pyrex containers
of gelatin dishes, Tupper Ware bowls of slaw, and a variety
of tossed leafy mixtures usually constitute the salad selec-
tions. For desserts there are the traditional pies and cakes,
and several choices of banana pudding, my favorite. Styrofoam plates and cups, picnic forks and spoons, and plastic
milk jugs of tea and Kool Aid complete the typical display.
After a long morning's service, that often has dipped one or
more hours into the afternoon, such a meal is always welcome, especially by the children, who rush back and forth
down the serving line, apparently fearful that they will over-
look one of their favorite foods.

At Mary Lou there are a few tables in the kitchen area,
but most people take their plates right into the church itself,
sitting on one of the pews in the member or visitor sections.

This is a time for fellowshipping, but it usually won't be long before someone starts lining a hymn, beginning an impromptu session of singing. Thus the day's events may close with thirty minutes or longer of "praising" through song, the crowd gradually dwindling; but it is not unheard of for some spur-of-the-moment inspired preaching to begin again at this point. Old Regulars are often reluctant to let their worship services end.[10]

A large number of family memorial services will be held each year throughout Old Regular country, with announcements being made in annual association meeting minutes. The following pronouncements, for example, were all published in the 1985 *Minutes* of the Union Association:

STANDIFER MEMORIAL—Third Saturday and Sunday [June] will be a memorial of Harrison Stanley, Salley Stanley, John Linton and others. Ministers requested to attend are, Elders, Hiram Standifer, Buford Brooks, Clyde Peaks, Billy Mullins, A. O. McKnight and Casby Conaway.

LUCAS FAMILY MEMORIAL—Third Sunday [June] will be a memorial of the Lucas family at Shelby Gap, Kentucky. Ministers requested to attend are, Elders, Frank O'Quinn, James O'Quinn, Freeland Yates, Toby Bailey, Carson Wright, Robert Kelley and Acie Rose.

MULLINS MEMORIAL— Fourth Saturday evening [September] at 4:00 o'clock will be a memorial of Brack and Samantha Mullins on Lick Fork. Ministers requested to attend are, Burley Mullins, Buford Brooks, Clyde Peaks, Billy Mullins, Hiram Standifer and Jim Mullins.[11]

The first family memorial I attended was proclaimed with this 1985 announcement:

LONESOME DOVE CHURCH — Second Saturday and Sunday [August] will be a memorial of Bro. Raymond Smith's family, his first wife, Clustena, Father Tom, Mother Gracie, brothers, Virgil and Edgar. Sister Maudie's family, her first husband, Ersel Williamson, father, Emzy Robinette, Mother Louisia Robinette, brother Estill, sister Gracie Francis and brother–in–law Caudle Francis. Ministers requested to attend are, Elders, George Baker, Billy Cochran, Arnold Clevenger, Dave Gibson, Bill Cotton, Jerry Thompson, Johnny Cline and Richard Staton. This meeting will be held at Bro. Raymond Smith's home on Straton Fork, Canada, KY. [12]

I have twice attended the Smith family memorial meeting, the first time in August 1986, and the second time in August 1987. As previously indicated, Elder Raymond Smith has been a strong supporter of my Old Regular field research. In addition, he has frequently urged me to visit his Canada, Kentucky, home and church, Lonesome Dove. Only on these two occasions have I been able to do so.

The traveler can reach Canada, Kentucky, and the Lonesome Dove Church by driving north out of Pikeville on Highway 119, heading toward Williamson, West Virginia. At about three miles northeast of Sidney, Kentucky, Route 3154 accesses Highway 119 from the right. The traveler should turn onto Route 3154 and drive up this road for approximately one mile. At this point the Straton Fork Road meets Route 3154 on the right. The last time I made this trip there was no road name or number displayed at this intersection, but there was a sign indicating this to be the way to a Kentucky highway maintenance facility.

Crisscrossing the creek for which it is named, Straton Fork Road runs up a narrow valley, passing the highway maintenance station and a small collection of homes. After about a mile and a quarter on this route the traveler will see Lonesome Dove Old Regular Baptist Church on the left. Elder Smith's home lies about two hundred yards farther up the road on the right, with the creek running between the roadbed and his house.

Brother Raymond's and Sister Maudie's home is reasonably modern, in good repair, and shows signs of having been extended a couple of times to accommodate a large family. A number of trees shade the lawn on both sides of the house, some of them apples, and on the left lawn there are two rough–structured kennels for Brother Raymond's coon hounds. Were you to visit this spot during the summer months you would find the front lawn festooned with numerous beds of colorful flowers planted by Sister Maudie and decorated here and there by brightly painted, flower bed windmills, assumably built by Brother Raymond. It is a simple home, but showing an above-average degree of loving care.

There is no mine in the hollow above the Smiths, so the small creek has not been polluted by runoffs. Still the hollow has flooded a number of times in the past, and at points people have placed large unattractive objects in the creek bed for stabilization. In fact, just below Smith's house someone has pushed an old car into the bank of the channel, apparently for that purpose. Rusting car bodies in creek beds or on hillsides are still one of the occasional factors of eastern Kentucky aesthetics.

Old Regular family memorials, held annually or at irregular intervals as called, serve not only as religious events but as family reunions. Sons and daughters, grandchildren, great-grandchildren, in-laws, aunts, uncles, cousins, nieces, nephews, and all manner of relatives gather to pay respect to deceased family members and just to socialize and catch up with the lives of each other. The event becomes a demonstration of family cohesiveness and shows deep regard for the reigning family matriarchs and patriarchs. These are happenings filled with a wonderful amalgam of worship, reminiscence, respect-paying, comparing notes on the progress of offspring, family problem solving, gossip, tale telling, consoling for losses, reestablishment of a sense of place, eating, laughter, bragging, tears, and general familial love.

Frequently elements of this extended family return to the homestead from several states, rebuilding the ties that may have grown tenuous through effects of time and distance. Appalachian Kentuckians and Virginians have often migrated to towns and cities in Ohio, Indiana, Michigan, etc., only to be pulled back for these moments of reestablishing roots. The old home, the church, the cemetery become potent symbols of place and belonging, and constitute lodestones that draw the wanderer back to the region from which he or she emanated.

Indeed, the Old Regular family and the Old Regular church

Brother Raymond and Sister Maudie's family gathered at their 1987 memorial.

community, when functioning at their best, may generate more of this cohesiveness and lodestone power than their typical counterparts in other divisions of contemporary American society. Both institutions possess a strong sense of patriarchy, a value system that says the family is of great importance (perhaps more important than the individual), a "May the Circle be Unbroken" hope for eternity, a strong tie to region, and, of course, a common religious base. The only crack in all this cementation is in the fact that the young people appear to be only minimally present within the functions of the Old Regular church, even though Elder Bill Campbell aruges that this is less of a problem today than it was twenty years ago.[13] Still, at least as indicated by the Smith memorial, these young people do seem to enjoy being a part of these family reunions, communicating through such involvements a love and respect for grandparents and other aging kin.

Old Regular family memorials tend to be extended weekend proceedings that involve at least two religious services —

at the home, at the church, or at both places. Since Elder Raymond Smith is moderator of the Lonesome Dove fellowship, he literally transfers the church's monthly Sunday meeting to his home, conducting the service on the side lawn. The Saturday morning business session and abbreviated worship service are conducted in the church. In the following account I will confine myself, for the most part, to my 1987 visit, since that trip was a two-day affair that allowed me to witness largely the full scope of this family memorial.[14]

The drive from Boone, North Carolina, to Canada, Kentucky, takes about five hours, depending upon the route of travel; but I left my home early enough that August Saturday morning to permit my arrival at the Lonesome Dove Church by 9:30, since that was when the monthly business meeting was to start. Attendance at the church was sparse that morning; only four men and four women in the member sections and just three (including myself) in the nonmember section. Nevertheless, the small group conducted a spirited introductory worship service, with singing and two preachings (Elder Smith and Elder Virgil Fields), before moving into the business section. Fields, of the Sardis Association, seemed to struggle with his sermon that morning, but Smith appeared particularly inspired, in spite of the small audience.

The only significant item on the business agenda that morning was to get ready for the annual association meeting, the third weekend in September. Discussion developed concerning the preparation of the church letter, a kind of annual report to the association, and this deliberation probably consumed more time than is usual simply because Lonesome Dove had a new clerk who had to be instructed concerning his duties in this task. There was also some discussion of the fellowship's contribution to the food fund for the association sessions. Although Old Regular women bring generous dishes to association meetings, there are always some supplies that must be purchased by the women who actually run the kitchens during these three–day events.

The final question for deliberation was whether the church's delegates to this session should be elected or appointed, with the decision being made that Moderator Smith should appoint these three males. Brother Raymond promptly performed this task, and the meeting was adjourned with prayer about 12:30.

I then went with Brother Raymond to his house, where Sister Maudie and one of her daughters (by her first marriage) had been cooking all morning. These two were quickly joined by two daughters from Elder Smith's first marriage, and then later by a couple of granddaughters. In fact, I was told that these women had cooked all of the day before. With only brief breaks in their activities, these women (joined later by Ganell Marshall) continued to bake, fry, broil, boil, stew, chop, and mix throughout that Saturday afternoon, getting ready for the big event the next day.

All of these cooking preparations for the memorial were temporarily suspended, however, when Brother Raymond, his brother, and I walked into the house. Attention was then immediately directed toward preparing lunch for the three of us. Throughout this weekend affair the women of the family worked in the kitchen or other areas of the house while the men sat in the front yard talking, periodically to be served tea, coffee, or other refreshments. Traditional gender roles prevailed, much — I thought — to the benefit of the males.

Saturday afternoon gave Brother Raymond and me a chance to talk extensively about Old Regular doctrines and practices. We sat in metal lawn chairs under a shade tree, watching the creek flow, and reviewed a number of theological concepts, worship procedures, and Old Regular social customs. One subject we discussed at length was that question about the proper degree of evangelism that should be found in Old Regular services. We also wandered widely over Old Regular redemption theology.

I first checked with Brother Raymond to see if he agreed with my explanation of Old Regular atonement doctrine: God calls man to redemption from original sin; the calls are individually issued but "general" in the sense that each man receives such a call; the calls (election) are "by grace," since sinful man cannot possibly merit the redemption offered; the calls are distinct from, and not necessarily accompanied by, any emotional experience that might occur during a church service; an individual may reject his or her call, but if truly heeded it results in a redeemed "saint" who never will "fall away." With one reservation, which I will discuss shortly, Elder Smith accepted this series of statements as his beliefs relative to atonement.

Concerning the call, Brother Raymond feels that any element of overt evangelism in Old Regular procedures would be improper. "God calls," he repeated, "not man." Therefore, any degree of urging to redemption carried out by man would constitute a usurpation of God's role, a point made in chapter 1. This would be particularly true, according to Smith, at the close of a service when the "church doors are opened," a position examined in chapter 2. It should be remembered, however, that Elder Bill Campbell qualified that prohibition by arguing that a man or woman should be implored to heed his or her call, even though it would be improper to urge the unredeemed to join the church.[15]

This sensitivity for the purity of a God-instituted call extends, for Brother Raymond, into the issue of emotionalism in the church service. If this emotionalism is purposefully "whipped up" by a preacher, Elder Smith charges, it feeds this problem of a man–manipulated call. On the other hand, emotionalism — coming from either the preacher or the congregation — that is a pure expression of remorse or joy, arising from the individual human passion, without being a creation of external stimulation, is not only acceptable but desirable. The purpose of this emotion, however, should not be to generate an environment within which a call would come to someone. That person might just get caught up in the emotion and not receive a true call. Speaking of some Old Regular preachers of whom he is critical, Smith argued that these elders use too much "sympathy," meaning that they try to play on the emotions of worshipers when they "open the doors of a church."

The distinction here is a fine one and involves a judgment

of motives or inner feelings present in a preacher (the question of whether he experiences emotion or generates it). Nevertheless, Elder Smith views it as an important distinction: the preacher who deliberately sets out to engender emotional responses could become guilty of artificially establishing an environment in which the perception of a call could occur, rather than a real call itself. Thus the entire nature of "election by grace" would be distorted.

Another issue discussed that afternoon was the question of the universality of calls: does *every* individual in his or her lifetime receive a call? Brother Raymond's first answer to this question was "Yes," indicating that the Deity eventually offers the blessings of atonement to every human creature. Then I asked him if this included, for example, peoples from the various oriental cultures. He then rather quickly said "No." When I asked him why this limited offering of "salvation," he simply added that God was an all-knowing Deity and would not issue a call where He knew it would not be accepted. Was this simply another form of particular election, I asked? "No," he announced, it wasn't a limited election, but just a case of God exercising good judgment and avoiding a "wasted call."

Later that evening, as the Smith family and friends gathered indoors for some hymn singing and other elements of social and spiritual interaction, I once again broached this "wasted call" topic and this time found Brother Raymond much more speculative on the issue, suggesting that he might be reassessing his position. I had the feeling that I had pushed Elder Smith into a deeper examination of Old Regular atonement doctrine than he — and perhaps a number of his fellow elders — had elected to pursue. To his credit, however, he never responded defensively to my probing.

The Gathering of the Men

Brother Raymond and I didn't have the front yard, the shade tree, the metal lawn chairs, or the conversation completely to ourselves throughout that Saturday afternoon. Several men — relatives and friends — dropped by during this period, particularly later in the day. And then the next morning there was an hour or two of male conversations in the yard before the service began.

Usually when a man arrived he had his wife with him, but she would quickly go inside to visit with the women around the kitchen area, leaving the lawn primarily as a male preserve. Here the men gathered in small clusters and talked about a myriad of things. They discussed various mining operations in the area. They talked about cars and sometimes machinery. There was one lengthy discussion about snakes in the mountains at that time of the year, and there occasionally were words about the weather, particularly about a flood that the area had experienced some three weeks earlier. Furthermore, the men had some thoughts to voice about politics and the general news of the moment. But the subject that appeared to get the most attention was coon hounds, primarily because Brother Raymond breeds these animals and had four in easy eyesight of the gathering men.

Each man felt compelled, it seemed, to make a trip out to the hounds, inspecting the lot with a critical eye of an experienced runner of coon dogs. I also made my trip and in the process was told something about coon hounds, the differences, for example, between blueticks, black-and-tans, and walkers.

During the two days I learned a few other things about these hounds. I learned, perhaps not totally to my surprise, that they cost a great deal, and that these men, who did not appear to have a large store of worldly possessions, are often willing to pay several hundred dollars, and perhaps one or two thousand, for a dog they will employ only to tree raccoons, from which the hunter often turns away with no killing involved. The joy, they often say, is in the chase, in observing the skill of the dog, and in listening to the deep-throated baying ("bawling") during the pursuit.

In fact, I learned that the quality and characteristics of

this baying might be the very factor making a dog especially attractive to its owner. I listened with some initial confusion, and then with some amusement, to one elderly gentleman who asserted quite vehemently — at least three times — that he didn't want any "bawler on a tree." Any good coon hound, he asserted, should "bawl" on the trail but "chop" on the tree. He reserved particular disdain for any hound of such poor breeding that it would reverse these responses.

During these two days of conversation I also learned something about the art of central Appalachian male discourse. It is a communication process that one does not rush indiscreetly. Thoughts are to be properly savored and meditated upon before being responded to. Any observation must be shown proper respect by allowing it to settle into the consciousness of all present before being answered. So one sits and speaks and waits a spell, and it helps to have something to do during the interims of thought — playing with a twig, carving, smoking or chewing, or just observing elements of nature. During my two-and-a-half-hour theological discussion with Brother Raymond Smith, I watched him carve a small stick down to a smaller one, smoothing it, tapering it, forming no particular object, but just sculpturing it into whatever shape pleased his aesthetic eye of the moment. This was something that could be done while carefully considering doctrinal issues of high import.

In the kitchen, when I caught glimpses of that environment, the women's talk seemed more spirited, animated, faster, even involving more merriment. While in the presence of their men, the women appeared to "hold back," to be reserved, to speak less. But around the cooking, without the men as inhibiting agents, the females "cut loose," and generated a discourse more energetic than that of the men, who — infected by their obligatory caution and stoicism — moved more deliberately through their dialogues on coons, dogs, automobiles, mining, and the rest of the world at large.

On Sunday morning guests started gathering at Brother Raymond's and Sister Maudie's house as early as 7:00. The first to arrive were several members of Brother Raymond's original family and a daughter from Sister Maudie's first marriage. The initial spouses of Maudie and Raymond died long before these two decided to join their families. Had there been a divorce in the situation, Brother Raymond would not have been able to remain an elder, and he and Sister Maudie probably would have been excluded from the church. But remarriage after the death of a husband or wife is fully acceptable to Old Regulars — and even encouraged — as long as there is no broken family somewhere in the picture.

The Marshalls and I had stayed the night with the Smiths, along with several other guests (how many I am not sure); and the evening had been spent discussing some Old Regular history and customs, pursuing a couple of doctrines in more detail (with Brother Raymond going to his Bible on a number of occasions), and with the family singing a few of their favorite hymns. Brother Raymond is especially fond of singing "the old songs of Zion," and he delights in doing the lining. For experiencing the nuances of Old Regularism, I found that evening to be one of the most rewarding intervals I have spent during this study.

Several of those early arrivals joined us for that Sunday breakfast: fried eggs, sausage, country ham, biscuits, grits, milk gravy, homemade apple butter — all of the traditional fare of an Appalachian morning table. As usual, men received the attention, with women — and especially Sister Maudie — joining the meal only after every male had been served, generally twice.

By 8:00 nonfamily guests had begun arriving, primarily members of the Lonesome Dove fellowship, settling into the living room for cups of coffee or bites of breakfast if they desired. It was still early. The memorial service itself wouldn't start until around 9:30. But prompt arrivals such as this would give plenty of time for the men to talk and for the women to join in clearing the kitchen and getting back to work with some of the other preparations for the noon meal.

When I walked outside I found that at one end of the

house Brother Raymond and a couple of men from Lonesome Dove had begun to assemble a large circle of church folding chairs, several wooden benches, and a number of Sister Maudie's lounge chairs, all being placed beneath a semicircle of shade trees. The arrangement, as first established, would have accommodated about fifty or sixty worshipers; but I noticed that as the morning wore on a number of late arrivals brought their own aluminum folding chairs, in anticipation of a scarcity of seating. By the time the service was well under way (10:00 to 10:30), there were approximately a hundred people in attendance, most of them sitting in this circle, but several clustered in front of the house around the tree under which Brother Raymond and I had held our theological discussion the afternoon before. Then there were always a dozen or so women in the house continuing the cooking chores of the morning, and perhaps a score of children running here and there.

General fellowshipping continued at various points in and around the Smith's home until approximately 9:00, when the crowd began to shift to the circle of seating within which the memorial service would be held. Sometime soon after one of the elders started lining a hymn, and the singing began. In keeping with the informality of all Old Regular services, no one called for people to assemble or announced the start of events. In fact, long after the singing commenced, and then throughout the service, small clusters of people continued to gather at other areas of the spacious yard and chat about whatever they had to chat about. This worship happening, like so many other Old Regular services, became a process with which one could engage and disengage at will; and during the singing and six sermons that were to follow folks moved to and from the circle, involved at times to the point of crying or shouting, but at other moments experiencing a need for other diversions. A wonderful informality prevailed, allowing each individual to experience the event as he or she wished.

For the most part, the ceremony itself fit the mold for all

Side yard of Elder Smith's House during memorial service.

Old Regular services — the singing of a number of hymns, an introductory sermon closed by a "sing down" and a round of handshaking and embracing, a prayer, then in this case five more sermons before another hymn, the "opening of the church door" (for Lonesome Dove), the announcing of appointments, and the final prayer and benediction. The only added feature of note was the formal reading of the memorial call that had been published in the Union Association minutes. Brother Raymond performed this task immediately before turning the service over to the first elder for the introductory sermon.

The Place of *"Place"* in Old Regular Worship

Earlier I mentioned the relative simplicity of Old Regular churches, the fact that they are clean and in good repair but functional. They tend not to be the things of worship themselves that the great cathedrals of our world perhaps have become, or even to take on that adulation which much less elaborate structures of our mainline Protestant faiths generate. The admired but expensive decorations simply are not there—the massive crosses, the lofty stained glass windows, the impressively polished soaring organ pipes, and the high arching rafters of dark wood.

Old Regulars like to feel comfortable and at home in any place they gather to worship. They apparently don't like to feel hushed, overawed, or intimidated by environment, wanting instead to be at ease, free, unshackled either physically or psychologically, able to move about if necessary. In addition, all the artificial symbols, they charge, are unnecessary, with even the stand and Bible being temporarily expendable. There are things that must go on, but the places in which they go on—church, home, cemetery, creek bank, yard—have no essential characteristics, other than the previously mentioned comfort and homeyness.

It would be unwise to say that "place" is not revered, for certainly these churches, cemeteries, and spots for baptisms are held in special regard; but they are not in themselves worshiped. Therefore, Old Regular services can be staged almost anywhere, with relative feelings of appropriateness. Preachers learn to adjust to distractions inherent in various settings, with the "stand" becoming almost any reasonably open space; and the fact that there may be preaching, singing, or shouting going on as a car passes on a nearby road seems to have no restraining effect.

For Old Regulars, therefore, the place of worship is to provide comfortableness, naturalness, some emotional affiliation with the specific service, and a degree of functionalism. Little else, if anything, seems essential.

It was close to 2:00 that afternoon when all of the sermons; the announcing of appointments; and the singing, praying, and benediction were ended. Long before that time the women had pulled all the children and young people into the house and fed them. That part of their chore would thus be over. But the food had been ready to serve since 12:00, and the expansive dinner-on-the-ground tables had been set up on the front lawn, covered with tablecloths, and arranged with those foods and other materials that could stand the wait. By 1:00, however, a few of the women seemed to be growing impatient with the length and number of the sermons, and one woman was heard to say, "Those men will preach forever. Don't they know some folk have to eat?"

Brother Raymond and Sister Maudie had called seven elders for the memorial, and all but one had met the call.[16] Thus Brother Raymond felt obliged to preach all of the remaining six, one of whom held the stand for over an hour. Therefore, it had indeed been a lengthy meeting, but protracted worship is very much in the Old Regular tradition. The women complained, but they did so with a proper tone of levity. Probably all of them had sat through meetings much longer than this one.

Communion and Footwashing

Old Regulars accept footwashing, communion, and baptism as "ordinances," meaning that these are procedures ordered by Christ and thus obligatory within the church's faith and practice. The following statement from the Union Association's articles of faith serves as one expression of this doctrine: "We believe that baptism, the Lord's Supper and feet washing are ordinances of Jesus Christ and that true believers are the only proper subjects of these ordinances. . . . "[17]

What this means, of course, is that individual Old Regular fellowships are obligated to stage communion and foot-washing services, and that true believers — and only true believers — should participate in these ceremonies. Footwashing, like communion, therefore is a "closed" event, involving only the members of the fellowship, members of other churches within the fellowship's association, and members of other associations with whom their association corresponds.

The ceremony is staged once a year, as an extension of the annual communion service, and the basic form for the event is provided in John 13:4–14, the only gospel account of this aspect of the Passover supper that Christ shared with his disciples just prior to the Crucifixion. A key phrase in this account is a statement that John attributed to Christ: "For I have given you an example, that ye should do as I have done to you." For Old Regulars and all footwashing Baptists, this statement became a commandment.

An Old Regular fellowship chooses one of its spring, summer, or fall regular meeting weekends for its annual communion and footwashing service and has that arrangement published in its association's annual minutes so that people from other fellowships will know when to visit. In most instances the communion and footwashing service will be an extension of that Sunday's meeting, but churches in the Sardis Association more frequently schedule their communions and footwashings on Saturday afternoons.[18] A few churches in Thornton Union Association stage their communion-footwashing services in the evening after a regular Saturday service.[19]

Traditionally a church's communion-footwashing meeting is the first or second most heavily attended service of the year, with only memorial or union meetings occasionally attracting a larger crowd. Two associations (Sardis and Old Friendship) combine their union and communion meetings, presenting an even greater likelihood that the service will be well attended. Old Regulars enjoy visiting each other's sacrament meetings not only because of the services themselves, but also because these will be the gatherings at which they are most likely to see people whom they may not have encountered for several seasons.

For those fellowships that make their sacrament ceremony a continuation of a regular Sunday service the church day will be a long one. First the congregation will experience a full standard set of proceedings, with the singing, the three or more sermons, and all the rest, taking the day up to at least 12:00, and more likely 1:00. Then there will be a brief intermission so the communion table can be set and the foot-washing articles arranged. During this break most of the men in the congregation will move outside to stretch, smoke, or converse. When the deacons and deaconesses have completed the physical preparations, the fellowship will be called to reassemble by the singing of a hymn.

Now the scene will reveal a table set behind, beside, or in front of the pulpit and covered by a white tablecloth. Under the covering will be a number of serving plates for the bread, the same number of cups for the wine, a decanter (sometimes just a quart jar) or two of wine (usually real in the case of Old Regular sacraments), and a platter of unleavened bread, looking much like a large thin and hardened pancake.

After the "call back" hymn the moderator will take charge and often carefully explain who can legitimately participate in the communion (primarily, it seems, for the benefit of those Old Regular visitors who may belong to associations not in correspondence with the association of the fellowship, but also, according to Elder Atlas Hall, because Free Will Baptists occasionally find their way into Old Regular services).[20] The moderator will then call to the stand the elder who will "introduce" the communion service.

This elder will preach ten to twenty minutes, and then there will be another round of handshaking and embracing before the moderator again takes charge. Now the moderator will call upon one or two deaconesses to "prepare the table," a ceremony which may become quite meaningful to the women involved — as we will see shortly — but which entails only a removal of the covering from the sacramental elements.

At this point the moderator calls forward all of the deacons and elders (both home church and visiting brothers), instructing them to prepare the bread and wine. This involves first the breaking of the bread into bite-size pieces and then the pouring of the wine into the serving cups, the actual pouring generally being done by the moderator.

At the completion of this step, the deacons move out from the table in pairs, one with a plate of broken bread and one with a cup of wine and a saucer to catch any spills. By now men and women of the church have established a clear spatial separation between the genders, with the men usually on the right as the stand is faced and the women on the left. Then there also will be a spatial break separating those eligible to participate from those who can serve only as spectators.

One or two associations (Thornton Union in particular) allow deaconesses to serve on the women's side, but this has been a real "bone of contention" within the more traditional Old Regular groups, with the result that the practice has become a justification for splits. In those associations that correspond with New Salem and Union the practice is not allowed.

Once the deacons have finished serving all of the eligible members of the congregation, they take turns serving each other and then return the plates, cups, and saucers to the linen–draped table. The moderator will carefully pour all of the remaining wine back into the larger container(s) and then step back as the deaconesses return to recover the unused bread and wine and the utensils. Care taken with the wine and broken bread is not motivated by any doctrine of transubstantiation. Instead there is simply a respect for these elements as symbols.

It is now time to start the footwashing, and the moderator may open this part of the service by quoting John 13:4: "He riseth from supper, and laid aside his garments; and took a towel and girded himself." While speaking these lines he will be removing his coat, if he is wearing one, and tying a long towel loosely around his waist, leaving one end to fall as far as it will go. Then he will secure a basin, usually from stacks placed by the communion table; partially fill it with water from a large pitcher or bucket; and then move to one of the other elders around the stand, often choosing the oldest of the lot or one who merits respect for some other reason. The moderator will then proceed to remove both shoes and socks of this individual and wash his feet, with a slow and sensitive attention to the rich symbolisms of the moment.

Once this first washing is completed other members of the congregation move forward, secure their own towels and basins, and commence the larger ceremony, usually changing roles after each initial rite. In only a short time the church is filled with crying, shouting, and praising, as these highly poignant exchanges unleash a flood of emotions. A fellowship that may have remained very solemn during the communion will now participate in a myriad of intense expressions of religious enthusiasm, and literally scores of high-pathos scenes will be played out in the raised platform area and among the first four or five rows of pews in the out-front section.

Footwashings now go on until all participants are satisfied, exhausting as much as an hour's time with this rite alone. Emotions will often peak, then fall, only to rise one or more times later, extending the day's worship activities to 2:00, 2:30, or later. Then there will be dinner-on-the-ground when this ritual is finished.

Little Martha Old Regular Baptist Church is located in Leemaster, Buchanan County, Virginia. Take Highway 83 southwest from Vansant, Virginia, and after about three or four miles turn left onto Route 619 and proceed to the Leemaster community. The church, a red brick structure, sits on the left as you enter this community and is identified by a small sign on the right side of its front.

Until 1986 this fellowship was moderated by Elder John Layne, who at that time was also moderator of the Union Association. Prior to his death on February 11, 1988, ill health had removed him from both positions. My visits to Little Martha occurred on June 8 and August 3, 1986. The first visit allowed me to witness the fellowship's communion and footwashing service. To avoid repeating information just provided

Front of Little Martha Church during break before Communion.

I will not review the entire sacrament meeting, opting instead to discuss selected high points in the activities.[21]

On June 8, 1986, Little Martha's regular morning service closed at 12:40, having included four sermons, the last by Elder Jimmy Dale Sanders of Draffin, Kentucky. Sanders is one of the more popular elders in the Union Association, and his sermon that morning generated a number of emotional responses from the women of the congregation. By the time the communion service began this audience had been well prepared for an exuberant culmination of this day's worship activities. The communion-footwashing expressions I subsequently observed may have matched the intensity I reported as characterizing the Bull Creek memorial service.

The Bull Creek fellowship had representation at Little Martha that morning in the form of Elder Fred Stiltner, whom I briefly discussed in chapter 2. Moderator Layne selected

Stiltner to introduce the communion service and then later chose this aging elder as the individual whose feet would receive that first ceremonial washing. But before this happened Layne called on two deaconesses (Sister Pollard and Sister Mitchell) to complete the final preparation of the table. All they had to do was remove the top covering of linen and reveal the wine, bread, and utensils; but the two women performed this task with high drama, crying even as they approached the table, and pausing in their course of travel to embrace several elders around the stand and a number of sisters to the right of the stand.

It must be remembered that events like this occur only once a year in each fellowship, and many of the elderly participants always wonder if they will make the next year's ceremony. In addition, just this small role of preparing the communion table is an honor for these deaconesses, one or both of whom also baked the sacramental bread.

I witnessed a comparable but somewhat more extended scene during a communion service at Lebanon Church near Clintwood, Virginia. In that instance only one deaconess was available for this role. The woman in question, appearing to be in her seventies, had been sitting at the back of the middle section behind the stand, and in her approach to the table she tearfully embraced several of the sisters in that immediate location. But when she began removing the linen covering she experienced a massive outpouring of emotion, sobbing profusely as she slowly and methodically folded the material into a tight rectangle before placing it on a table beside the stand, twice pausing during this entire process just to allow her joy to have full expression. When she had finally completed this uncovering chore, she embraced the moderator and began moving slowly around the entire raised area, making tactile contact with every individual in the member sections before she arrived back at her original seat, crying forcefully between each human encounter. In respect for the deaconess's role, the moderator waited patiently with the service, not willing to move any farther until she had finished her movements to and from the table.[22]

Returning to the Little Martha service, the next moment of special poignancy occurred when Elder John Layne called for all "ordained authorities" (elders and deacons) to prepare the bread and wine for serving. It immediately became obvious that there were more of these men present than were actually needed for this limited task. Still the group was careful to see that each man (more than a dozen deacons and elders in all) received a piece of bread to break, thus allowing all to become involved symbolically in this stage of the service. This included one aging gentleman whose infirmities would not permit him to move from his pew to the table. A fragment of the unleavened loaf was taken to him on a plate, and help was provided in steadying his hands as he struggled to break that one piece of sacramental bread. Elder Atlas Hall has informed me that the large pancake of stiff bread is usually perforated for more even breaking but that its toughness often necessitates forceful tearing, something that the elderly gentleman was having trouble doing.[23]

Emotions at Little Martha ran high during both the communion and footwashing segments of their service, with some demonstrations breaking out on the women's side even before the servers arrived in that area. Shouting and praising at this point in the ceremony, however, struck me as being atypical, because the only Old Regular communion meeting I had observed prior to this moment (one at Bethany Old Regular in Kingsport, Tennessee) had been generally reserved during the sharing of the sacrament. Only after the footwashings began did passions explode. Here at Little Martha, on the other hand, the scenes of tearful joy, in mere anticipation of the sacrament, were immediate and unreserved. I learned later that it is dfficult to predict exactly when emotions will be unleashed in an Old Regular service.

An additional observation: the shouting and praising I witnessed at Little Martha involved more hand-clapping than I had seen on other occasions. The typical clapping-shouting scenario would develop something like the following. One woman would start shouting, her arms thrown high above her head, wrists bent sharply back, fingers spread — much in the same posture I described when reporting the Bull Creek service in chapter 2. Then she would quickly bring her arms down in front of her, execute four or five rapid claps, shout a line of praise, and then hurl her arms high above her head again. The process usually was repeated a number of times in quick succession, with (in each cycle) the woman proclaiming something such as "We're drinking from the fountain!" or "Oh, what a wonderful kingdom!" One such shouter frequently would engender another, with the second woman taking over while the first momentarily brought her emotions into a more moderate form of expression. On these occasions, seldom did I hear more than one shouter at a time, giving a slightly orchestrated effect to the drama.

I also noticed several women who were not shouters but who tended to play support roles during the joyous episodes. These individuals would move toward their more exuberant friends, perhaps embrace them or literally undergird them physically during the dramas, or just stand close and draw unto themselves some of the passionate energy being expended. Frequently I had the impression that these support persons had difficulty letting go of their own emotions in this fashion, but still benefited from the unbridled demonstrations of their more expressive friends.

Later, during the footwashings, these shouting scenes did not become more intense, for there was no way for them to climb any higher in drama than they already had reached, but they did become more general. In addition, throughout this segment of the service the men — if not preaching or singing — were inclined to join the overall emotional displays, not by shouting and clapping or by mingling with the dynamic scenes on the women's side, but through their own tearful embraces following footwashing exchanges.

One observation, however, that must be made concerning the respective male and female contributions to the emotionality of these services is that men are active and women are reactive—men initiate, orchestrate, and direct; women respond. The result is an unwritten rule of female decorum which says that no woman should ever completely take over a service. With the possible exception of those moments when the one or two deaconesses uncover the table, males somehow always stay in control of the scene, if by no other means than being "in the stand."

The entire nature of the footwashing rite is extremely personal, humbling, sensitive, and interpersonally cathartic. At the beginning of these events participants generally move to individuals with whom they have particularly close relations. In fact, many of the worshipers never participate in any exchanges beyond these initial ones. As emotions climb, however, some worshipers may bathe several pairs of feet, while others may involve themselves symbolically in a large number of exchanges by moving about embracing pairs of washers or by slipping a hand into a basin while another brother or sister is formally doing the bathing.

But there is a certain type of footwashing exchange that invariably occurs somewhat late in the ceremony and becomes far more meaningful than the average for these potent interactions. I am thinking of those situations in which one person finally decides to approach, basin in hand, the one church member for whom he or she holds the most antipathy, or that estranged family member toward whom profound bitterness has in the past been directed. These are the encounters that typically produce the highest drama and from which the most needed therapeutics may be derived. They are not uncommon during these annual footwashing rites.

Generally speaking, cross-gender footwashing exchanges do not occur in Old Regular churches: men wash the feet of other men, and women wash the feet of other women. In some fellowships this separation of the genders for this rite is so serious a matter that a violation of the rule results in a severe reprimand.[24] I have, nevertheless, witnessed scenes (notably at Lebanon Old Regular Baptist Church) in which a woman joins a male-male footwashing rite by dipping a hand into the basin and scooping water over the foot of the recipient of the ablution.[25] My experiences, however, tell me that such variations in the accepted decorum are rare in Old Regularism.

Little Martha's communion-footwashing meeting ended at approximately 2:15 that Sunday afternoon, and then the women of the fellowship served dinner-on-the-ground. After such impassioned services congregations tend to be extremely relaxed and sociable, ready for the capstone experience of a fellowship meal, having had many of their tensions drained away by the fervor of the various interpersonal exchanges. There is a kinship, I believe, between such traditional religious practices and the psychology of T-groups and encounter sessions; therefore, footwashings undoubtedly play a vital role in maintaining interpersonal harmony in these small religious communities.

Union Meetings

For most Old Regular fellowships there are three special annual services, two of which I have already discussed (memorials and communion-footwashings), and the third of which is the union meeting. There will be no need to spend time describing the actual structure of this final special worship event, because — as practiced today — there is no significant difference between a union meeting and a regular Sunday service, with the exception that the preachers for the day are "called," making the morning one during which the congregation will hear their favorite ministers from other churches.

I have previously mentioned that Sardis Association and Old Friendship Association have deemphasized their union meetings by staging them on the same weekend with their communion-footwashing service. What needs to be added here is that for all Old Regular associations the original purpose of these special gatherings may have been substantially lost.

In 1793, when first considering an affiliation with the South Kentucky Association (Separates), the Elkhorn Association (Regulars) passed a resolution stating that "nothing is to be more earnestly desired among the people of God, than union and fellowship."[26] This concept of "union" apparently became even more critical during the early nineteenth century, when the relative harmony of Kentucky and Virginia Baptists was being ravaged by discord generated as a consequence of the antimission and Campbellite movements. Furthermore, the problem was augmented by the fact that so many fellowships were highly isolated, having only infrequent contacts with other churches of their "faith and order." Thus it became easy for the various congregations of an association to develop divergences in both doctrine and practice.

Writing sometime before 1886, the year he published his *A History of Kentucky Baptists*, and expressing his remarks in the past tense, J. H. Spencer briefly discussed union meetings as he understood them to have developed on the Kentucky frontier. Spencer first described a "quarterly meeting," saying this had been a three–day gathering held not for business, but as "a reunion of brethren" and as "a happy season of worship." He then observed that the term "union meeting" was simply another name for "quarterly meeting." He also stated that these affairs "were of much value to the churches, at the early period in which they prevailed. . . . The meetings of the Associations were great occasions, and often afforded opportunity for hearing from churches in all parts of the State. But all could not attend these gatherings, besides which they were too infrequent to satisfy the demand for a knowledge of the condition of the churches, or to afford the desired intercourse between the preachers who were laboring in a common cause."[27]

Within Old Regularism emphasis may have fallen upon this "knowledge of the condition of the churches" and this "desired intercourse between the preachers" as factors necessary to discouragement of heretical doctrines and practices; for the prevailing view within this subdenomination is that union meetings originally were used, at least in part, to "check out" the beliefs of elders who were called to preach on these occasions. Darvin Marshall tells me it is his understanding that at these early union meetings it was not uncommon for the home–based elders and the visiting elders to question each other on basic doctrine. Elder Atlas Hall supports this interpretation, noting that he "observed this [the questioning process] when he was a teenager." Elder Dallas Ramsey introduced the 1988 union meeting of Ash Camp Church by telling his congregation that such interrogations had been the original purpose of this special service.[28]

The first mention in New Salem Association minutes of a union meeting was recorded in 1848. During that session a motion was passed agreeing that a union meeting be held at the Joppa Church, with four elders and one brother requested to attend.[29] From that point on there was a slow but steady development of this tradition, with only one such meeting a year for about a decade; then with the number expanding to two or three, then five or six, and holding there until the practice really caught hold after the turn of the century.[30] Throughout this period, however, nothing was ever recorded in the New Salem minutes as explanation of these events. Still there were notations of reports being given by elders called to the meetings. Such an agenda item still exists in contemporary association meetings, but the moment is used primarily as a time when elders can, if they so chose, report to the association on their travels.

Apparently none of the original purpose remains in the present-day Old Regular union meeting, unless inadvertently so. Instead, the gatherings provide, as suggested above, opportunities for hearing favorite exhorters from other fellowships within the association or within corresponding associations. A popular preacher may find himself traveling to churches in four or five associations during the peak union meeting months of the spring and summer, and audiences for these occasions will swell beyond attendance records for regular meetings.

A Special Healing Service

On January 31, 1988, I attended a "fifth Sunday" service at the Little Sarah Old Regular church on Big Ridge near Haysi, Virginia. The church is one of two Old Regular fellowships in the Haysi vicinity that, at the time of this writing, are moderated by Elder James O'Quinn, mentioned in the introduction of this work as having been particularly supportive of my research. The invitation to witness this service, however, came from Elder Bill Campbell, who wanted an opportunity to confer with me after the meeting about some Old Regular doctrinal matters we had been discussing.

As mentioned earlier, fifth Sundays present Old Regular congregations with the opportunity to do something special, to stage a meeting that emphasizes a theme not necessarily present in any regular monthly service. One option is to conduct a worship event focusing upon infirm members of the fellowship. Such happenings are not healing services in the tradition of Holiness-Pentecostal practices, but are meetings in which the concentrated supplications of a congregation are directed toward the needs of the sick, with the main feature of the morning's activities being a reading of names — church members, relatives, and friends who are experiencing physical or mental maladies.

I have witnessed two such readings, one at Stone Coal Old Regular Baptist, Garrett, Kentucky, February 15, 1987, and the second at the Little Sarah meeting. In each case there was no special ceremony that sought to call down spiritual powers on individual disabilities by, for example, a laying on of hands or an anointing with oil. Instead, there was simply a focusing of prayers, supported by preaching that played upon the healing theme.

At the conclusion of the Little Sarah service, nevertheless, I did get a chance to witness that aspect of laying-on-of-hands healing that does exist in Old Regular practices. Elders Bill Campbell and Toby Bailey invited me to accom-

Little Sarah Church, Haysi, Virginia.

pany them to the nearby home of a Little Sarah member
who was to enter a hospital the next day. The man had can-
cer and was facing a decision concerning a proposed pro-
gram of heavy radiation therapy.

The visit was pleasant but uneventful until we started to
leave. At that moment the man's wife asked the two elders
if they would "lay hands on" her husband. This aging gentleman, once a person of commanding physical stature, immediately began to cry softly, posturing himself as if in expectation of some highly significant event. The scene I then
observed was dignified, touching, and imbued with deep religious conviction; and it in no way mirrored the artificially
staged, high-drama showmanship of those media-event healing services to which we have grown accustomed as a feature
of some televangelism. Instead, the mood was quiet, sensitive,
and personal, accompanied by a deep, jointly shared sense of
hope. Touch, the laying on of hands in which Old Regulars

place so much emphasis, became the key element, the magic of a collective connectedness, as the wife, husband, and two elders sought to focus a mutually accepted faith on an insidious infirmity, a deep-running malignancy that threatened this man's life. The moment was a powerful one, and I flinched slightly — or quivered might be the better word — as I watched the scene, not knowing what to expect from such intense passion and belief. A full and honest description of my reaction to this episode would report, perhaps not unexpectedly, that I found myself hoping for the miracle.

4. Seated in Peace and Love

In chapter 2 of this work I mentioned my initial dismay at the apparent formlessness of Old Regular worship, observing that only after a number of visitations did I discover liturgical and sermonic structure. Such was never my reaction to the business meetings of this subdenomination of Baptists, either at the local fellowship level or at the association level. Old Regulars follow fixed business procedures inherited from their eighteenth- and nineteenth-century forebears, and a set of "rules of decorum" that—when stringently enforced, as they most often are—infuse in their meetings an admirable degree of order, discipline, and fair play.

In qualification of this fair play claim, however, it must always be remembered that Old Regular governance is essentially male dominated. A number of fellowships do allow women to vote in the selection of church officers, and some of the more liberal fellowships have permitted women to serve as clerks or treasurers (particularly when males were not available for these roles). But no association, according to Elder Atlas Hall, gives females the right to move or to second motions; and, with one highly divergent exception (one of the Mountain associations), delegates to annual association meetings are always men.[1]

Therefore, except as Old Regular women (in some fellowships) are allowed to vote for church officers, and except as these women (in all fellowships) exert informal influences over their husbands and other male family members, the female voice is not operative in those processes that determine substantive policy and doctrine. That indirect leverage just mentioned, however, is undoubtedly very powerful at times,

particularly as it might be applied to questions with strong female relevance (dress code debates, for example); but since Old
Regular women never move or second legislative proposals, are
not permitted (in most fellowships) to vote on such proposals,
are not allowed to hold major offices, may not serve as delegates to association meetings, are restricted from leading any
form of worship (prayers, singing, etc.), and in general are not
permitted to speak during church deliberations, they are left
largely under the dominance of their male counterparts. In
fact, at one time the Pauline directive, "Let your women
keep silence in the churches," was applied so strictly that a
female could not argue in her own behalf when charges were
brought against her, having instead to use a male spokesper-
son. Apparently, this more extreme restriction has now been
dropped by most fellowships and associations.[2]

This chapter discusses policies and procedures applicable
to Old Regular church governance. First, attention is directed
to local church business meetings; and next, analysis is made
of annual association sessions. The chapter's title, "Seated in
Peace and Love," was selected because this communicates an
attitude considered essential to all Old Regular deliberations
and has become a phrase (along with "seated in love and fellowship") routinely employed by moderators to describe a
church's interpersonal conditioning at the beginning of any
business meeting.[3]

Monthly Business Meetings

As indicated earlier, Old Regular churches devote one
Saturday morning a month to a shortened worship service
and the fellowship's business meeting. These sessions often
become high-drama happenings, because they are the moments during which these small religious communities not
only conduct the mundane affairs of church government,
but also make the harder decisions necessary to maintenance
of a cohesive church family—who is admitted, who is ex-

cluded; whose cause is sanctioned, whose is condemned; which party to a quarrel is supported, which is denounced; what will be the social standards to which all will adhere, what will be the behaviors and attitudes all will eschew?

Undoubtedly, much of what is suggested above is applicable to all religious groups, but few members of other denominations are willing to assign to the larger fellowship as much influence over their lives as do Old Regulars. The latter part of this statement is true simply because Old Regular churches have continued to play a quasi-judicial role in the lives of their members, a situation which was common to the Kentucky-Virginia frontier of the nineteenth century, but which is considerably less prevalent in this age when the civil courts have become the arbiters of society's every problem. As families, churches, schools, and other institutions have gradually withdrawn from their roles in the maintenance of social mores, morals, and ethics, Old Regular churches have held tightly to their "right" to "make straight the crooked."

They assume this right, they argue, from biblical mandates — from Paul's own advice to the early Christian church at Corinth:

> Dare any of you, having a matter against another, go to law before the unjust, and not before the saints?
> Do you not know that the saints shall judge the world? and if the world shall be judged by you, are you unworthy to judge the smallest matters?
> Know ye not that we shall judge angels? how much more things that pertain to this life? (I Cor. 6:1–3)

Members of this Baptist subdenomination also reason — once again with Paul as their authority — that what makes going to the courts of the "unjust" so unacceptable is that it often becomes Old Regular brother against Old Regular brother or sister against sister:

> I speak to your shame. Is it so, that there is not a wise man among you? no, not one that shall be able to judge between his brethren?

But brother goeth to law with brother, and that before the unbelievers.(I Cor. 6:5-6)

Old Regulars also declare, as do numerous traditional Christian groups, that scripture has prescribed for them a precise set of actions to be taken when one of their number believes himself or herself to have been wronged by a brother or sister:

Moreover, if thy brother shall trespass against thee, go and tell him his fault between thee and him alone: if he shall hear thee, thou hast gained thy brother.

But if he will not hear thee, then take with thee one or two more, that in the mouth of two or three witnesses every word may be established.

And if he shall neglect to hear them, tell it to the church: but if he neglect to hear the church, let him be unto thee as an heathen man and a publican. (Matt. 18:15-17)

All of the above, of course, means that quite a number of issues are dealt with in Old Regular business meetings that would not come before deliberative bodies of other religious groups. If one member declares "nonfellowship" with another member, then the division between the two must be healed before they can sit together "in peace and love." And there are endless varieties of human problems that could result in "nonfellowship": separation or divorce, remarriage after divorce, nonpayment of debts, drunkenness and other forms of social disorderliness, criminal behavior, gossiping and general troublemaking, general immorality, inappropriateness in dress and hair styles, the voicing of heretical doctrines, obvious neglect of fellowship obligations, and a host of similar wrongdoings and misconduct.

For Old Regulars, Paul's admonition, "let him be unto thee as an heathen man and a publican," translates into "exclude him," the ultimate punishment these churches take against one of their number who has violated some basic tenet of their faith and order. "We can't force any individual to behave as we wish him to behave," they reason, "but we can push him away from us if he refuses to adjust to our way."[4] So exclusion is a formal pushing away, a casting out, a nullification of fellowship affiliation, and thus an expulsion from the entire association to which the church belongs. Indeed, each church in an association and in all correspondent associations honors the exclusion powers of every other church in that brotherhood, to the effect that the only way to obtain membership (after exclusion) in one of these other fellowships is to go back to that original congregation, to be reinstated, and then to transfer by letter.[5] An excluded brother or sister might, depending upon the grounds for expulsion, find a fellowship in a noncorresponding association that will accept him or her, but generally not without rebaptism. More often than not, the expelled individual will leave Old Regularism altogether.

Although not as severe as "shunning" (practiced by the Amish), exclusion (or the fear of it) can become a significant deterrent to deviance from fellowship when a believer cherishes not only his or her faith but the friendships thereof; and Old Regular communities, while slowing down somewhat in this practice, still employ this correctional method with a moderate degree of frequency. A glance at statistical tables in 1986 association minutes shows this to be the case. Among the ten fellowships of the Old Friendship Association there were thirteen exclusions that year. Thirteen exclusions also came from the seven churches of the Philadelphia Association. The fifty-six affiliates of New Salem were responsible for twenty-three exclusions, while Union's seventy-two churches produced sixty-four exclusions, and Thornton Union's twenty-seven fellowships voted through eighteen exclusions. Bethel (eight churches) and Old Indian Bottom (fifteen congregations) reported only three and four respectively.[6]

So each year there are numerous Old Regulars who are expelled from their fellowships, and many of these expulsions are imbued with intense individual and familial pain as loved ones fall from grace, occasionally with a resultant bitterness that will never be eradicated. This, therefore, becomes one of the prices paid for fellowship cohesion, but it is my impression that those memberships that are the happiest are also those that employ this form of discipline the most sparingly.

Since local fellowships deliberate issues as fraught with emotion as these questions of exclusion are apt to be, it becomes essential that some kind of procedural rules be adopted to govern the debates. All of the associations mentioned in this work have approved a set of such rules, applicable both to each association and to the member churches. There is, in fact, a strong commonality between these various associations' "Rules of Decorum," so much so that several of the documents are word-for-word copies. This would be expected, since all Old Regular groups (with the possible exception of the two Mountain associations) trace their origins, directly or indirectly, to the New Salem cluster. But Old Regular roots, of course, go back farther than 1825, with the result that the subdenomination's rules of decorum also usually look very much like similar documents found in minutes of Primitive, United, Regular, Separate, and Missionary Baptist associations.[7] As the Old Regular example for discussion, I will use the body of rules adopted by the Union Association fellowships. Union local church meetings are subject to the same procedural regulations.

1. The Association shall be opened and closed by prayer.

2. The Association shall elect the officers by vote of the delegates present, and shall vote for a Moderator, Assistant Moderator, Clerk, and Assistant Clerk.

3. Only one member shall speak at a time and shall rise from his seat and address the Moderator when he is about to speak.

4. The person thus speaking shall not be interrupted in his speech by anyone except the Moderator until he is done.

5. He shall strictly adhere to his subject and in no wise reflect on the preceding speaker, but shall define his ideas on the proposition for debate so far as he can.

6. No person shall abruptly absent himself from the Association without leave to do the same.

7. No person shall rise to speak more than three times on any one subject without permission from the Association.

8. No member of the Association shall have the liberty to laugh during the sitting of the same, nor whisper in time of public speech.

9. No member shall address another in any other form or term than that of "brother" or "sister."

10. The Moderator shall not interrupt a brother or prohibit him from speaking until he gives his views on the subject unless he shall violate the Rules of Decorum.

11. The names of the several members of the Association shall be enrolled by the Clerk, and called over as often as the Association may require.

12. The Moderator shall be entitled to same privilege of speech as any member, provided the chair be filled, but he shall have no vote unless the Association be equally divided, in which event he shall give the deciding vote.

13. Any member who willfully and knowingly violates any of these rules shall be reprimanded by the Association as it may think proper.[8]

It doesn't take much imagination to visualize the deliberative misbehaviors these codes were designed to prevent—a number of people speaking at once, participants interrupted before finishing their thoughts, derision directed toward the arguments of others, disgruntled debaters stamping from the room, one speaker mocking another, shouting comments before being recognized—all behaviors that occur within some of the world's most lofty legislative bodies. But to persist in such miscreant conduct in Old Regular business meetings is to court exclusion, especially under the leadership of a strong moderator.

The moderator of a local fellowship is obviously an important figure. He not only presides over all of the church's business meetings, but he also, as indicated earlier, directs the worship services. What may be most significant, however, is that this man is expected to play a wide range of authority-figure roles, including the establishment of a high moral and spiritual example within the fellowship. When he grievously errs—and some of these leaders occasionally do, violating the most basic Old Regular prerequisites to moral character—his fall and subsequent exclusion tend to produce far more drama than is the norm for such happenings. Indeed, charges against these figures occasionally result in split fellowships, since the charismatic power of these men can be significant. An example of this type of problem will be briefly discussed later in this chapter.

The Form of a Church Business Meeting

This discussion now will focus on an examination of traditional structure in these local fellowship business meetings, and I will use as my prototype example a business session I witnessed at Ash Camp Old Regular Baptist, August 16, 1987. The church can be reached by taking Highway 23 northeast out of Jenkins, Kentucky, turning right onto Route 197 at Shelby Gap, and then continuing to a point just past the junction (on the left) of Route 195. These maneuvers will place the traveler in the small community of Ashcamp (spelled as one word), Kentucky, and the meetinghouse in question will be found sitting above the road on the left. Elkhorn Creek will be on the immediate right.

At the time of this writing the moderator of the Ash Camp fellowship is Elder Dallas Ramsey, a short, wiry, energetic man in his midsixties. Ramsey is a Navy veteran of World War II, bearing a tattoo on his right arm; and although he is a warm and caring person, he carries into his leadership at Ash Camp some blunt and matter-of-fact management techniques he may have learned during his military experience. Brother Dallas is held in high regard by the Ash Camp membership (101 in 1987), and he appears to be generally respected throughout the Union Association, with which Ash Camp is affiliated.[9]

After the abbreviated Saturday morning worship service, an Old Regular business meeting is opened by first determining whether the fellowship has removed all major interpersonal barriers to the orderly and dispassionate conduct of business. All visitors who may be sitting in the raised areas

Elders Dallas Ramsey and Bill Campbell (far right) in an after-church discussion, Ash Camp Church.

around the stand are asked to vacate these pews until the local fellowship is established to be functioning in "peace and love." In fact, after the visitors have left the stand area the moderator specifically asks his congregation if they are in "peace and love," telling them their silence will indicate an affimative response. According to Elder Atlas Hall, another manner in which all this is done is for the moderator to ask members to stand who can attest to being in "full love and fellowship," followed by the same request for those who cannot proclaim "full love and fellowship."[10]

If all is not well with the congregation — if some individual declares "nonfellowship" with another brother or sister — then the charge or charges against that brother or sister must be heard and all disputes resolved before the fellowship can invite their corresponding brethren back to sit with them. Of course, if "peace and love" do exist, which was the case during the Ash Camp session, then the Old Regular visitors file back to the raised area and the rest of the business meeting begins.[11]

The first thing that the moderator now does is to call on the clerk for any "back references," items of old business carried over from the previous meetings. These are brought forth and deliberated, and then the moderator moves to reports from the treasurer and clerk. Some fellowships apparently delay the seating of visiting brethren until after these "back references" have been dealt with or carried over to a future meeting.[12]

A good portion of the morning's business probably will be generated by the clerk's report, as he reads any letters having come to the church — letters requesting official release of membership to another corresponding fellowship, letters beseeching restoration to membership after exclusion, letters asking special dispensations relative to church rules, letters from other fellowships concerning matters of common interest, etc.

On the morning of August 16, 1987, three letters were read to the Ash Camp fellowship, the first of which precipitated the most discussion. A woman had written the church asking not to be excluded from the fellowship. She had cut her hair, a violation of the traditional Old Regular rule by which Ash Camp females consistently abide. The woman explained in her letter that she had cut her hair (apparently trimming it very close) because she had developed a scalp problem. The implication was that she had been advised to shear her head for medical reasons.

From the beginning of the subsequent discussion there appeared to be no real opposition to granting this dispensation, but the concern was for the precedent involved and for how the fellowship's letter should be written. One factor complicating the matter was that the woman's mother-in-law had been excluded for cutting her own hair, and what had colored this earlier incident was that the mother-in-law had at one time influenced the church to exclude yet a third woman, only to violate the no-haircut edict herself a short time later. In fact, the story of the mother-in-law's exclusion was one that Elder Ramsey obviously enjoyed telling.

As indicated, the mother-in-law had become heavily influential — apparently through her badgering of the voting males — in the exclusion of the third female of this story, who allegedly had periodically trimmed her hair. But no sooner had this particular exclusion been voted through than Elder Ramsey spotted the accusatory mother-in-law at the local post office, noting with dismay that she not only had cut her own hair but had frizzed it into an Afro. According to his account, the duplicity had so angered Ramsey that at the very next business meeting he brought charges against the mother-in-law himself. Now he only wanted the church's letter to make clear to the petitioning woman that as soon as her scalp problem was corrected she was to let her hair grow and keep it growing.

The remaining two letters read by the clerk were requests from other churches, one in the Sardis Association and one in the Union Association, for donations to offset building or remodeling costs. As mentioned earlier, fellowships occasionally make such solicitations of nearby corresponding churches, with the rationale that their facilities frequently will be visited by members of these other churches. On this particular occasion the two requests were set aside for the next business meeting because the church treasurer was not present and no report on finances had been heard.

A final element of business came up at the urging of Elder Ramsey. He noted that the present body of deacons was somewhat small, that some of these men were becoming quite old, and that the work of the deacons within the church community (visiting the sick and the elderly, attending to the needs of the widowed, etc.) was not always being done as completely as it should be. Therefore, he suggested that the fellowship consider ordaining another deacon, naming a young brother whom he considered to be worthy of this recognition. A motion was soon offered to this effect, and it was decided that at the October business meeting this brother would be "set aside" for examination by the presbytery (pronounced "pres-bat-try" by many Old Regulars), preparatory to his being ordained.[13]

These were all of the major issues of the morning's deliberations, and the meeting was soon brought to a close by prayer. But I need to add a note about the motion and voting process, since it is not procedurally in line with what most people might expect. In both local business meetings and association sessions, motions and resolutions pass simply by a "move and second," if no objection is heard. In other words, if a motion is made and seconded no actual vote is taken unless an objection to the motion is voiced. In that case discussion is called and a vote is eventually taken, with — for most matters — a simple majority prevailing. For Old Regulars this is procedurally legitimate, but it does appear to place presumption on the side of the motion: one has to object in order to force a discussion and vote, and this could become intimidating to anyone who feels the majority to be solidly in favor of the action. Elder Atlas Hall read one of my earlier statements of this concern and responded as follows: "I concur with your opinion of intimidation relative to this subject. Elder Clayton Montgomery was ordered to be seated and silent by Elder Wardie Craft at the Thornton Union Delegate House for insisting that we follow *Robert's Rules of Order*. They applied when he was a Free Will Baptist but not as an Old Regular, which he discovered, and he stayed away from the Delegate House for three years after that."[14]

Ordination of a Deacon at Tivis Chapel

Before closing this discussion of the local church business meeting, I need to report my observations of a very special local meeting, the ordination of a deacon. Elder Ramsey's action at Ash Camp concerning that fellowship's need for another deacon provides my bridge to such an examination.

On Saturday, May 23, 1986, I met Elder Bill Campbell in Vansant, Virginia, and traveled with him to Tivis Chapel, an affiliate of the Union Association. Campbell had invited me to accompany him on this occasion because the Tivis Chapel was set to ordain a new deacon, Brother Ted DePriest.

Tivis Chapel sits on a high ridge on the south side of Virginia Mountain near Haysi, Dickenson County, Virginia. In environmental attractiveness the site of the church exists in my mind as second only to that of the Mary Lou church. For example, I vividly recall sitting in a back pew that May morning and looking out a window down an extended vista of steeply sloping mountain meadows and wooded coves; and what I saw was two deer grazing in an idyllic setting that seemed as if it might have been chosen by a landscape artist to stand in relief against that delicate, softly rippled, ridge-layered horizon of bluish haze so familiar to early morning travelers of Appalachian mountain roads. Ironically this was my view as I listened to this small congregation of Old Regular Baptists sing:

> O come angel band,
> Come and around me stand.
> O bear me away on your snowy wings
>   to my immortal home.
> O bear me away on your snowy wings
>   to my immortal home.[15]

Tivis Chapel is that second church I mentioned as being moderated by Elder James O'Quinn, a man of genuine warmth and friendliness who not only has personally supported my field research but has maintained a spirit in his congregations that is strongly receptive to my visitations. It has been my observation that Old Regular moderators exert commanding influences over the moods of their memberships, creating atmospheres either of insularity or openness. It is for this reason, more than any other, that I have felt so indebted to men such as Bill Campbell, James O'Quinn, Raymond Smith, Wardie Craft, Dallas Ramsey, Jimmy W. Hall,

Edwin May, the late John Layne, and others. Such men are secure enough in themselves not to be frightened by an outside investigator such as I. On this particular occasion, Elder James O'Quinn demonstrated his positive attitude to my work by carefully explaining each step of the ordination process, largely, it seemed, for my benefit.

At the close of the abbreviated worship service that morning, Elder O'Quinn called the business meeting to order. Following the procedure described above, he first requested all visiting brethren to step down from the stand, leaving only Tivis Chapel members in that section. Then he asked his church if they were "in peace and love." There was a brief pause as the congregation considered this question, but no member broke the silence to speak against another. O'Quinn subsequently declared the fellowship to be in a proper spirit and invited the visiting brethren to rejoin the home membership on the stand.

Following some preliminary discussions, Elder O'Quinn moved the gathering to the main business of the morning, the ordination of Brother DePriest. It was first moved and seconded that this brother be turned over to the presbytery for examination and ordination. The presbytery was then convened, an action that resulted in all the elders and deacons (local and visiting) shifting to that side section of pews on O'Quinn's left.

After this shuffling of the seating arrangements, the presbytery came to order and elected a moderator and a clerk. Elder O'Quinn was chosen moderator, and his election precipitated some discussion as to whether this would now require that a temporary moderator be elected for the church, in view of O'Quinn's titular absence from that role. One visiting elder reported this to be the procedure followed in the fellowship to which he belonged. Nevertheless, no additional moderator was chosen, and the presbytery was considered to be instituted and seated.

Brother Ted DePriest and his wife were then officially turned over to the presbytery and seated in folding chairs in front of this body. At this point Moderator O'Quinn called for the reading of three documents (the Union Association's articles of faith, constitution, and rules of decorum), preparatory to the presbytery's quizzing of the candidate about his acceptance of these doctrinal and procedural codes.

The reading of these official statements precipitated a series of questions and comments concerning the various rules and doctrines. Apparently any member of the presbytery was now able to interrogate Brother DePriest concerning his understanding and acceptance of these pronouncements, and several elders asked the brother if he could support particular codes. The questioning was not harsh, and emphasis seemed to be on instruction.

As a continuation of this process, Moderator O'Quinn asked one of the visiting elders, Dallas Ramsey of the Ash Camp fellowship, to read passages from Acts and I Timothy that are interpreted as relating to the appointment of a deacon:

> And in those days when the number of the disciples was multiplied, there arose a murmuring of the Grecians against the Hebrews, because their widows were neglected in the daily ministration.
> Then the twelve called the multitude of the disciples unto them, and said, It is not reason that we should leave the word of God, and serve tables.
> Wherefore, brethren, look ye out among you seven men of honest report, full of the Holy Ghost and wisdom, whom we may appoint over this business.
> But we will give ourselves continually to prayer, and to the ministry of the word.
> And the saying pleased the whole multitude: and they chose Stephen, a man full of faith and of the Holy Ghost, and Philip, and Prochorus, and Nicanor, and Timon, and Parmenas, and Nicolas a proselyte of Antioch;
> Whom they set before the apostles: and when they had prayed, they laid their hands on them. (Acts 6:1–6)

> Likewise must the deacons be grave, not doubletongued, not given to much wine, not greedy of filthy lucre;
> Holding the mystery of the faith in a pure conscience.

And let these also first be proved; and let them use the office of a deacon, being found blameless.

Even so must their wives be grave, not slanderers, sober, faithful in all things.

Let the deacons be the husbands of one wife, ruling their children and their own houses well.

For they that have used the office of a deacon well purchase to themselves a good degree, and a great boldness in the faith which is in Christ Jesus. (I Tim. 3:8–13)

Members of the presbytery now questioned DePriest and his wife concerning their willingness to live up to the duties and requirements set down in these scriptures, and when satisfied they dismissed Sister DePriest from her chair. Twice Elder O'Quinn observed that DePriest's wife was not there to be ordained herself, but that her answers would testify to the fitness of her husband for the role he was seeking.

A hymn was now sung, and during the singing all the elders and deacons pressed about Brother DePriest, laying hands on him, and shaking his hand or embracing him, some tearfully. There was no apparent order to this process, with all these men milling around the stand area, engaging in other fellowshipping after laying hands on DePriest. Women, from their more distant positions, added to the emotionality, as the church reveled in this advancement of one of their most respected members.

Following this formal ordination, the entire congregation engaged in another prayer. O'Quinn, still acting as moderator of the presbytery, then returned the new deacon to the hands of the church. Subsequently a move and second were made by the congregation to receive the work of the presbytery and to discharge them. This concluded the official work of the Tivis Chapel membership that morning, and the service ended with a general round of handshaking and embracing.[16]

"Association Time"

In Old Regular country, the months of August and September are devoted to "association time," the annual three-day sessions during which the various associations combine business, worship, and fellowship into wonderful amalgams of fun, politics, and spirituality. Ranging in attendance from the forty or fifty delegates and visitors that the tiny Mud River Association (only three churches) can muster to the three thousand to four thousand participants of a New Salem Association annual gathering, these events become the culmination of a church year and capture in both their significance and size a degree of excitement that makes them irresistible to the typical Old Regular member — so irresistible, in fact, that large numbers of people regularly return from homes in Michigan, Illinois, Indiana, Ohio, North Carolina, Georgia, Florida, and points in between to reestablish their roots in Old Regular country. Thus these events are the homecomings of Old Regular tradition, drawing the faithful to their sites for large dinners-on-the-ground, spirited preaching and singing, exciting deliberations of the association delegates, and the annual reinstitution of social ties.

Dates for these weekend events become traditional, but corresponding associations try to avoid conflicts in scheduling so that members from all the affiliate churches can attend every other association's gathering. In the case of the seven clusters in correspondence with New Salem that no-conflict ideal works out for all groups except Old Friendship and Mud River. In that particular case, however, although both alliances correspond with New Salem, they don't correspond with each other, and thus are not motivated to avoid a conflict. Nevertheless, the following represents a schedule that could be followed by an Old Regular wishing to attend all but one of these eight gatherings:

> Northern New Salem (three days) — convening on Friday before the first Saturday in August.

Philadelphia (three days) — convening on Friday before the
second Saturday in August.

Old Friendship and Mud River (both three days) — convening
on Friday before the fourth Saturday in August.

Indian Bottom (three days) — convening on Friday before the
first Saturday in September.

Sardis (three days) — convening on Friday before the second
Saturday in September.

Union (three days) — convening on Friday before the third
Saturday in September.

New Salem (three days) — convening on Friday before the
fourth Saturday in September.

In 1986 I attended three of these affairs (Old Friendship,
Union, and New Salem); in 1987 I managed four annual sessions (Thornton Union, Indian Bottom, Union, and New Salem); and during 1988 I again visited these same four association meetings. In addition, on August 29, 1987, I witnessed
the reorganization and fifth annual session of the Original
Mountain Liberty Association, Little Freedom Church, Vansant, Virginia.[17]

Probably very few Old Regulars make more than three or
four of these meetings a year, but numerous families do plan
vacations to coincide with at least two annual sessions. Indeed, parking lots at the gathering areas (especially for Union
and New Salem) give evidence of the long-distance travel involved, filled as they usually are with cars, pickups, and recreational vehicles from a dozen or more states. In the world
of Old Regular Baptists association meetings rank among the
peak experiences of life, and events which transpire in annual sessions are not only vital to the operations of the faith,
but also provide topics for excited discussions during the suc-
ceeding twelve months.

Among the associations there are several variations in the
physical arrangements for business sessions and the preaching and singing services. Since 1984 the Union churches have
met at the fairgrounds in Wise, Virginia, where they use two
gathering areas, a large tent that accommodates between
800 and 1,000 people and a permanent covered arena, used

Crowded parking at the 1986 Annual Session, Old Beaver Church, and the New Salem Association Building.

during fairs for outdoor concerts. This second facility will seat 1,500 to 2,000 spectators. Delegates conduct their business under the tent, while the sideline preaching and singing transpires in the concert arena.

New Salem possesses perhaps the best facility for such arrangements, a large metal "Association Building" that sits adjacent to Old Beaver Church in Minnie, Floyd County, Kentucky. Delegates meet in the church, while nondelegates gather in the larger structure. The only difficulty with this situation is that Old Beaver Church is too small to seat many more than the official delegates and the "messengers" from other associations, thus allowing only a few nondelegate spectators to witness the sessions. At Union's annual meetings nondelegate spectators crowd under the tent until there is no space remaining. Only then will some individuals go to the preaching-singing area. Old Regulars take a deep interest in association business.

Elder Wardie Craft moderates the 1987 Thornton Union Annual Session.

Indian Bottom also has a permanent association building, a three-story former high school in Sassafras, Knott County, Kentucky. Many of the original room partitions have been removed from this structure, allowing a spacious area in the basement to become the delegate chamber, the middle floor to be employed as the dining facility, and the entire third floor to constitute the preaching and singing auditorium.

Thornton Union has built its "Delegate House" across the parking lot from Thornton Church in the small community of Mayking, Letcher County, Kentucky. Preaching and singing takes place in the church, business is conducted in the delegate house, and association meals are served in a long kitchen and dining facility attached to the church.

The other associations, as far as I have been able to determine, rotate their annual meetings among their member fellowships, unless a particular church is either too small or too distant from the geographical center of the cluster. The meetinghouse of the host congregation usually becomes the space for business meetings, while other arrangements are made for the sideline worship activities. For example, the 1986 session of the Old Friendship Association was held at Mary Lou Church, discussed in chapter 3. Business sessions were conducted in the church sanctuary, while the accompanying services of preaching and singing were staged up the road at the Mary Lou Cemetery, using the covered stand described earlier.

In much earlier times horses provided the main form of transportation to and from these gatherings, and so there would be large collections of these animals on the periphery of the meeting areas. This eventually gave rise to the "jockey grounds," spots near the association meetings where horse trading would be going on during the three-day meetings, a practice that soon developed many highly objectionable aspects. In 1914 the New Salem Association passed a motion condemning this practice:

> Resolved that we, the New Salem Association . . . denounce the practice of horse jockeying and the so-called Jockey Ground near any of our annual sessions, and we positively declare the said practice to be a public nuisance, endangering human life, destruction to the peace and good order of the community and injurious to the morals of the people.[18]

The "Jockey Ground" tradition may not have disappeared entirely even today. When leaving the 1987 New Salem gathering, the Marshalls and I spotted a temporarily cleared, side-of-the-road horse trading area less than two miles from the New Salem Association Building.

For the larger associations preparation of meeting areas begins early in the week. In the case of the Union annual session, for example, workers gather at the Wise fairgrounds on Monday morning, one male group to raise the tent, another male contingent to ready the grounds, and a female crew to clean and arrange the kitchen and food-serving facility. Then all week, as some of this initial work continues, other clusters of people arrive to deliver folding chairs for the tent (loaned by affiliate churches), to set up trash barrels around the grounds, to bring food products to the kitchen, to establish a concession stand, to string electrical wiring to the tent, or just to mingle with the growing crowd of Old Regular folks who gradually are drawn to the scene, much as crowds once were attracted to the setting up of an annual circus.

In addition, throughout this week people arrive in their recreational vehicles and campers, parking them in a long row on the far side of the grounds. Toward the middle of the week this movement has produced a small on-the-grounds community which may gather in the evening to sing "the old songs of Zion," getting in the spirit for the weekend events.

Women groups in particular are busy during a week before an association meeting. For the annual sessions of the smaller groups these sisters have continued the tradition of each preparing several miscellaneous dishes to be arranged on an outside common table or an inside serving counter. But the larger gatherings (those of Thornton Union, Indian Bottom, Union, and New Salem) have begun to demand a more planned approach, since between a thousand and four thousand people may be fed in a two- or two-and-a-half-hour period. This of course requires a large quantity of food, a systematic way of preparing it, and a somewhat lockstep method of serving it: the basic dishes prepared in mass quantities (mashed potatoes, chicken and dumplings, fried chicken, corn, beans, etc.), staggered serving shifts, multiple well-managed serving lines, and considerably more regimentation than in the informal serve-yourself arrangement. Even in these much larger affairs, however, the systems have preserved some elements of the bring-a-dish tradition, especially for desserts: during meals in the New Salem dining area one will find shelves along both side walls laden with servings from several hundred pies, cakes, custards, and cobblers that individual women have baked for the occasion.

The Three-Day Events

In general, the three days of an association's annual meeting will go something like the following. On Friday morning the crowd will gather between 8:30 and 9:30 in the larger of the two assembly areas available. There will be thirty or forty minutes of singing, and the introductory sermon will be preached, followed by the opening prayer. Then, depending upon the arrangements, either the delegates will be dismissed to another structure or the spectators will be dismissed to wherever the sideline preaching and singing takes place. In this area a steady stream of elders (from the particular association or visitors) will conduct a nonstop worship service, which often, with the crowds involved, becomes highly spirited.

Some individuals may wander back and forth from the preaching arena to the delegate conclave, in one instance trying to catch an especially exciting bit of debate in the session and in another being drawn to the preaching talents of a certain elder. Then throughout the day small clusters of people will gather around the concession stand, in various open areas, or just anywhere to discuss events of the moment.

The association's business meeting, to be examined more closely later, will continue until 12:30 or 1:00, at which time delegates break for the noon meal. But the women probably will have started serving by 11:00, trying to get as many people through the lines as possible before the larger crowds hit.

When this meal is completed delegates may return to their meeting, depending upon how many of the traditional agenda items were covered during the morning session; but the afternoon usually is devoted just to committee meetings. Then in the evening both delegates and spectators may return to the larger gathering facility for another round of preaching and singing.

On Saturday the same procedure is followed, except that there will be different items of business to be considered by the delegates. Indeed, the Saturday session is traditionally the longest, the most complicated, and potentially the most heated, involving as it does deliberations that are more likely to engender controversy. The Sunday session, on the other hand, includes no business, becomes the time for unification and inspiration, and focuses solely on worship, with the three or four preachers chosen for both their eminence within the association and their speaking abilities. Unless health or some other factor prevents him from doing so, the association moderator delivers the sermon that closes the worship.

Thornton Union seems to place the most emphasis upon the preaching and singing part of this annual happening. Starting on the Sunday of the previous weekend, this association stages seven evening services that lead to and include Friday night and Saturday night of the session weekend, calling four preachers to fill the stand each evening.[19] The Sunday through Thursday evening services are viewed as spiritual "warm-ups" for the main event, and crowds tend to grow as the week develops.

Annual Business Sessions

The actual business sessions of typical association meetings develop something like the following. On Friday morning, following the introductory singing, preaching, and prayer, the association's moderator calls for the "church letters." As the roll of fellowships is called, a delegate from each congregation moves to the stand and presents that church's letter, a combination annual report, statement of the fellowship's "love and peace," and documentation of legitimacy. Each of these letters also contains names of the three delegates and their alternates. At some earlier time all of these letters may have been read to the assembly, but today the tradition is, at least in the larger associations, to select only one of the letters and read it as representative of all the others.

Once all these lists of delegates have been presented to the clerk, the moderator can proceed to seat the assembly, which sometimes means an actual reshuffling of the crowd so that delegates are positioned in a particular area of the facility. Now the moderator appoints a committee of tellers whose job it is to collect and count delegate votes for the session's officers: moderator, assistant moderator, clerk, and assistant clerk. Since this counting can become politically sensitive, a tradition has developed that the moderator select as tellers three or four leaders from corresponding associations. These men, in turn, take their task seriously, knowing that session elections are potentially explosive. Ordinarily Old Regulars are loyal to their leaders and return them to office year after year, but occasionally a moderator must step down due to age or infirmities. Then there are the years when true dissatisfaction with a moderator develops, giving this point in the convention the chance to become the first moment of real devisive tension and controversy. If a new moderator is elected the subsequent transition may also become destructive to "love and peace," for the various fellowships may not coalesce around the new leader, even resulting in another new moderator being elected the next year.

Once the election has been completed and the chosen brethren have formally accepted their positions, the doors of the association are opened to the receiving of any new churches, with each application being debated separately. During the 1986 Union meeting three fellowships sought and were granted affiliation with the association. One, Little Marie of Litchfield, Ohio, was a newly constituted church; while the second, Little Jewel of Ashland, Kentucky, had been granted a letter of dismissal from the Northern New Salem Association, specifically to enable them to affiliate with Union. The third fellowship, Bartlick Church of Haysi, Virginia, was "restored to fellowship" after having withdrawn from the association at an earlier time.[20]

Brother John Morgan Mullins, Clerk of the Union Association, reads a church letter during the 1986 Session. Moderator John Layne listens.

Traditionally the next items of business are (1) to receive letters from each of the other associations with which the alliance corresponds, (2) to seat the delegates sent by these corresponding associations, and (3) to call for requests from other Old Regular associations wishing to correspond. Regarding this third item, there usually is not much action, at least not among the seven clusters corresponding with New Salem. First, the relationships between most Old Regular groups have been relatively static for some time, and, second, there has been only one new association formed in recent years, the Original Mountain Liberty Association. Furthermore, it seems unlikely that the Original Mountain Liberty group will seek correspondence with any of the Union or New Salem corresponding clusters, since the present leadership of Original Mountain Liberty views these other groups with some degree of antipathy.[21]

Controversy occasionally occurs when the moderator moves

to the next major item of business, consideration of a formal motion to maintain correspondence with the particular group of associations recognized by the cluster. At this time some delegates may argue to drop correspondence with one or more groups on the grounds of doctrinal impurity or irregularity in practices. At one time, for example, Thornton Union and New Salem corresponded, but during the 1950s and 1960s New Salem frequently expressed concerns about the behaviors of certain Thornton Union fellowships, even on two occasions demanding that Thornton Union bring those churches in line with traditional Old Regular practices. New Salem's main concern, apparently, was the allegation that some Thornton Union fellowships were allowing their women members to lead prayers and to "bob" their hair. Finally, in 1969, New Salem dropped correspondence with Thornton Union altogether.[22]

In more recent years the larger Indian Bottom Association has been in trouble with some of its correspondents. At the time of this writing Old Friendship and Philadelphia, two groups corresponding with both New Salem and Union, don't recognize either of the Indian Bottom clusters, and have not done so for a number of years; but in 1986 Northern New Salem also voted to drop correspondence with the larger Indian Bottom alliance. As has often been the case in such situations, the charge was that the latter's churches were allowing women to "bob" their hair.[23]

Routine agenda items will consume the remainder of Friday's agenda, including appointment of a committee on ministry (charged with determining who will fill the stand during the preaching and singing services) and a committee on arrangements (responsible for setting the agenda for Saturday's business session). If the delegates dispense with these matters by noon or thereabout, as mentioned earlier, then they will not convene again until Saturday morning, but if debate has become protracted, then the delegates might recess for lunch and reconvene around 2:00. In the Union Association the committee on arrangements will have their meeting on Friday evening.

On Saturday morning, following the roll call of delegates and a report of the committee on arrangements, the first item of business ordinarily is to hear the "Circular Letter," read by its author and submitted for publication in the minutes. This is a moment of significant honor for the Old Regular elder who has been chosen to compose and present this document, an honor that may come only once in a lifetime, if at all. The elder in question will have had a full year to ponder and compose the thoughts he most wants to express to his brothers and sisters in the association, and the final composition should not only be expressed in the best form of which the elder is capable, but it should also embody a message significant to the association's needs. Darvin Marshall has observed that the original purpose of this document was to "clarify a point of doctrine that was not understood" or which had become a focal point in "differences of opinions among the churches."[24] Again, this is one of those traditions reaching far back beyond the origins of Old Regularism, and the practice undoubtedly has passed through a number of transitions in purpose and style. My impression, however, drawn from reading a large number of these documents, is that they are either primarily didactic in goal or primarily inspirational in goal. Elder Fred Stiltner's letter to the 1987 session of the Union Association fell into the latter category, praising as it did the generations of Old Regular leadership; while Elder Clayton Montgomery's letter to the 1986 Thornton Union session was clearly didactic, scolding the association for a large number of practices — both by preachers and by congregations — that he viewed as destructive of effective worship. Included in Montgomery's list of distractions were several of the informalities in behavior that I have felt give charm to Old Regular services.[25]

At the 1986 annual session of Union Association, Elder Garland Mullins of Lloyd, Kentucky, presented the circular letter and at one point during its reading became very emotional, experiencing, I surmised, the full impact of the honor of being chosen for this role. However, perhaps anticipating some of the conflict that would be present in that session later in the morning—to be covered shortly—he drew his message from the Beatitudes of the Sermon on the Mount, stressing in particular the "blessed are the peacemakers" proclamation.[26]

Following the presentation of the circular letter, the delegates take up a series of matters that generally stimulate no extensive discussions: the treasurer's report, motions to publish several traditional items in the minutes (such as the obituaries of deceased members), motions to establish certain committees, the consideration of letters to be addressed to corresponding associations, and the naming of messengers to deliver these correspondences.

But after all these items of business the session moves into an area of deliberations during which controversy may run high, and generally does at least once. This is the point at which the committee on arrangements clusters any "queries," "requests," and special issues that may have arisen earlier in the session which could not be dealt with at the time of inception. Queries relate to points of doctrine or policy, and requests most frequently express the desire of individual churches to change their calendar of services or to modify their role of ordained ministers.

An example of a query could be the one placed before the 1985 session of the Sardis Association: "Shall we receive into fellowship men or women having more than one wife or husband?" This is a question that had been asked numerous times in the various associations, and it does not relate to bigamy but to the act of remarrying after a divorce. It was phrased this way because, as was established in chapter 1, Old Regulars traditionally don't recognize a divorce unless it is achieved on the particular ground of adultery. In continued support of that policy, the response of the Sardis delegates went as follows: "We advise the Churches not to receive into their fellowships any such [persons], except those who have put away their companion for the cause of fornication, such cases to have Gospel or Church evidence of same."[27]

Example of requests would include, among others, the asking of permission to change the date of a communion meeting; requests to drop a name or names from the association's roll of ministers; and requests to alter wording in the articles of faith, constitution, or rules of decorum. The first of these items is fairly routine and rarely would involve any dispute. The second, dropping names from the roll of ministers, relates to the right of an individual fellowship to withdraw from this roll any man whom that church has ordained. Again there is generally no debate over these requests, unless in one instance the fellowship itself has been split on the issue. In such cases the association traditionally supports the majority local church position. Controversy often does arise, however, when an attempt is made to alter one of the key documents of the association, unless it involves a request like one advanced during the 1987 Northern New Salem annual session. In that instance Antioch Church and Little Flock Church both asked the delegates to amend the articles of faith so that the wording "We believe the scriptures of the Old and New Testaments are the written words of God" be changed to "We believe the scriptures of the Old and New Testaments of the 1611 Authorized King James Version of the Bible are the written words of God." That request was granted simply by a motion and a second.[28]

Concerning questions that earlier came before the assembly but which were not acted upon at the time of inception, the best example I can give is from the 1986 Union meeting. On Friday morning, when letters were being submitted by the member churches, one fellowship — the name of which I will not give, because of the sensitivity of this issue — presented two letters, meaning the fellowship had split, with each remnant seeking to represent itself as the legitimate church. Moderator John Layne had no choice but to postpone this matter until later in the session, since he had to seat the delegates before any issue could be considered; and by presenting two letters the church had also represented two sets of delegates. Consequently, Layne referred the matter to the committee on arrangements for placement on the agenda. He then announced that no delegates for that fellowship could be seated until the issue was resolved.

On Saturday morning, when the question of the two letters reached the floor, the spectators and delegates under the Union Association tent were exposed to an intense and highly sensitive debate. Briefly, here is what had happened at the splintered church: the fellowship's moderator had been accused of adultery; not all members of the church, however, had believed the charge; the result was that the membership had split to both sides of the issue, one faction led by the moderator, and the second led by his assistant. Eventually each group composed a letter for presentation to the association.

The issue debated that morning under the Union Association tent, before an audience of over eight hundred spectators, was not, in the language of Paul's first letter to the Corinthians, "the smallest of matters," nor was it the least provocative of matters; nevertheless, it was discussed with unusual decorum, considering the emotions inherent in the issue. As a manifestation of the tension present, about ten minutes into the deliberations the entire audience stood and remained on their feet, in relative silence, during the remainder of the discussion.

Moderator John Layne had only one immediate goal, to get the issue off the floor and into the hands of an investigating committee, and he stated this goal repeatedly. But it was obvious that a number of delegates wanted to decide the question then and there. With the instinct of a leader who was aware of the explosive passions of his people, Layne still did his best to stay away from the substantive charges of the case, steering the debate toward procedural questions and hoping for the motion that would refer the matter to a committee. Only once did he recognize a speaker who moved into the adultery issue, and in that instance simply to provide a scriptural base – again from Paul – for excluding an individual guilty of this charge:

I wrote unto you in an epistle not to company with forni-
cators. . . . But now I have written unto you not to keep
company, if any man that is called a brother be a fornicator,
or covetous, or an idolater, or a railer, or a drunkard, or an
extortioner. . . .

                                                I Cor. 6:9 and 11

Only once, also, did Layne lose his temper during this debate, and that was when a woman, in one of the spectator
sections, shouted a comment, which from my position in the
tent I could not understand. "You shut up! You just shut up!"
Layne retorted. "We have enough trouble up here without
you talking!" The woman did "shut up," and there was no
laughter or similar response from the crowd. There appeared
to be general agreement within the audience that this woman
had greatly overstepped her bounds, giving Layne every justification to lash out at her in the harshest of tones. Indeed,
had Layne not responded as he did he probably would have
lost much of his male and female support.

After about twenty minutes of extremely tense discussion,
Moderator Layne did get a motion to refer the matter to a
committee, and the motion carried. Whereupon, Layne appointed to this body five elders who were instructed to visit
the church, ascertain the truth, and attempt a reconciliation
of the factions if at all possible.[29] At the 1987 annual session
the committee made a report to accept the exclusion of this
fellowship's previous moderator and the letter presented by
the faction supporting the assistant moderator.[30] The committee's recommendation was accepted.

Before this episode erupted I had been at one side of the
raised platform that constituted the stand, taking photographs. The high sensitivity and tension of this debate had
caused me to close my camera case and make it as inconspicuous as possible. However, when the discussion ended I
moved around to the front entrance of the tent to get some
head–on shots of various individuals on the stand, and I then
had my camera exposed. It was at this moment that one delegate rose and started to exit the tent but stopped when he

saw me. The expression I first observed on his face simply suggested that he might have had some involvement with the previous issue, but when he saw my camera he assumed a very stern countenance and asked, "What are those pictures for? You're not with a newspaper, are you?"

The response I gave apparently satisfied him, since he quickly relaxed. Still this was not the most comfortable interpersonal confrontation I have experienced during my studies of Appalachian religious traditions, and while the adultery debate was transpiring there were moments when even I questioned the propriety of my presence.

Old Regulars do have a reason to be cautious about outsiders, for the subdenomination has not always been treated with the minimal respect due its religious traditions. Members of the Bethel Old Regular Church in Dunham, Kentucky, tell of a Sunday when a television crew barged into one of their services, without any request or warning, and began taping the worship proceedings.[31] Such disrespect for any religious service is difficult to excuse. Elder John Layne knew of my presence and had given his blessing to my camera usage. During the 1987 Union Association meeting, however, I was asked to remove a tape recorder that I had set up in front of the stand. That was one instance in which I had overstepped my bounds.

Returning to the discussion of typical proceedings, I will just add that after the consideration of these queries, requests, and special issues, the delegates usually have only two or three brief items of business before adjournment, including approval of the minutes. Following the procedure adopted for local church business meetings, minutes for a session are approved before that session closes; however, there usually will be a motion to omit the actual reading of the minutes. By late October or early November member churches will receive their requested supply of the printed minutes, and individual members will have plenty of time to scrutinize the work of the association's clerk before the next session. If something has been incorrectly recorded a motion of correction will eventually be moved.

On Sunday morning the service will be emotional and unifying. Every effort will be made to mend any divisions that might have developed as a consequence of the debates, and the annual meeting will close on a note of "love and peace," with, as mentioned, the moderator delivering the final sermon. Generally, it will take thirty minutes or more after the close for the stand to clear, as officers, delegates, ordinary church members, and the wives of everyone go through a round of warm embraces and final expressions of fellowship.

When placing a record of this service in the annual minutes the clerk will usually write in glowing terms, praising not only the harmony of the event but the beauty of the "old hymns of Zion," the eloquence of the speakers, and the sadness of another season's farewell:

> The last day of the Session of the Union Association was a day of thanksgiving and also sad farewell, when so many would travel to distant homes, going their separate ways after the Sunday Service comes to a close. It was a day of sweet memories for some and sad goodbyes for others.
>
> Several met out early and soon the area was filled with the sound of many happy voices singing the good old hymns of Zion in praise of our King.
>
> Elder Fon Bowling came forward and was blessed to introduce the service with much humbleness and thanksgiving expressed through the humble Spirit of the Lord.
>
> Elder Jimmy Dale Sanders was second on the stand. The Sweet Spirit carried him out on wings of love as he was blessed to preach the Gospel in its purity. Many of the hearers rejoiced as he pursued his subject under the guidance of the Sweet Spirit of Peace.
>
> Elder Franklin O'Quinn was third to come to the stand. With his humble manner and tender expression, he seemed to capture the attention of the congregation, as the Lord blessed him to preach the Gospel of the Kingdom. His extra blessing seemed transferred to those around him, and many shouted the praises of the Lord through a great part of his sermon.

Our beloved Moderator, Elder John C. Layne, though in pain and ill health, he seemed to forget his discomfort and spoke wonderfully and with much humbleness, he brought to a close this, the 127th session of this Grand Old Association. Brother John was tender and humble in his discourse as he bade goodbye to the congregation.[32]

There are two narratives I want to record before concluding these observations concerning annual sessions, and both relate in some way to the Union Association. The first tells of Sister Rena Caudill and New Hope Church, the only Old Regular Baptist fellowship in North Carolina; and the second treats the funeral of Elder John Layne, mentioned above for his moderating of Union Association.

Homegoing, a Sense of Place, and Sister Rena Caudill

As a transition to my Sister Rena narrative I need to mention again the drawing power of annual association sessions. I remarked earlier that association meetings are often used by Old Regulars as homecomings, creating a profound sense of loyalty for these yearly events. During the 1986 New Salem "association time," for example, I met a woman from Virgie, Kentucky, who told me that the occasion was her thirty-fourth consecutive annual New Salem session, and she added that she did not intend to miss any future ones as long as her health permitted. Unfortunately, I didn't record the woman's name, nor did I encounter her again at the 1987 New Salem session; nevertheless, she still represents for me both that group of Old Regulars who are so faithful in annual session attendance and the lodestone effect that keeps pulling them back year after year. My guess is that this personal achievement of thirty-four "association times" is far from any record, that some Old Regular senior citizen could be found who has made it to fifty of these events.

What might be of equal significance, however, is the fact

that so many of these people are "returning," in the sense that they have moved completely out of the region but still make their pilgrimages back to Old Regular country in sense-of-place home goings, pulled by the magnetic attractions of family, friends, geographical area, and religious faith. It is understanding of that reality that must precede this introduction to Sister Rena Caudill of Winnabow, North Carolina.

When I began my initial work with Old Regulars I was intrigued by the fact that the only Old Regular church I could locate in North Carolina was in Winnabow, Brunswick County, over four hundred miles away from her nearest sister fellowships, Mt. Ararat in Galax, Virginia. As indicated earlier, there are a number of Regular Baptist churches in this state, but New Hope Church, situated in the southeasternmost county of North Carolina, is the only Tar Heel contribution to the Old Regular tradition.

The New Hope church can be reached by traveling south from Wilmington, North Carolina, on Highway 17, moving toward Supply and Shallotte. Drive past the small community of Winnabow; turn left onto Highway 87; proceed to the junction with Route 1518 and again turn left; move on to the junction with "Pretty Pond Road"; and this time turn right. From this point New Hope Church is approximately three miles down Pretty Pond Road, on the left. The meetinghouse can be clearly identified by its large sign on the front of the structure. A beach vacation in July 1987 provided me the opportunity to visit this church and to conduct the first of two interviews with Sister Rena Caudill.[33]

New Hope Old Regular Baptist Church was established primarily through the efforts of the late Elder Emmitt Caudill and his wife, Sister Rena, both from Letcher County, Kentucky, the small towns of Eolia and Partridge respectively. Emmitt had begun work in the Kentucky coal mines in the mid-1930s and had continued through the 1940s, laboring at one time or another in Harlan, Letcher, and Perry counties, and experiencing the Harlan County labor wars of the 1940s.

New Hope Church, Winnabow, North Carolina.

But he was afflicted with an early and severe case of black lung and by the 1950s had retired from coal mining.

Embittered by his respiratory problems, and disturbed by general labor conditions in the coal industry, Brother Emmitt declared in 1953 that he never wanted either of his three sons to work the mines; but he reasoned that if the family remained in the region he might not be able to prevent that eventuality.

Sister Rena had family members, including a brother, who had already moved to Brunswick County, North Carolina, where farming and other occupational opportunities looked much better than in Letcher County, Kentucky. So after a visit to these North Carolina tidelands to confirm these opportunities, Brother Emmitt and Sister Rena moved their

*Sister Rena Caudill on her porch in Brunswick County,
North Carolina.*

family away from the coalfields and out of Old Regular country. It was in this new location that Emmitt would die in 1986.

Before her marriage Sister Rena had been a Maggard, and she was also a granddaughter of Elder Dave Maggard, one of the patriarchs of Old Regularism and a man important in the history of the Indian Bottom and Thornton Union associations.[34] Therefore, she was strongly imbued with the beliefs and customs of Old Regularism and was a member of the Oven Fork fellowship while in Letcher County. Emmitt, on the other hand, at the time of this move was not a member of the Old Regular faith.

Now living in the coastal tidelands of North Carolina, Sister Rena suffered an immediate and severe sense of cultural dislocation. She tried a few of the Baptist churches in and around Winnabow. One was Free Will; another was Missionary; and the third, according to her description, was "just plain Baptist." But she found the beliefs and worship practices of these fellowships to be sharply alien to everything she had experienced in an Old Regular church. There was no lined singing; there was none of the richly rhythmical or plaintively chanted preaching to which she had grown accustomed; and there were few of the customs of fellowship she had learned to love—the rounds of handshaking and embracing at various intervals in the service, the intensely emotional interchanges at footwashings and other Old Regular ceremonies, and the touchingly communal memorial services, creek baptisms, and dinners-on-the-ground. There were, however, Sunday schools, musical instruments, songs sung in harmony, plates passed for money, very young children being baptized, paid ministers, and a host of other practices which bothered her considerably. It was going to be difficult for her, she thought, to practice her religion there on the coastline of North Carolina.

The several members of Sister Rena's family who were already living in Brunswick County had been members of

Old Regular fellowships back in Kentucky and Virginia, but these memberships were scattered, not only among different churches, but also among different associations. The thing that needed to be done, Sister Rena decided, was to collect this handful of memberships in one church, and then have that fellowship establish an "arm" in Winnabow, North Carolina. That was precisely the plan followed, all under the direction of Sister Rena.

As noted earlier, Emmitt Caudill was not a member of an Old Regular fellowship when he first moved his family away from Kentucky, but the services that his wife occasionally arranged in their North Carolina home (conducted by visiting elders from Virginia, Tennessee, and Florida) ultimately resulted in the 1970 baptism of Emmitt and his oldest son, Fred. These additions to the Brunswick County cluster encouraged Sister Rena to make her final push toward the establishment of a new church.

Before the actual foundation of the fellowship there was discussion as to what to name the new church. Some members of the group wanted to name it "Little Rena," in honor of Sister Rena's almost twenty-year effort to organize the fellowship, but Rena Caudill would not accept that recognition, sensitive as she was to her female position in all these activities. Instead, she argued for "New Hope," primarily because there had been a time when it looked like efforts to organize the fellowship and acquire a piece of ground for the church building would not be successful, a time followed, she said, by "new hope."

Bethany Old Regular Baptist, Kingsport, Tennessee, became the mother church for New Hope, arming off a small congregation of nine North Carolinians, in June 1972, nineteen years after Brother Emmitt and Sister Rena had migrated to their new home. Emmitt eventually became an elder of the nascent congregation, but his black lung problems increased to such an extent that he could no longer be of much service to the fellowship. Elder Caudill died May 24, 1986, after a prolonged confinement that included constant connection to a respirator. His obituary, published in the 1987 Union Association minutes, will be provided later in this work.

Sister Rena's three sons and one daughter all married in the Brunswick County region and have provided her, at the time of this writing, eleven grandchildren and nine great-grandchidren, all of whom she hopes will continue to populate New Hope Church. In 1987, however, the fellowship still could claim a membership of only ten, but each year the small church sends their three delegates to the Union Association meeting.[35] Sister Rena Caudill, of course, can never be one of those delegates, even though she was largely responsible for the establishment of this one-and-only North Carolina Old Regular Baptist fellowship; but annually she travels the six hundred miles between Winnabow, North Carolina, and Wise, Virginia, to attend these Union Association meetings. It was there, on September 18, 1987, under the Union Association's large tent, that I was able to conduct my second interview with Sister Rena.

I have devoted this space to Sister Rena's story primarily because she represents that group of Old Regulars who have been instrumental in establishing isolated fellowships of this Baptist subdenomination far from the geographical core of Old Regular country, but who regularly return to that geographical core for annual reunions of the faith.

Two factors of this phenomenon need to be mentioned. First, it appears that Old Regulars, once having migrated away from central Appalachia, are not easily assimilated into the established Baptist churches of their new regions: the variances between Old Regularism and some of the other Baptist groups are simply too great. Second, there seems to be an inextricable tie between this faith and the region in which it originated: although Old Regular fellowships may be instituted in Michigan, Indiana, Florida, North Carolina, and elsewhere, the true mother country of the faith remains that dozen or fifteen counties of central Appalachia where

the roots of the subdenomination were first planted. The
first of these phenomena may cause Old Regular churches to
be formed outside this mother country, but the second pre-
cipitates those annual pilgrimages to such places as Wise,
Virginia; and Sassafras, Mayking, and Minnie, Kentucky.
Thus a magnetic pull is always present, drawing the faithful
back to the Cumberland, there to sing an old hymn that has
become traditional as an opening anthem, "Brethren, We
Have Met Again":

> Brethren, we have met again,
> Let us join to pray and sing'
> Jesus as the Savior reigns,
> Praise Him in the highest strains!
>
> Many days and weeks are past,
> Since we met together last,
> Yet our lives do still remain,
> Here on earth we meet again.
>
> Many of our friends are gone
> To their long eternal home.
> They have left us here below,
> Soon we after them shall go.
>
> Brethren, tell me how you do,
> Does your love continue true?
> Are you waiting for your King,
> When He shall return again?
>
> Gracious is the Lord indeed,
> To my soul in the time of need;
> Surely He hath won my heart'
> May I choose Him for my part?
>
> Jesus is my glorious King,
> May our hearts be tuned to sing:
> Praise Him, love Him evermore,
> He's the God whom we adore.[36]

The Funeral of Elder John C. Layne

Elder John C. Layne moderated the Union Association of Old Regular Baptists from 1968 to 1987.[37] His length of service was exceeded only by the tenure of Elder J. C. Swindall, who led the association from 1896 to 1938.[38] During Layne's years of leadership, Union Association grew from sixty-four to seventy-three churches, but actually decreased slightly in total membership, 3,518 to 3,225; however, his period in office appears to have been highly successful in keeping all of these fellowships together under one organizational structure. As we will see in chapter 6, Old Regulars are capable of being very contentious, and it takes a strong and politically astute leader to maintain any significant degree of association cohesion.

I watched Elder Layne in action during that heated 1986 Union Association annual session and developed an immediate appreciation for his ability to handle a potentially explosive gathering. As a man of strong voice and even stronger physical demeanor, Layne proved able to maintain order and decorum when persons of lesser skill and stature surely would have failed. An Old Regular association moderator must always stand ready to employ his physical imagery and his voice to overpower recalcitrant delegates or spectators, particularly under the Union Association's tent where tradition forbids the use of any sound system.

John Layne met those physical requirements of voice and stature very well, and he always reminded me of the stereotypic union boss — tough, decisive, and unhesitant in the wielding of power, but stealthily political and closely in touch with the wants and values of the people he led. Furthermore, he was capable — so his Old Regular people always said — of remarkable kindness and sensitivity. He was, after all, a religious leader, and that required that he exhibit what his followers would perceive as moral and ethical character.

Although Elder Layne engendered some controversy dur-

ing that 1986 annual session (through his handling of the
adultery debate and subsequent committee action, and by
his support for the readmittance to fellowship of a church
that had left the Union Association with considerable bitterness), it seems likely that he would have been reelected to his
moderator's role in 1987 had he not experienced a rather severe heart attack.[39] So on the morning of September 18, 1987,
John C. Layne stood before the assembled Union Association
and emotionally requested that the delegates not reinstate
him to leadership. Whereupon, they followed his wishes, ele-
vating instead Layne's long-time assistant moderator, Elder
Fon Bowling.[40]

On February 11, 1988, after yet another heart attack, Brother
John Layne died, setting the stage for what I have been told
was one of the largest Old Regular funerals in recent history.
Indeed, several individuals expressed to me their judgment
that it would have been even a larger affair had it taken place
during a spring or summer month when more people could
travel. Still, as it was, the funeral became the three-service
event that attracted approximately two thousand respect-
payers from several associations and several states.

An ordinary Old Regular funeral tends to be what some
might view as a drawn-out affair, with one or two nights of
service in the home before the main event at the church. Furthermore, the home services usually include as full a slate of
singing and preaching as will occur in the church, thus allowing the bereaved to call upon a contingent of six, eight, ten,
or more preachers if family protocol or individual wishes
so dictate. In the case of Brother John's funeral, the family
home could not contain the crowds wishing to attend; therefore, all three services (Friday evening, Saturday evening,
and Sunday morning) were held in Bethlehem Old Regular
Baptist Church on Poplar Creek near Grundy, Virginia. Sister
Kathryn Layne, Brother John's wife, got word to me through
Elder Bill Campbell that the family would welcome my attendance at one or all of the services, and so the Marshalls
and I drove to Grundy that mid-February Sunday morning

to pay our own respect to a man who had given his full support to this study of Old Regularism.

It had snowed in Buchanan County, Virginia, during the evening of that Thursday Elder Layne died, and on Sunday a small residue of that whiteness still clung to the shadowed coves of the hills around Poplar Creek. This, plus the winter-barren limbs of native hardwoods, lent a starkness to the region that would not have been present during spring, summer, or fall months. I have periodically had to remind myself that I was experiencing Old Regularism primarily during those lushly foliaged intervals of the Appalachian year. It makes a difference, I think.

Bethlehem Church is one of the larger Old Regular meetinghouses, a building that when filled will seat well over six hundred people. That Sunday the church was filled, and folding chairs had been tucked in every available open space, particularly on the raised section, where all of the visiting elders wanted to find a spot as close to the stand as possible. Outside another hundred or more adults, young people, and children milled around the front of the church throughout the morning service.

Directly in front of the stand Elder Layne had been laid out in an opened casket, surrounded and partially covered by an abundance of floral sprays. In a front pew, three feet away, sat Sister Kathryn, receiving the steady flow of condolences given by those who made their way down to the casket. It was a quiet and properly dignified affair, but members of the family seemed genuinely pleased by the occasional appearance of someone who had driven several hundred miles to honor this past leader of Old Regularism.

There are at least two factors making Old Regular Baptist funerals different from their counterparts in mainline Protestant churches, the first of which is the reading of the obituary. Singing-preaching formats for these services are essentially the same as those for standard Old Regular meetings, following the basic organizational pattern described in chapter 2. But before the introductory sermon is preached one el-

Crowd outside Bethlehem Church during the John Layne funeral service.

der (usually the moderator of the fellowship) will read the deceased's obituary, the same document that later will be published in the association's annual minutes, if submitted by the family. In the case of John Layne's obituary, Elder Paul McClanahan, moderator of Bethlehem Church, performed the reading. Since obituaries will be briefly discussed in chapter 5, I will simply note here that in Elder Layne's case this document naturally stressed his contributions to the Union Association.

The second difference alluded to above deals with the number of preachers. While the mainline churches will usually have only one funeral sermon, Old Regulars will have the obligatory three, four, or more, depending upon the wishes of the family. On February 14, 1988, the Layne family kept the number down to three, since they did not want an inordin-

John Layne's casket being carried up the hill to his burial site.

ately long service, and because six preachers had already been heard during the evening services.

The last of these preachers was a young elder from Haysi, Virginia—Freddie Ramey. Brother Freddie is a leader in Bartlick Church, the fellowship that John Layne was instrumental in bringing back into the association in 1986, much to the disgruntlement of some factions in both Union and her corresponding associations.

The Bartlick controversy went back to a 1972–73 Union Association split that resulted in the formation of the Mountain Liberty Association, organized during a September, 1973, meeting at Bartlick Church.[41] Though relatively minor in consequence, this split was a particularly bitter one, involving some strong personalities on both sides. Thus, thirteen years later when the Bartlick fellowship sought to reestablish affiliation with Union Association, there was considerable opposition to the proposal, so much so, in fact, that representatives from the Old Friendship Association walked out of the session after the readmittance vote was taken.[42]

The achieving of this affirmative vote constituted one of the severest tests of Moderator Layne's leadership and culminated at least two years of work with the Bartlick fellowship and Elder Freddie Ramey. In the process the young elder apparently became a favorite of Brother John, thus causing the latter, before his death, to request Ramey's participation in this funeral service.[43] These were the circumstances making Ramey's remarks particularly poignant, both for the audience and for the speaker, who obviously had viewed Layne as his mentor.

Elder John C. Layne was buried just outside Bethlehem Church in the Stiltner Cemetery, only two hundred yards from his house. For a number of years Brother John had held his membership at Little Martha Church in Leemaster, Virginia, apparently because he was the moderator of that congregation. But in the last year of his life he had relinquished that role at Little Martha and had lettered back to the Bethlehem fellowship so he would be attending service nearer his home.

5. *"Brothers and Sisters in Hope": The Old Regular Baptist Fellowship*

As should be obvious by now, the typical Old Regular congregation is a vital element in the total dynamics of this subdenomination's services. Unlike some mainline, high-church faiths in which the churchgoer is primarily a spectator, participating only in a very controlled manner through choir-assisted hymn singing and creeds recited in unison, the Old Regular worshiper views every Saturday or Sunday service as an opportunity for his or her own self-expression. There may be three, four, or five elders who will do the preaching on these mornings, but their contributions will be considered flat and somewhat sterile without the congregational behaviors that complete the impassioned cycles of reciprocal responses.

As partners, therefore, in the total expression of Old Regular "praising," these assemblages merit their own chapter, an examination of the Old Regular congregation as a dramatic persona, a participating agent in "glorifying." In this examination three components of these congregations will be discussed: the formal membership of the church, the visiting members of affiliated fellowships, and the nonmember regulars or visitors. The chapter will be closed with a discussion of black-white relations within Old Regular congregations. "Brothers and Sisters in Hope" has been chosen as the chapter title simply because, as was established earlier, this is a phrase Old Regulars apply to themselves.

Local Memberships

Discussions in this chapter examine memberships not so much as responsive agents in worship, a phenomenon that was touched on in chapter 1, but as social, political, and spiritual entities, the blood and tissue of the individual churches. Emphasis is placed upon a few basic characteristics of these memberships, again with the idea of identifying a typical collective persona.

In this regard, the first thing that must be noted about local memberships is that they are small, giving the impression of belonging to a religious breed that is slowly but surely passing from the contemporary scene. Whether that is actually the case will be examined in chapter 7.

According to statistics reported in association minutes, the largest Old Regular local church membership belongs to the Thornton church in Thornton Union — 396 in 1986; while the smallest apparently is that of the Philadelphia church in the Philadelphia Association — only 4 in 1986. A more complete picture of these sizes can be gained, however, from Table 1, showing the smallest, largest, and average local fellowship sizes for seven representative associations. The figures were drawn from statistics reported in 1986 association minutes. They should be contrasted with the enrollments of the megachurches of the moment.

These figures suggest that the average Old Regular fellowship will have between 35 and 45 members, with only an exceptional church here and there having a membership above 100. Therefore, this average church will have no problem in seating all of its members in the raised stand area, probably with enough space left to accommodate a number of visiting Old Regular church members. This smallness in size, however, does present some problems which will be examined later.

Although no statistics exist to show precise male-female distributions, my general impression is that these memberships are weighted heavily toward the female side, a logical

Table 1 Local Fellowship Sizes, Old Regular Baptist Associations, 1986 Statistics

Association	Smallest	#	Largest	#	Average
Bethel	Trimble	13	Bethel	90	34.2
Mud River	Sarah	14	Mt. Zion	28	24.3
New Salem	Mt. Juda	4	Old Beaver	170	51.7
Old Friendship	Mountain Home	18	Bee Branch	100	66.7
Old Indian Bottom	Little Daniel	5*	Little Home	69	24.3
Philadelphia	Philadelphia	4	Mt. Olivet	44*	25.4
Union	Little Marie	8*	Russell Prater	196	50.2

*Others this size

consequence of two facts: women live longer and these congregations are aging. A few of the smaller fellowships have reached a point at which their gender imbalance is so great that they don't have enough males to fill the various offices of the church, particularly in those associations that do not permit women to serve even as clerks or treasurers. To meet this problem, the associations have allowed small fellowships to "borrow" males. Here, for example, is the record of such an action, as taken by the 1985 session of the Old Friendship Association:

> In answer to the question from the Mountain Home Church.
> We would like the Association to allow our churches to adopt the practice of borrowing male members from our sister churches in our association when one of our churches does not have enough ablebodied male members in their church to carry out the necessary works of the church. Request was granted.[1]

The Mountain Home fellowship currently has only eighteen members, most of them women; yet the church still must have four officers, a reasonable supply of deacons, and three delegates for the association meetings, with all of these positions filled by males. Although there can be situations in which a man assumes several roles, a small membership like that of Mountain Home usually experiences an acute shortage not only of "ablebodied" males, but males of any type, the consequence being that the fellowship reaches a point at which it cannot transact business. The clerk of the fellowship, to be specific, is not allowed to move or second a motion approving his own work, so at least two other male members are needed for the church to approve, carry out, and record business. One of these cannot be the moderator, since he does not vote, except in the case of a tie.

When a fellowship reaches one of these impasses, it is forced to "borrow" male members from a cooperative church in the same association or in one of the corresponding associations.[2] Thus contact is made with specific men in a nearby fellowship to see if these individuals are willing to serve in this capacity. For the affected males this arrangement means that they will, for the duration of the agreement, serve as members of two churches, regularly attending both business meetings and being empowered to vote and to hold office in both. They are not, therefore, temporarily removed from the roll of their regular church. These procedures have been practiced by Union Association for many years.[3] Old Friendship, as far as I can tell, just initiated this policy.

Will this shortage of males eventually force Old Regulars to allow women to serve in leadership capacities? My inclination is to answer, "Probably not," at least never in an association as traditional as Old Friendship. Thornton Union has permitted a few women to serve in clerk or assistant clerk positions, when sufficient male talent was not available, and so apparently have Sardis and Indian Bottom.[4] But Old Friendship, Union, New Salem, and other more traditional associations are not inclined to yield on this point of both custom and doctrine.

As in most organizations, religious or otherwise, the obtaining of formal membership in an Old Regular fellowship brings to the individual a certain degree of status within that social, political, and religious structure. Although this subdenomination prizes humility, insisting upon this virtue as a factor of almost every aspect of faith and order, it is hard to escape the fact that membership lifts one up and sets one apart.

The stand area itself becomes a potent symbol of status, raised as it is above the primary floor level and facing out toward the nonmember sections. Then there are status zones even in this broader area, especially that inverted "U" of seats immediately yoking the pulpit. Here the moderator and all other elders sit, particularly those who will be speaking at the service. Furthermore, proximity to this zone of power appears to be one of the most dependable indicators of recognized rank and position.

But there is status even in having one's special place to sit, one spot in either the men's section or the women's section of your home church. I recall the situation at Bethel Church in Dunham, Kentucky, for example. The pews of the stand areas, like those elsewhere in the church, were unpadded, plank-backed, homemade benches, uncomfortable to sit on for any great length of time. To make this seating less vexatious, members brought pillows, leaving them in place after each service. So the cushions not only became aids for comfort, but territorial markers, reserving an owner's seat until next month. This seemed to be especially true on the women's side.[5]

But flagging with pillows or other personal items is not really needed to make such reservations of space. In those churches I visited more than once (Sandy Ridge, Little Martha, Ash Camp, Bull Creek, Bethany) I was able to observe a general respect for long-held territory, a natural tendency within any human setting. So fellowship members tend to have "their places," and the mere possession of a spot implies a certain recognized status that the visitor or nonmember probably will not have.

This "status on the stand" phenomenon is certainly present during association meetings, since only the more prominent of the association's leaders are able to possess space on the raised platform. Consider this problem as it relates to the Union Association's stand area during their annual sessions, an under-the-tent platform, three feet high and approximately thirty feet square, that accommodates the speaker's lectern, a long table for the clerk and assistant clerk, and chairs to seat forty or fifty officers and association dignitaries. The Union Association has 213 elders (1987 statistics), so there is no way that all of these individuals could sit on this platform, were they (or any significant portion of them) to be in attendance.[6] Furthermore, the problem is intensified by the fact that protocol demands that visiting leaders of corresponding associations — at least the moderators and assistant moderators of these sister groups — be welcomed to the stand. Even if the association were to limit the honor of sitting on the platform to the moderators of the seventy-three churches, room would still not be available for all. So some system has been needed to dictate protocol for this situation.

The system which has evolved appears to be nothing more than an informally structured status hierarchy, one which permits on the stand those who, because of longevity in service or preeminence for other reasons (preaching skills perhaps), have been able to thrust themselves forward in this fashion. In addition, there is a constant sensitivity to the patriarchial status of others who should be on the stand in your place, so much so that individuals frequently leave the platform to urge aging elders or men of similar respect into their vacated stand seats.

One tradition that has developed within the Union Association's annual session is that on Sunday morning wives of the association's leaders assume positions on the platform. The result is an extension of the stand area status system, with the ranking of the women determined by the ranking of their men.

I even noticed a stand-area status sytem being honored at the funeral of Elder John Layne. Long after the space immediately around the pulpit had become completely filled, Union Association leaders would still enter the church and immediately be provided a spot within that inverted "U" of power; and when each new person sat down another had to rise and vacate the area. Subtleties within an informal ranking system controlled these movements.

In addition to status, formal membership guarantees some other privileges: publication in association minutes of obituaries and family memorial announcements, addition to the church's annually read memorial roster, and attention from the fellowship's deacons in times of need. There is variance from association to association — and even from church to church — as to the rules or customs governing these privileges, but formal membership always grants access to these benefits.

Union Association allows members occasionally to submit for publication obituaries for their nonmember loved ones, especially deceased infants and children. However, it still takes membership to facilitate the processes of this privilege, even when the deceased was not a member. Sardis Association, on the other hand, limits the publications to obituaries of former members:

> By motion and second, it is ordered that Obituaries of our deceased Brothers and Sisters that are in good standing with the Church at the time of death be printed in our Minutes. These are to be presented to the Clerk at the end of the Association. A charge of $10.00 will be made for a picture with the obituary, except that pictures of an Elder or his wife will continue to be published free.[7]

I addressed this custom of printed obituaries in some detail in *Giving Glory to God in Appalachia*, but I will touch on it again here for clarity and continuity.[8] Each year when the clerk of an association publishes the minutes of its annual session, he also includes obituaries (and picutres if submitted) for all individual members who have died the previous year. Written by loved ones of the deceased or by elders or clerks, a published-in-the-minutes obituary becomes a prized family possession and is just one of a series of recognitions usually bestowed upon the "passed on to glory" individual, including the annual family or church memorials. Occasionally obituaries are framed and displayed in the family homestead. Sometimes they are reread during special memorials, but as a minimal treatment they are preserved among pictures and other family memorabilia.

Manuscripts for these documents, along with any pictures and requisite moneys, are usually collected by the church's delegates and then submitted to the association's clerk at the time church letters are presented on those Friday mornings when annual sessions begin. Making certain that these statements then make it into the published minutes becomes one of the major responsibilities of the association's clerk and assistant clerk.

The following is the obituary published for Wayne Bryant, a long-time elder of the Old Friendship Association who died in 1985. It is somewhat longer than the average such document, most likely because the deceased was a highly respected elder; still it serves as a good example of the general content of these statements and of the sentiments involved. I am including the obituary in its entirety in order to preserve the totality of its message and nuances. I am also preserving the copy exactly as originally published, for the same reasons.

Elder Wayne Bryant of Panther W. Va. was born, the son of the late James and Elizabeth Peaks Bryant, in Pike Co. Ky. Nov. 7, 1904, deceased this life Dec. 10, 1985, being 81 years of age, he was a retired coal miner and an Elder in the Old Regular Baptist faith, a member of the Panther Creek Church. He was married to Sister Elsie Collins Bryant and to this union was born two sons and five daughters, one son Sebert and one daughter Eunice preceded him in death, also three brothers and two sisters.

He is survived by his wife Elsie of Panther and one son James H. Bryant of Hurley, Va., four daughters Mrs. Ruth Allen of Morehead, KY. Mrs. Louise Hall of Dahlgren, Va., Mrs. JoAnn Lester and Mrs. Evelyn Anderson both of Panther, WV; four brothers Toby Bryant of Fort Royal, VA. Jarvie Bryant of Oceana, Jessie Bryant of Roderfield, Kimbo Bryant of Northfork, two sisters Opal Michalski of Mentor OH, and Ella Branham of Panther; 19 grandchildren; and 19 great-grandchildren, all who knew not the depth of their love until the hour of separation. And today you are sorrowful, for in your heart you are weeping for that which was once your delight, one that gave so much without knowing that he had given at all, for it is only when you give yourself, as he did, that you give at all.

Bro. Wayne joined this old church many years ago and soon after that he, with much humility, accepted the call to preach. I knew him in good times and in bad, I saw him open his home to many, who shared his beds and sat at his table. I saw him many times stand in the pulpit and proclaim the name of his God, he had a strong faith and firmly stood on what he believed. He often went when called on, when he was not able, thinking it his duty to serve in anyway he could. One of the things I admired about him was he never expected, nor demanded, to be put on a high seat and be praised, he, rightly so, believed that all praise belonged to God. He endured his share of tribulations in his life as well as his joys. Some of his joys was the church that he put so much of his life in, his wife and children, his grandchildren and many friends, and they in turn honored him to the end and still do. Some of his heartaches was when the church was in trouble, he hurt, when children or grandchildren or friends hurt, he hurt, and we saw part of his life slip away with the death of two of his children, Eunice and Sebert, that left a void space in his life and an expression of pain on his face that remained the rest of his days.

As we sat outside his door at the hospital and knew that his life was slipping away, I thought of what it is to die and knew that we were born to die and do daily, each day brings us a little closer to our homeland until the day comes that our breath is released from a tired body that it might rise to meet God, for many years ago Bro. Wayne tasted the Lord and saw that he was good.

Psalms said, "weeping may endure for a night but joy cometh in the morning." Bro. Wayne has wept his night in this life and the joy he has longed for will be his when he wakes up in the morning, for precious in the eyes of the Lord is the death of one of his saints.

He loved his children and blazed a path for them to follow and I feel that it would be safe to follow Daddy.

And now the earth shall claim his limbs and death shall hide him in the grave, but for a moment, until his wrath has passed and Jesus calls, then Bro. Wayne will answer for he that has found grace shall lie down and be not afraid; and his sleep shall be sweet.

Sister Elsie and all his children and friends stood by him until the end, he knew that you were there, and I'm sure it made his last moments easier. I knew when I shook his feeble hand for the last time that it would most likely be the last, and he whispered goodbye I hope to meet you in a better world. His destiny is sealed his face here we will see no more but memories, precious memories how they linger.

He has gone home with a friend.

Bro. Roby Raines[9]

Old Regular obituaries not only provide writers opportunity to praise deceased individuals, but they permit a certain amount of sermonizing; and because these documents are often written by church laymen, as opposed to the ordained elders, their closing statements frequently violate the anti-evangelism doctrine that is so much a part of the faith's theology. The following excerpts, for example, have been taken from closing remarks in obituaries published in the 1986 minutes of Union Association. Although no such examples are provided here, for reasons of discretion, these admonitions occasionally name specific individuals who, according to the obituary's writer, should change their ways.

> So children if you ever want to see mom again you had better fall out with sin and into the merciful hands that she fell into.[10]

> So to my brothers and sisters if you want to see mom again fall out with sin and look to the Lord where all our help come from.[11]

> We can be with Dad again if we listen to what the Lord asks of us, and if we follow the path of righteous. Then God will once more fill our hearts with gladness, and never again will we suffer the path of parting.[12]

> We would like to say to the children, if you want to see mother and dad again, you will have to come to the Lord the same way they did. For there is only one way from earth to glory. You will have to fall out with sin and be borned again.[13]

The smaller associations will have only a few of these obituaries in their annual minutes, but Union and New Salem minutes ordinarily devote fifty or more pages to these statements, with each document supplying not only information about the particular deceased, but also rich glimpses at Old Regular values, beliefs, and philosophies. Since I discussed such values, beliefs, and philosophies in *Giving Glory to God in Appalachia*, I will avoid doing so again here; however, I will give one more complete example to illustrate the tone and substance of these works, and also to complete the account I gave of Emmitt Caudill in my last chapter.

BROTHER EMMITT H. CAUDILL

It is with much sadness I write an obituary of Elder Emmitt H. Caudill. Brother Emmitt was born in Letcher County, Kentucky on August 12, 1912 and was the son of the late George Washington and Nannie Bell Caudill. He was married to Rena Maggard on October 16, 1936, and to this union were born 6 children, two of which preceded him in death.

Brother Emmitt joined the Old Regular Baptist Church the second weekend in April, 1970, and was later called to preach and to moderate as an assistant at the Little New Hope Church at Winnabow, North Carolina where he was a faithful member until his death on Saturday, May 24, 1986.

I became acquainted with Brother Emmitt and Sister Rena around the year 1970 when I heard about the little meetings they were having in their home at Winnabow, and what joy I received on my first trip to their home. You could feel the good spirit flow from breast to breast as we sang and shouted and embraced each other, and I believe that meeting and other[s] which followed are recorded in Heaven. Brother Emmitt and Sister Rena along with others prayed and worked hard and helped to establish the New Hope Church of Old Regular Baptist, and it is evident that their work was not in vain since the 4 remaining children, Ted, Fred, Ned, and Doris Creech, who survive him, profess a hope in Christ. Three had their membership with him and Sister Rena in the New Hope Church.

Brother Emmitt leaves Sister Rena, the children, grandchildren, and a host of relatives and friends to mourn his passing, and I am confident that they would agree with me that the words of the Apostle Paul would apply to Brother Emmitt, "To be absent in the body is to be present with the Lord." I believe that Brother Emmitt is now at rest.

Written by Brother Jim Frazier,
A Brother in the Lord,
and Assisted by Sister Rena Caudill, Wife[14]

Membership and the Doctrine of Salvation

According to Elder Raymond Smith, Old Regulars believe neither church membership nor baptism to be essential to redemption, meaning they accept the possibility that there are individuals who have received and accepted their calls but never gone through the ceremonies of immersion and church affiliation.[15] By the same token, they reason that baptism and church membership are not absolute guarantees of salvation, since individuals are capable of going through rites without honest or clearly understood conviction. In other words, people can fake a call or misinterpret human emotions for "an experience." Either way, the result is the same: no true redemption.

On the other hand, if the call is true and the acceptance is pure, proclaims the mainline of Old Regular doctrine, there is a true "regeneration of the soul, sealed with the Holy Spirit of promise, and none such shall fall away and be lost."[16] The clear meaning of a backsliding, therefore, is that the individual involved was never redeemed in the first instance. This Old Regular belief represents a clean doctrinal split from the tenets of Free Will Baptists, who accept the possibility of backsliding and reconversion.[17]

A corollary to all of the above is the "brothers and sisters in hope" doctrine: since for Old Regulars redemption is ultimately a God-controlled factor, there is no way for individuals to be certain of salvation, either for themselves or for others. So the best a person can do is act upon a "hope," directing his or her life accordingly. It is a humbling theology and retards, it seems, inclination to judge dogmatically the "redeemed" or "unredeemed" status of others.

Membership and Behavior Within the Fellowship

Although church membership may not be considered essential to redemption it does become a condition that automatically makes one vulnerable to the heavy influences of the fellowship, simply because to be a member makes one subject to exclusion. This reality leads us naturally to a discussion of membership responsibilities.

Most of the associations mentioned in this work have never officially codified any list of membership responsibilities, at least not in the sense of having such understandings placed in writing.[18] But the Old Friendship Association is different in this regard, having adopted a set of regulations governing membership obligations that are in addition to "Rules of Decorum," those procedural codes applicable to church deliberations.

These Old Friendship codes of behavior are important because they express in definite terms many of the understood but unwritten rules operating in churches of other associations. The first rule given here, of course, just governs admittance into the fellowship, but the remainder deal with duties and responsibilities assumed after that act:

1. Members may be admitted or received into our body by experience and baptism or by presenting a letter of commendation from a sister church of our faith and order, also members who have been excluded may be restored by a satisfactory acknowledgment. All matters coming before the church shall be decided by a majority of the members present.

2. Any members of our body having aught against a brother or sister of said body shall first make it known to him or her alone; if satisfaction is not obtained, then take one or two members as witnesses; if the offender fails or refuses to hear them, the grievance shall be told unto the church. But all public offenses contrary to a Christian profession shall be brought before the church by the members knowing the same.

3. It is the duty of any member knowing himself guilty of an offense against his brother or sister to come forward and make satisfaction without waiting for an application from the member or members grieved.

4. For the purpose of keeping the unity of the Spirit in the bonds of peace and for the upbuilding and cleanliness of Zion, it is our duty to speak the truth in sincerity at all times and under any circumstances which may surround us.

5. We should always be armed with the helmet of salvation so as to defend our brethren and sister when they are traveling in the pathway of rectitude and right, even if they are evilly spoken of.

6. The disputes of controversies arising among us shall

be settled by our body the church, and the decision shall be binding that we may not go to law before the unjust.

7. Any member or members using spiritous liquors shall be dealt with in accordance with the crime, or it may more plainly be understood in the following words, "We will not tolerate drunkenness in our church."

8. It is in accordance with God's word that we watch over one another for good. Be it resolved that we do so.

9. We as Christians must refrain from all appearances of evil, and we do hereby pledge our word one to another that we will endeavor, God being our helper, to remove all idols from before us and worship the One Only, the true and living God, in the beauty of holiness.

10. It is the duty to live in obedience to the laws of our country, unless they conflict with the laws of God.

11. It is our duty to follow Peace with all men, to render good to all men, more especially the Household of Faith.

12. If our male members fail to attend more than three church meetings in succession without being providentially hindered, they shall be notified; if they shall then fail or refuse to attend they shall be excluded from our membership after having been notified three times in succession.

13. When grievances arise between Brethren, the same coming to the knowledge of the Church, the Church will, if possible, have said grievance settled within two months after knowing or having knowledge of the same; and any member bringing a trouble before the church which has been passed for two months and not having tried to settle the same, the said member shall stand as a violator of church decorum and shall be dealt with as the church directs.[19]

Some of these behavioral codes need to be examined more closely. Note, for example, in rule number 2 that each church member is made responsible for reporting to the fellowship the improprieties of any other member: " . . . all public offenses contrary to a Christian profession shall be brought before the church by the members knowing the same." Furthermore, take special note of rule number 8: "It is in accordance with God's word that we watch over one another for good." Finally, consider rule number 11: "It is our duty to follow Peace with all men, to render good to all men, more especially the Household of Faith."

When the first of these statements is considered in isolation, it appears that members are being asked to monitor each other's public behaviors for the purpose of reporting to the fellowship all "offenses contrary to a Christian profession." Viewed one way, that rule smacks of cultural tyranny, a brother-watches-brother type of climate that would breed suspicion, fear, hatred, and endless retributions; and perhaps in some extreme fellowship environments that does occasionally happen. But the rule seems to be strongly tempered by the last two codes I highlighted: " . . . we watch over one another for good," and " . . . our duty [is] to follow Peace with all men, to render good to all men, more especially the Household of Faith."

Undoubtedly there are times, in the Old Friendship Association or in other associations holding to these codes, when individuals have trouble keeping these duties in balance, thus adopting oppressive, big-brother-is-watching modes of conduct; but any individual falling into this pattern of behavior may become so disruptive and such a general threat to a fellowship's "peace and love" that he or she eventually will be excluded. Equally possible, it seems, is the opposite consequence: a church falls into a pervasive attitude of mistrust and disunity. My own impression — limited as it is to the fellowships I have visited — is that more often than not Old Regulars manage to avoid the latter of these possibilities. The strongly cathartic nature of their worship practices bleeds off many ill-humored interpersonal attitudes before they infect entire fellowships.

Visiting Members

One factor that determines the vitality of any Old Regular church is the number of visitors attracted to its Sunday services, particularly visiting members of other fellowships. It has already been observed that Old Regulars do a great deal of traveling to meetings of fellowships with which they have agreeable relations, sister churches of their own association or of corresponding associations. On Sundays when their own churches don't meet, members of the faith are expected to do their best to attend services elsewhere, as long as the church to be visited is recognized as being legitimate in "faith and order."

Therefore, every Sunday, but especially during the spring, summer, and fall, thousands of Old Regulars are on the road to the services of sister fellowships. Attracted by favorite preachers, friends of long standing, special services (memorial, union, or communion meetings), the general spiritedness of certain fellowships, or just the location of the church to be visited, these roving congregations frequently make the difference between gatherings that stay low key and ordinary and those that soar to emotional peaks of expression. Thus, on special occasions attendance at a particular church may double or even quadruple official membership numbers, creating such happenings as the Bull Creek service I described in chapter 2.

Take for example the communion meeting I witnessed at Little Martha Church, June 8, 1986. This church's membership in 1986 was seventy-four, but attendance that morning was probably three hundred or higher, the many visitors having come to observe or participate in the intense emotionalism that accompanies such an annual event.[20] During the break between the main service and the communion rite, when the deacons and deaconesses were preparing the table and the footwashing utensils, I strolled among the cars parked tightly around the meetinghouse and then among those along the road, discovering license plates from five states (Virginia, Kentucky, Tennessee, West Virginia, and Ohio); and I was not certain I had seen them all.[21]

Many of the visiting worshipers at the Little Martha sacrament service probably come to the event annually, knowing that a large crowd will be attracted and that some of the Union Association's most effective preachers will be on the stand. They always know when the service will take place because the sacrament meeting for each church is made a part of the statistical table published in the association's minutes. These minutes also include, as mentioned earlier, dates for memorial and union meetings, the other two big services of a church's year.

The major difference between the visiting members of other churches and the visiting nonmembers is that the visiting members will become full participants in the church service. They will sit in the stand area, if there is sufficient room; they will participate in communion and will help serve it if they are visiting "ordained authorities"; they will involve themselves in the footwashing; and, if elders, they may preach, line hymns, or lead in prayer. Indeed, if male members of other churches visit on Saturdays, when business meetings are in session, they will be invited to sit in council with the home male members, and even deliberate and advise.

In one sense, however, these visiting members of other churches can be threatening entities: it is possible that one or more of them will scrutinize the practices or doctrines of the host church and judge that fellowship to be in some kind of error. If the error is sufficiently grievous, then an account of it generally will be taken back to the visitor's home church. Leaders of the second church might then approach the membership of the first church, asking for a correction of the error. If an amicable solution is not reached, the second church could approach the association with a request or query, thus bringing the issue before this larger body.[22]

Consider, as a possible example of the above, a 1972 request presented by Robinson Creek Church to the New Salem Association, most likely precipitated initially by a visiting Robinson Creek member who observed that Pikeville Church, a sister fellowship, had accepted into membership an individual excluded by Robinson Creek, a procedure unacceptable in all Old Regular associations. To carry out New Salem Association policy, the Pikeville fellowship should have sent the individual back to Robinson Creek to make amends there first. To compound the problem, Pikeville Church apparently refused to dismiss their new member after their sister fellowship pointed out the error. Thus Robinson Creek turned to the association:

> Request from Robinson Creek Church. August the first Saturday, 1972. We, the Robinson Creek Church of Old Regular Baptist of Jesus Christ met in regular session. After prayer, the moderator called for love and fellowship. Same being found we proceeded to work. The committee sent to labor with the Pikeville Church made their report and after some discussion a move and second was made to ask the New Salem Assn. to advise the Pikeville Church to comply with item no. 4 in the 1925 Minute and also item no. 12 in the 1958 minutes, concerning members excluded from one church taking up membership with another sister church, Brother Tommie Thacker being the member in question. Done and signed by the order of Robinson Creek Church.
>
> Elder Woodrow Dye, Moderator
Bro. Clint Reed Damron, Clerk
>
> Moved and seconded to advise the Pikeville Church to exclude Bro. Tommie Thacker. Objections was filed. Vote taken, carried to advise the Pikeville Church to recant their work of giving the Bro. a letter of dismission, to call him back and exclude him.[23]

Frequently such requests develop from one or more visits to a church in another association, with the discovery that fellowships of this sister group of Old Regulars are allowing some practice considered improper. Requests recorded in New Salem minutes have often emerged from such scenarios, with the improprieties usually centered upon the behavior of women — cutting their hair, dressing in men's attire, assuming a male's role in church.[24]

Regardless of their occasional disruptive influences, all these visitations undoubtedly have maintained strong ties between individual churches and associations and perhaps ultimately brought more unity than disharmony. I have noticed within the larger Old Regular family less inclination to restrict one's involvement and loyalty to just one church than I think I have seen in other denominational groups. Because these members of the faith may be at another church about as much as they are at their own, their sense of belonging has a tendency to become much broader than is usual, encompassing a number of fellowships and the association at large. Recall the practice, already mentioned, of fellowships going to each other for financial assistance in enlarging their physical facilities, and also the policies concerning the franchising of visiting males and the "borrowing" of males. These practices tend to reduce significantly the dividing space between churches, moving them toward a true sisterhood relationship.

Visiting Nonmembers

In the first chapter of this work I suggested that this subdenomination's total number of reasonably regular nonmember churchgoers might be as great as the total number of members. Remember that individuals occasionally wait for years in the nonmember section in expectation of their personal calls to redemption. This waiting is not considered wasteful, since the preaching, singing, prayer, and personal expressions of joy to which nonmembers are exposed are supposed to help in keeping them to the good life.

There is some variance among the Old Regular associations as to how these nonmember churchgoers are viewed and treated. It has already been established, for example, that the Sardis Association does not permit obituaries for nonmembers to be published in their annual minutes and that the Union Association does publish such nonmenber obituaries. Some Union Association families, in fact, use these documents to express vague and thinly disguised arguments or expressions of hope that the individuals involved had been "redeemed."[25] Some churches of the Union Association, as already illustrated by the practices of Bull Creek Church, also include names of their deceased nonmember former regulars on memorial lists, reading their names each year in the same fashion that names of deceased former members are read. Fellowships in all of the associations, nevertheless, welcome the nonmember churchgoer, not only because he or she might eventually express a "conviction," be baptized, and join the church, but because he or she becomes a vital part of the general spirit and total dynamics of the services.

So this collection of nonmembers (both local and visiting) must be added to the members-of-other-churches visitors when conceptualizing the greater Old Regular congregation, with the understanding that this total nonmember entity fluctuates from fellowship to fellowship, dependent upon a great variety of factors in worship service dynamics, not least of which are the size of average crowds, the spiritedness of typical services, the popularity of the preachers who frequent the particular church, the exuberance of the singing and praising, and the general warmth of the regular congregation.

Preaching is certainly one of the most important elements in this formula for crowd attraction, and elders exercise a great deal of individual volition in determining their traveling schedules. Unless the preacher's home fellowship is in session, and unless he is "called" for a union or memorial service, he is himself free to visit any service he pleases (within his association or within corresponding associations), with the possibility that he will be requested to preach. Furthermore, it appears that when free to float the more dynamic preachers are attracted to churches where there are apt to be large congregations and where the dynamics of this larger crowd are likely to turn the morning's activities into an exciting religious event. In addition, part of the subtle politics of advancement in association power, influence, and position is to be noticed by a large number of Old Regulars, and the more broadly attended meetings provide this opportunity.

One result of all this is that once a fellowship begins to slide in numbers a variety of factors tend to maintain that slide or to hold the congregation at its lower base. Unless specifically called, the most popular preachers seldom visit, and without these dynamic preachers the visiting laymen and laywomen do not materialize. Soon the fellowship's worship services are attended only by that church's members,

Lebanon Church, Clintwood, Virginia.

with few of the expressions of vitality necessary to attract new blood.

On July 27, 1986, I visited the communion-footwashing service of Lebanon Church and recorded in my notes that this particular fellowship appeared to be suffering the problems described above. When I interviewed the young licensed preacher, Danny O'Quinn, he told me that he remembered, in the not-so-distant past, Lebanon Church as being always filled with visitors on meeting Sundays and the services as being some of the most energetic to be found within the Union Association. On that sacrament meeting Sunday, however, the aging congregation was very sparse, less than forty people (including Darvin, Ganell, and me), and was assembled in a building that would have accommodated well over three hundred.[26]

Lebanon Church lies between Coeburn and Clintwood,

Virginia, on Caney Ridge in Dickenson County. It can be reached by taking Highway 72 north from Coeburn, traveling four miles before turning right onto Route 649, and then moving along this road for another ten miles. The church will be seen resting on the rib of the ridge, with a view that looks northward down a network of hollows toward the community of Clintwood. It is a structure that gives every indication of having been the home of a vigorous Old Regular membership. Larger than is usual for an Old Regular church, the building is tastefully designed and projects an image more akin to that of a mainline denomination house of worship than to the wood-framed, concrete-block, or brick-veneered rectangular box meetinghouse image that prevails for most Old Regular churches. Exterior trim, window frames, and front entrance decorative units show much more ornamentation than one traditionally expects from such structures.

The well-kept grounds of the church are adjoined by the "Mullins Cemetery," a beautifully fenced and landscaped burial area that looks somewhat out of place in these Cumberland hills, very unlike the rugged primitiveness of the Mary Lou Cemetery described in chapter 3. In general, this cemetery, the grounds, the attractively finished church exterior, and the spacious and well-appointed interior, all carefully maintained, initially suggest the presence of a membership that is vital and growing. Nevertheless, at the time of this writing, that does not seem to be the case for Lebanon Church.

In contemporary times, Lebanon's membership appears to have peaked in 1979 with an enrollment of fifty-three, increased that year by three baptisms and seven transferals by letter; but from that year the membership has steadily fallen to its present (1987) low of thirty. What perhaps is most telling about the Lebanon statistics, however, is that from 1980 through 1987 there were no baptisms and only one individual was received by letter; while during this same period there were eleven deaths within the membership, six exclusions, and six dismissals by letter. Therefore, for eight years this church appears to have been dying by slow attrition.[27] Given the apparent age of the present membership and this trend toward diminution, unless new blood is pumped into the fellowship, Lebanon Church will soon die. Keep in mind, however, that there are presently Old Regular fellowships being kept alive with membership enrollments of ten or less. Union Association's 1987 statistical tables show six of that cluster's churches falling into that category.[28]

My point is not merely to show that Lebanon is in trouble because of a membership drain, but to suggest that this membership drain may have something to do with a lack of the general vitality that normally is maintained through visitations. When I attended Bull Creek Church in June 1984, for their annual memorial service, the fellowship had only 117 members; but the building was crammed with 300 to 350 worshipers.[29] On the other hand, when I witnessed Lebanon Church's communion-footwashing in 1986, the church officially had 38 members; but the total attendance was less than that number, with the congregation being somewhat lost in a structure that would seat well over 300.

I feel compelled to soften these observations about Lebanon Church by reminding the reader that I have at other places in this work focused on two touching episodes from that July 27, 1986, Lebanon service, episodes that demonstrated the continuing presence of an inordinate fervor in that small congregation: the one-legged footwashing efforts of the late Elder Billie Mullins and the impassioned display of religious conviction exhibited by the deaconess who removed the linen covering from the communion table. This fellowship has been diminishing in size but not necessarily in faith.

Black-White Relations
in the Old Regular Fellowship

A number of years ago when I first read in *Southern Exposure* Ron Short's essay "We Believed in the Family and the

Old Regular Baptist Church," the one paragraph that lingered longest in my mind was the following:

> As long as I can remember, there have been black preachers and members in the Old Regulars. I think it is important to point out that while this country has labored under the burden of continued racial strife, this Church has maintained the equality of people as a natural part of the Christian ethic, not as defined by the legal limits of a person's civil rights.[30]

I will close this chapter on the Old Regular congregation by examining Short's thesis, at least regarding practices I have witnessed.

Unlike most Southern and border state Protestant denominations, Old Regular Baptists have never formally maintained two separate but parallel traditions, one for whites and the other for blacks. To the degree that blacks have found their way into this faith they appear to have been fully integrated into the structure, frequently becoming deacons or elders (if male) and also frequently developing strongly positive reputations for their preaching, singing, or praising. One black elder, George Hagans of Vicco, Kentucky, served as assistant moderator of the Indian Bottom Association for several years prior to his death in 1958.[31]

Although I have not seen Old Regular blacks in any great numbers, those whom I have seen appear to function within their fellowships not only as equals but as beloved equals. Indeed, my observations have led me to accept Short's general thesis: black-white relations within the Old Regular tradition are open, fair, warm, and honest. In support of that judgment I will discuss the Little Home fellowship in the Old Indian Bottom Association, a church I visited on May 3, 1987.

Little Home Church is located in Red Fox, Knott County, Kentucky. This small community can be reached by traveling northwest from Whitesburg, Kentucky, on Highway 15.

Shortly after entering Knott County the traveler will reach Red Fox, a collection of small business establishments, garages, and service stations on both sides of the highway. The church will be on the left, some two hundred yards off the highway.

Little Home is occasionally spoken of as a "colored church." In truth it is integrated, with a membership that, at the time of this writing, appears to have about a 50-50 distribution between blacks and whites. Elder Claren Williams, the present moderator of the fellowship, is black, and so is the church's clerk, Elder Lovel Williams; but the membership has been evenly mixed, apparently since the church's foundation in 1911. The gallery of pictures of the fellowship's deceased leaders — on the rear wall behind the stand — contains photographs of both races, an even mixture, it seems. One of the photographs, apparently the oldest in the lot, is of Elder David Crockett Church (a white), who has been previously mentioned as having been important to the history of both Indian Bottom associations and of the Union Association.

One picture of the integrated nature of this fellowship can be gained simply by examining obituaries published in the Old Indian Bottom Association minutes. The 1986 minutes of this Old Regular cluster, for example, include four obituaries for late members of the Little Home Church — Brother Eulice Smith (white), Brother Arthur Madden (white), Brother Joe Bates (white), and Sister Estella Adams (black). Madden served the fellowship as a deacon from 1947 until his death in 1985.[32]

My main intent in visiting the May 3, 1987, service of Little Home Church was to witness this Old Regular principle of equality in operation, and I was not disappointed. Indeed, I was genuinely impressed by the apparently uninhibited, caring fellowship I saw demonstrated within this racially heterogeneous congregation, a spirit shown in the actions of both Little Home members and visitors. Black and white women embraced and kissed each other — and each other's children — and black and white men shook each other's hands

Little Home Church.

and embraced, all of this during those warm greeting encounters I have grown accustomed to witnessing in Old Regular churches.[33] I was told by Darvin Marshall that this fellowship weathered the bitter storms of the late 1950s and the
early 1960s with relative good will and fellowship, a statement that impressed me considerably, given the fact that
some of my own study of Southern Protestant traditions had
documented such opposite behaviors among that era's more
mainline and Deep South white denominations.[34]

The service I witnessed at Little Home was this fellowship's
annual union meeting, and six elders from other churches in
the Old Indian Bottom Association had been invited to be
available for preaching. Five of these "called" elders (all white)
did speak, but all of the elders on the stand insisted that Elder Williams, the black moderator of Little Home, close the
service. I soon saw why they had insisted, since Elder Williams turned out to be by far the most dynamic speaker of
the morning, inciting as he did considerably more audience
response than had been demonstrated during earlier parts of
the service.

Elder Williams is very dignified looking, and at the time
of this writing appears to be in his early to midseventies.
When in the stand he takes full charge of the occasion, structuring the mood as he sees fit; and it becomes obvious that
he is a favorite speaker with both Little Home members and
visitors. He maintains a speaking mode, however, that is characteristic of traditional Old Regular preaching, and the readers of this work should not visualize a pulpit style similar to
that adopted by rural black preachers of the Deep South.
Williams is simply a black Old Regular preacher, following
the traditional wailing delivery patterns of most Old Regular preachers, a little more talented than most at what these
exhorters do, perhaps, but still very much within the Old
Regular mode.

A similar statement needs to be made about the black Old
Regular congregational responses. Again the reader should
not envision the jazzy clapping, singing, swaying, arm-waving,

black-gospel, congregational responses common to black worship in the Deep South and elsewhere, exciting and artistic as that style is. As in all Old Regular fellowships, the black women of Little Home occasionally break into those highly emotional episodes of shouting and praising, but when they do so they follow the traditional style of Old Regular shouting and praising, the elongated, upward soaring wail I have earlier described. At least to my ear, there is no distinctly black Old Regular sound, either in the preaching or in the shouting. This factor, joined with those scenes of brotherhood and sisterhood I witnessed at Little Home, gave me a feeling of real integration, confirming in my mind the judgment Ron Short advanced, at least for Old Indian Bottom Association.

6. *"We Declare Nonfellowship":* *Disunity within Old Regularism*

Up to this point these depictions of Old Regularism have been characterized primarily by loving fellowship and congregational harmony, highlighted by images of handshaking and embracing. There is, nevertheless, another side of the picture, one which shows a subdenomination frequently engulfed in argument and disunity. The mere fact that there are so many divisions of this brand of Baptists, with no one association in correspondence with all the other groups, gives evidence of past and present disagreements. There are two Indian Bottom associations, two Friendship associations, and two Mountain associations. There are pairs of associations in which each corresponds with a common third, but not with each other (Mud River with New Salem, Old Friendship with New Salem, but not Old Friendship with Mud River). There are two associations (Old Indian Bottom and Bethel) that correspond with no other cluster. And there is no one alliance that fellowships with more than half of the total Old Regular associations.

The Union and New Salem clusters (in correspondence with each other, and together controlling 130 churches) constitute the dominant center of Old Regularism, and the size and strength of these two groups do provide some unity within the basic core of this subdenomination of Baptists; but almost every year there is movement in or out of this core, precipitated by differences over one or more of a wide variety of traditional dividing issues. As has already been suggested, Old Regulars have fought over the propriety of female involvement in church government; over dress and hairstyle codes; over variations in doctrine; over procedures for reestablishing fellowship with disordered individuals, churches, or associations; over notebook singing; over preaching with elders outside the established faith and order; over regulations governing divorce and remarriage; and over a host of other issues that perpetually generate debate. When such disputes erupt and then fail to be resolved, the only recourse is to split from the individual, the church, or the association perceived to be in disorder. In addition, because Old Regular associations are usually in correspondence with two or more other alliances of the same faith and order, it has been difficult to contain these fights within one church or one association. The more severe arguments, as we will see, often infect the love and peace of two or more associations.

Troubles at the Association Level

Examination has already been made of the role of exclusion in the local fellowship, the expulsion of a member who for one reason or another has become highly objectionable to the other church members — because of drunkenness; immorality; dereliction of membership duties (failing to attend meetings when in good health); violations of personal appearance codes (length of hair or modes of dress); heretical beliefs and practices; criminal malfeasance; and even gossiping, lying, cheating, backbiting, and assorted antisocial practices that bring discord to the fellowship. Exclusions become the ultimate means by which congregations maintain peace and fellowship, clearing out those elements that might shatter "faith and order" harmony.

At the association level the same type of process is put in operation when dealing with deviant churches. If any congregation "falls into disorder," adopting doctrines or practices not in accord with established codes, that church probably will be given a prescribed period in which to correct its errant behavior, with the ultimate consequence of ejection from the association when demanded adjustments are not made. In such situations the typical sequence of events is for (1) charges to be brought at an association meeting, (2) an investigating committee to be appointed with instructions to visit the accused fellowship, (3) the respective committee to report findings and recommend actions during the next association session, and (4) the association to prescribe remedial actions to be taken by the dissident church, establishing a timetable for the carrying out of these instructions, and perhaps formulating another committee to see that the demands are met. At the end of this process, perhaps three or four years later, the particular fellowship, if still in disorder, will be expelled from the association.

My examination of the New Salem Association minutes (1825 to 1983) has suggested, however, that more often than not an "out of order" fellowship will make the demanded correction rather than suffer exclusion from the association, a punishment affecting every member of the affected church, and one not to be taken lightly. Consider, for example, a series of developments that threatened the Pilgrim's Rest fellowship between 1967 and 1972, arising out of the Old Regulars' ongoing argument over the proper length of women's hair, an issue that often embarrasses the more moderate factions of Old Regularism.

In 1955, as a factor in the big Indian Bottom-Thornton Union dispute (to be examined shortly), New Salem Association had voted through a very stringent resolution relative to "bobbed hair."[1] The resolution technically is still in effect in this association, even though there are some fellowships that interpret the ruling quite liberally:

> We, the New Salem Association as an advisory council hereby wish to say to all churches in the bounds of this association that we hereby advise all our churches to not receive into your fellowship any woman with bobbed hair unless she agrees to not have it bobbed any more and after you receive them to exclude from your fellowship all those who violate this agreement or continue to have their hair bobbed and to not restore them back to fellowship except by an experience of grace.[2]

This was a less equivocal and more detailed version of a statement that had been adopted just the year before:

> In answer to a request for advice concerning sisters who cut their hair, we as an Advisory Council advise all the churches, we do not think sisters cutting their hair is a public crime, such as fornication, lying, or getting drunk. But such practice is a trespass against the church. If any sister cuts her hair, exclude her, and if when she proves she has stopped such practice, then the church from which she was excluded for this trespass, may restore her to fellowship.[3]

What made the 1955 version of this policy considerably more stringent was its closing phrase: " . . . and to not restore them back to fellowship except by an experience of grace." This allowed a church to demand not only a new "experience of grace" but perhaps a rebaptism. This last demand can become quite humiliating to an Old Regular, who generally looks back at his or her baptism as a moment of great personal truth. Rebaptism places a brand of error and falsity upon that original moment.

In 1968, however, New Salem appeared to take a less adamant stance in responding to the request of one of its Washington state fellowships. At that time there were three such churches in that northwestern state (Western Union, Mt. Olive, and New Home), and these congregations were having trouble maintaining consistency in their enforcement of this "no bobbed hair" rule. At least that is what was suggested by the request of one of these fellowships: "Request from Western Union Church in Washington about the doctrine and practices in the churches in Washington." The session's response was recorded in the following language: "It was moved and seconded for these brothers to labor with their members and ask their sisters to let their hair grow."[4]

This advice, "to labor with their members," sounded much less forceful and less precise than did the language of the 1955 resolution; and some elders in the association strongly objected to the softened tone and lack of an absolute order, as indicated by the fact that in 1969 Prilgrim's Rest Church requested a recantation of the advice given Western Union, with the added stipulation that the 1955 resolution be reprinted in the 1969 minutes. It appears, however, that the session issued no official recantation, even though the 1955 statement was ordered republished, suggesting somewhat of a variance, or at least an ambiguity, in official policy.[5]

New Salem's reluctance to apply, in a more forceful manner, this 1955 resolution to her Washington state fellowships continued to rile the leadership of Pilgrim's Rest, so much so that two of this church's elders began to criticize the association in a rather scathing fashion. This, in turn, resulted in the following 1971 request by Stone Coal Church:

> We the Stone Coal Church of Regular Baptist, met on our regular meeting time, the second Saturday of August, 1971, in the evening.
>
> The following subject was brought before the church, namely the preaching of Bro. Mack Tuttle concerning the remarks that he made at Mt. Olive Church criticizing or pertaining to the order of the New Salem Association.
>
> Witnesses, Elder[s] Estill Slone, Jerry Campbell, Troy Sparkman, and others stated that Bro. Mack Tuttle preached that the order of the New Salem Association was rottener than Hindman [in Knott County, Kentucky], and you all know how rotten Hindman is, and wouldn't stand up in the Hindman court.
>
> We the Stone Coal Church request the Association to send a committee to the Pilgrim's Rest Church requesting that the Pilgrim's Rest Church take action in said church to stop Bro. Mack Tuttle from criticizing, [and] the Pilgrim's Rest Church to stop Bro. Troy Nichols from preaching that a woman cannot pray with short hair.
>
> If, Pilgrim's Rest Church refuses to take legal action, by a move and second concerning the two above mentioned Bros. and the subject mentioned, we the Stone Coal Church request that the Pilgrim's Rest Church be dropped by the New Salem Association until they become willing to abide by the orders of our Association.
>
> We the Stone Coal Church request that this action be

done by the Pilgrim's Rest Church concerning the two aforementioned Brothers on their regular meeting time, the second Saturday in November, 1971.
    Done and signed by the order of Stone Coal Church
                            Elder Banner Manns — Moderator
                                    Hawley Scott — Clerk

    Moved and seconded to grant the request and send a
committee to the Pilgrim's Rest Church. Committee sent:
Elder Luther Conn, Mitchell Chaffins and Coy Combs.
Brother Mack Tuttle made an acknowledgement before the
Association.[6]

Elder Atlas Hall reports that both Nichols and Tuttle were
indeed highly "incensed" by the association's response to Western Union Church and had made their views known with
considerable regularity. Regarding the charge that "a woman
cannot pray with short hair," Nichols argued that "the prayers
of a 'bobbed-haired' woman were 'bottled' up by God." If
she had already received her call, but had not made her "travel
from nature to grace," then God would not hear her prayers
and thus not permit her to pass through her "travail" to redemption — until such time as she let her hair grow long again.
Nichols also charged that were the woman ever to cut her
hair after being redeemed, she "would be 'lost' and that for
eternity."[7]
    The association's committee did visit Pilgrim's Rest to in-
vestigate the actions of Tuttle and Nichols, but the atmosphere
at this church was so antagonistic that the investigation could
not be completed. Thus at the 1972 New Salem annual session the committee recommended that this church be dropped
from the association until the membership excluded the two
errant elders. The resulting heated responses (perhaps on
both sides of the issue) apparently grew so disruptive (including, I have been told, a fight between two women) that the
session had to be adjourned temporarily.[8] When reconvened,
the delegates agreed to follow the committee's recommendation: "On move and second . . . we drop Pilgrim's Rest Church
from our fellowship until they set their house in order. . . ."[9]

That action was taken on September 23, 1972, and a week later, on September 30, Pilgrim's Rest met and excluded the two elders.[10] That allowed the fellowship to inform the 1973 session that the association's order had been honored, thus permitting the church to be reinstated.[11] The entire situation had resulted in four years of New Salem discord, two exclusions (from Pilgrim's Rest), a great many angry words, and the disruption of an annual session. In addition, Elders Tuttle and Nichols left the Old Regular ranks to organize a new fellowship, in Kite, Knott County, Kentucky, naming their organization the True Baptist Church, no longer extant.[12]

During that 1973 session another issue was resolved that could have resulted in actions detrimental to the correspondence of Indian Bottom with New Salem. The dispute in question had been precipitated by Pilgrim's Home Church, a New Salem fellowship, that had accepted into membership an individual previously excluded from Powell Church, one of the Indian Bottom fellowships. Such admissions to membership of excluded persons are not permitted between churches of the New Salem Association or between a church of the New Salem Association and a church within one of New Salem's corresponding associations. Thus the violation resulted in the following 1973 request:

> Request from Indian Bottom Association: The Indian Bottom Association of Old Regular Baptists now in session with the Little Dove Church do hereby send this request to our sister, the New Salem Association when convened in her 1973 session. We your sister, the Indian Bottom Association, with much love and tenderness, request that you deal with the Pilgrim's Home Church as you deem proper and necessary for her transgression against the Powell Church and the Indian Bottom Association, by taking into her fellowship Perry Tackett who is excluded from the body of the Powell Regular Baptist Church for crime.
>
> May God help us to understand and respect each other's views as we continue our journey together in this good old time way. May He richly bless and guide you in all your undertakings.

> Done and signed by order of the Indian Bottom Association,
> Elder Manus Isom, Moderator
> Elder Olus Baldridge, Clerk[13]

The situation was so threatening, both to the Pilgrim's Home fellowship and to the Indian Bottom and New Salem relationship, that the errant church immediately issued an apology to Indian Bottom and Powell Church, apparently in the process agreeing to reverse the offending action:

> The Little Pilgrim Church of Old Regular Baptist, the Church of Jesus Christ met, seated and found to be in love and at peace with another. It was unanimously agreed that we send this apology and ask forgiveness if we have offended you by trying to help a brother to get recognition and to have his fellowship restored to him by our sister Association and we, the Little Pilgrim Home Church further extend this apology to our sister, the Indian Bottom Association and whomsoever we may have offended. Done and signed by order of Church.
>
> Elder Alonzo Allen, Moderator
> Brother Kelly Day, Clerk[14]

Troubles Between Associations

Disputes that involve two or more associations can have serious repercussions for the broad sweep of Old Regular fellowships, locking individual churches (and thus individual members) into fixed relationships of unity or discord with other individual churches (and individual members) — unity or discord that remains for years as an officially defined reality, controlling, among other things, who visits which churches, who preaches in which stands, and who may move his or her membership to which fellowship.

This officially defined reality — association "X" does or does not correspond with association "Y" — largely controls the flow of visitors from one church to another, from one association meeting to another, and perhaps even from one home to another. Indeed, the officially defined reality of "correspondence" can possess a tyrannical edge, determining, for example, which two or more preachers can be invited to preach together at a funeral and which two or more churches can establish close ties of sisterhood.

Three terms become critical in all this, "faith and order," "fellowship," and "nonfellowship." Churches and elders are constantly admonished not to interact, in any official capacity, with churches and elders divergent from the "faith and order" of the respective association. "Faith and order," however, and the judgment that any particular church or association is in alignment with the respective concept, are malleable factors, subject to changes from year to year. In addition, there is not always a clear understanding of what precise practices and doctrines come under the essentials of "faith and order."

In some instances associations have pronounced the "holds the key to its own door" principle when ruling on issues of "order" or "practice," meaning that the local church ultimately determines the questions of to whom it will grant membership, for whom it will deny membership, or from whom it will take away membership. Furthermore, this "key to its own door" is usually understood to fall under one particular clause that occurs — with only slight variations in wording — in the constitution of every one of these associations. "The members thus chosen and convened [the association delegates] shall have no power to lord anything over God's heritage nor shall have any clerical power over the Churches, nor shall they infringe on any clerical, internal rights of any Church in the Union."[15]

The clause just cited, however, is tempered — if not contradicted — by another traditional clause: "The Association shall have the power for the general union of the churches; to preserve inviolable a chain of communion among the churches; to give churches all necessary advice in matters of difficulty; to inquire into the cause of the churches failing to represent themselves at any time in the Association; . . . *and they shall have the power to withdraw from any church in the Union which shall violate the rules of our order to a seat with us.*"[16]

So by one clause the association cannot "Lord anything over" the local church and must not violate that church's "internal rights"; but by the other clause the association can "withdraw from any church in the Union which shall violate the rules" of the association. Obviously, therefore, the issues that are always critical are: (1) is the church somehow being "Lorded over" to the detriment of her "internal rights," or (2) is the association merely preserving "inviolable a chain of communion among the churches" and in doing so protecting the essential rules of their order?

To bring the problem inherent in these questions into sharper focus, consider two sequential items published in the Sardis Association's 1982 minutes. The first item dealt with the frequently debated issue of a dress code for women: "Does the Sardis Association believe in Sisters wearing pants, slacks, or shorts?" In this instance the association accepted a committee report that spoke in general terms about dressing "soberly and modestly" but turned the main question back to the individual churches with the following statement: "We believe, and the Association has so stated in the past, that each Church in the Sardis Association holds the key to its own door and is the sole judge of the conduct of its members as long as they follow the orthodox principles of religion and keep up a Godly discipline according to the rules of the Gospel as laid down in the Scriptures."[17] In contrast to this statement, however, the language of the second resolution was far more absolute: "The Association, by regular move and second, said that if a Sister has cut her hair, she should be asked to let it grow; if she fails to do so and cuts her hair again, she will be exluded."[18]

What appears to be obvious, at least for Sardis Association, is that dress regulations don't become serious enough to be considered among the absolutes of "faith and order," but that hair regulations for women do reach that level of seriousness. Very shortly we will see that judgment to have been operating in the various disputes leading to the Indian Bottom split.

But those "holds their own key" judgments (rulings on practices outside the essential requirements for "faith and order" agreement) are to some degree temporary and subject to shifts, with the result that all associations are not of the same mind at the same time. Thus two or more associations who once were in close correspondence may no longer "fellowship." "Fellowship" allows full interassociational relations, while "nonfellowship" makes all formal interassociational relations illegitimate.

Associations that are in correspondence with each other send delegates to each other's annual sessions, recognize the lettering of members from a fellowship in one of the associations to a fellowship in the other, accept the movement (when properly dismissed) of an entire church from one association to the other, acknowledge the legitimacy of each other's doctrines, allow each other's elders to share stands, and just generally encourage cross-associational interactions. Old Regular clusters that do not correspond engage in none of these exchanges.

One example of a complicated series of events that reshaped relationships between several associations is the chain of actions and reactions that split the original Indian Bottom cluster of churches and that left Thornton Union, both Indian Bottoms, and the collection of associations currently corresponding with Union and New Salem in realigned relationships. The following narrative examines that chain of events, drawing upon information supplied in various annual minutes from 1953 to 1961. Because there is still some bitterness connected with elements of this story, I need to assure my Old Regular friends that I am reporting these happenings from a totally objective and dispassionate point of view. These friends should forgive me if I do not include in my narratives any particular detail they personally consider essential to the story. Readers not within the Old Regular family should realize that the following accounts don't relate the full story, in the sense that these disputes have involved numerous strong personalities, whose individual motivations are not examined.

The Indian Bottom Split

In 1955 New Salem was in correspondence with seven other associations: Union, Indian Bottom (before their split), Sardis, Mud River, Friendship (before their split), Philadelphia, and Thornton Union.[19] Northern New Salem had not as yet been organized: it would be "armed" by New Salem in 1957 and come into correspondence with the mother association in 1958.[20]

Relations between these eight associations, however, were not completely harmonious even at this time, since Indian Bottom was soon (1956) to declare nonfellowship with Thornton Union on the grounds that the latter had not met demands of Union and New Salem concerning "bobbed hair"; and New Salem was soon (also 1956) to reject the letter of correspondence from Thornton Union.[21]

Nevertheless, in 1955 none of the other associations named above had broken correspondence with Indian Bottom, Thornton Union, or each other. Thornton Union fellowships, however, had become the focus of a general controversy, with charges being leveled against this cluster that several of its churches were regularly allowing sisters to cut their hair.[22] In fact, acting on these grounds, the 1953 New Salem session had almost ended that association's correspondence with Thornton Union, only backing out of the move at the last minute.[23]

During the mid-1950s Indian Bottom Association apparently was experiencing some divisiveness among its own fellowships, with a number of its more traditional churches growing impatient with New Salem's and Union's reluctance to declare nonfellowship with Thornton Union. These more traditional Indian Bottom elements — evidently centered in the Clear Creek and Little Rose fellowships — even wanted Indian Bottom to break correspondence with Union and New Salem because elders of these associations were "sharing stands" in

Thornton Union churches and then preaching in Indian Bottom churches. This practice, so declared the traditionalists, placed Indian Bottom in "indirect fellowship" with Thornton Union.[24] The more moderate elements of Indian Bottom seemed willing to treat the entire situation less stringently, and leaned in the direction of a reestablishment of fellowship with Thornton Union.

During its 1956 session, however, New Salem yielded to pressure from without and from within and voted to break correspondence with Thornton Union, joining an action also taken by Union Association.[25] In 1957 New Salem again rejected Thornton Union's letter, and for two years after that the Thornton churches made no formal attempts to reestablish this correspondence.[26] It was not until 1960 that New Salem renewed fellowship with Thornton Union.[27]

Union Association, however, was not quite so stern with its former associate, in the sense that in 1959 it voted to welcome Thornton Union back into correspondence, apparently without conferring with New Salem to assure a united set of actions.[28] One consequence of the failure of these two giants of Old Regularism to act in unison was that the two warring elements in Indian Bottom were able to interpret the Thornton Union situation from different perspectives.

During Indian Bottom's 1959 annual session (held two weeks before the Union session that rerecognized Thornton Union), Big Cowan Church (one of Indian Bottom's more traditional congregations) advanced a question concerning the mechanics of receiving into Indian Bottom fellowships the "orderly part" of Thornton Union churches: "In regard to request from the Big Cowan Church concerning members and churches that has been dropped from our churches and association and gone into churches and associations in disorder. What can be done to receive orderly part of the above mentioned members and churches?"[29]

That year's minutes recorded the following as having been the answer to this query:

It was moved and seconded that we adopt the same answer as our sister — the Northern New Salem Association
which reads as follows:
We, the Northern New Salem Association, as an Advisory
Council, say to all our churches that we do hereby agree to
follow the footsteps of our Mother, the New Salem Association, and our Sister, the Union Association in whatever decision that they may make pertinent to this question.[30]

That action was taken on September 5, 1959. When on
September 19, 1959, Union Association — in session at the
Bold Camp Church in Pound, Virginia — voted to reestablish
correspondence with Thornton Union, a series of actions en-
sued that drove a wedge between the two Indian Bottom
factions.[31]

What happened was that during the winter, spring, and
summer of 1959–60 the divergent elements of Indian Bottom
Association viewed their September 5, 1959, resolution from
widely differing interpretations. The moderates, led by Moderator J. W. Pratt, apparently saw the motion as allowing the
reestablishment of fellowship with Thornton Union if and
when New Salem and/or Union reopened such correspondence, a requirement they judged to have been met when
Union, on September 19, 1959, reestablished fellowship with
the Thornton churches. Those more traditionalist, who co-
alesced around Elder Frank Fugate of Clear Creek Church,
viewed the motion solely as treating the question of how to
"rescue orderly members and churches from the Thornton
Union Association."[32]

By the time Indian Bottom convened its sixty-fifth annual
session, Elder Pratt had already taken some actions conso-
nant with an Indian Bottom-Thornton Union state of full correspondence (allowing Thornton Union members to sit in
council with Indian Bottom fellowships, permitting Indian
Bottom elders to share the stand with Thornton Union elders, and sanctioning the transferal of members from one of
these associations to the other). These procedures greatly disturbed the Fugate side in the controversy, and on September

2, 1960, when the two factions came together at Little Rose Church in Hindman, Kentucky, they were primed for a controversy. Fugate's position was that Pratt was in disorder because he violated the 1959 Indian Bottom resolution governing the reinstatement into fellowship of Thornton Union. Pratt's position was that he did follow the spirit of that resolution and that the Fugate forces were in disorder because they did not follow his "legitimate" instructions relative to the reestablishment of correspondence with Thornton Union.[33] The two most significant consequences of all this were that the Fugate-side churches gained control of the 1960 annual session and elected Elder Frank Fugate moderator of Indian Bottom Association, while the Pratt-side churches met at another location, in a kind of "rump session," declared themselves to be the true trunk of the association, and elected Elder Pratt as their moderator.[34]

One factor greatly complicating the entire affair was that during the years Thornton Union was declared to be in disorder there had been members moving from Indian Bottom to Thornton Union or from Thornton Union to Indian Bottom, depending upon which side of the moderate-traditionalist division these individuals favored. Since these two associations were not in correspondence, these membership movements were not "by letter." Instead, they were "by recommendation," a transfer method used by Old Regular fellowships to "rescue" individuals from a church or association judged to have fallen into disorder. A member of the fellowship to which the transfer was being made simply vouched for the legitimacy of the individual's faith and former membership, recommending his or her acceptance by the receiving fellowship.[35]

The sanctioning of such a method for transferals usually has been accomplished by a formal motion "moved and seconded" during an association session. In fact, that apparently was what the more traditional Indian Bottom churches thought their association was doing in 1959 when the September 5 resolution was adopted.

Anyway, when Indian Bottom split, both Union and New

Salem immediately entered the situation as would-be concil-
iators, trying to bring the two factions back together and to
establish fellowship between a reunited Indian Bottom and
a reinstated–to–correspondence Thornton Union. At their
1960 session New Salem established a committee to work with
the Fugate and Pratt sides of Indian Bottom, promising to "letter up" to them the next year if they would get back together.[36]
Concurrently, Union approved a plan which it advised Thornton Union and Indian Bottom to follow in handling the memberships that had crossed from one association to the other
during the times these two were not in fellowship.[37]

The Fugate side of Indian Bottom, however, still viewed
Thornton Union to be in disorder. In addition, they considered Elder Pratt and his Indian Bottom following to be in
disorder because they "abruptly broke away" from the 1960
session.[38] By Fugate's argument, Union and New Salem could
deal only with his faction of Indian Bottom, with the Pratt
churches being completely out of the picture until such time
as they might reestablish fellowship with the "legitimate"
Indian Bottom Association.

New Salem and Union didn't agree with this Fugate-side
rationale and proceeded to recognize the Pratt side of Indian
Bottom, on the grounds these churches had followed procedures recommended (by New Salem and Union) for reestablishing harmony with Thornton Union.[39] These actions,
supported by other associations, such as Philadelphia, Sardis, and Northern New Salem, tended to widen the split between the two Indian Bottom groups, largely because the Fugate side believed these other associations had recognized
the "disordered" faction of Indian Bottom in order to establish "love and fellowship" with another "disordered" Old Regular group, Thornton Union. Thus the end result of all this
controversy was that this Fugate side (earlier identified as
Old Indian Bottom) became a maverick Old Regular association, corresponding with no other cluster of this subdenomination of Baptists. That, as mentioned earlier, is still the
status of Old Indian Bottom at the time of this writing.

Two addenda need to be affixed to this Indian Bottom narrative. First, New Salem and Union didn't long remain in correspondence with Thornton Union. Acting on charges that several Thornton Union fellowships were again allowing women members to cut their hair and that one of these churches was even using women to close services by prayer, New Salem severed this correspondence in 1969.[40] Union lingered in fellowship with Thornton Union until 1972.

The second addendum concerns recent efforts by Old Indian Bottom to reestablish correspondence with some of the other Old Regular associations. When this Fugate-side Indian Bottom met for its 1986 annual session, the delegates passed the following resolution:

> Regarding the request from the Crab Orchard Church requesting that we send letters to the Sardis, Northern New Salem, Old Friendship and Philadelphia Associations asking what can be done that the Indian Bottom Association may have correspondence with them. It was moved and seconded to grant this request and for the Clerk to prepare the letters.[41]

At the time of this writing responses to this Old Indian Bottom request have not been positive. First, it should be noted that the letter in question was not sent to New Salem and Union, suggesting that either Old Indian Bottom had no interest in reestablishing correspondence with these associations or believed there was no chance of doing so. This fact that no letter went to either New Salem or Union, in turn, makes the 1987 resolution passed by Northern New Salem particularly interesting: "That we refer their [Old Indian Bottom's] letter of request concerning advice in obtaining correspondence to our mother the New Salem Association or our Sister the Union Association."[42] The effect of this statement, of course, was to pass the question on to New Salem and Union, even though these two had not been approached by Old Indian Bottom. Philadelphia Association's response was more mixed and less clear, but the last sentence of that statement also appears to have referred the issue to New Salem and Union:

> We the Philadelphia Association received a request from the Frank Fugate side of the Indian Bottom Association, asking for advice on the steps to be taken to obtain correspondence with the Philadelphia Association.
>
> We as an advisory council say we believe the first thing that you must do is to be unified among your own brethren in the desire to obtain correspondence.
>
> We feel that the second thing you must do is to comply with the orders of the Philadelphia Association.
>
> We would require that you would "consider" all our correspondent brethren and the advice they would give.[43]

The point here is that as "correspondent brethren" New Salem and Union would again be brought into the picture, forcing Old Indian Bottom to satisfy whatever demands these power blocks of the subdenomination might impose upon the situation. Were these two (New Salem and Union) to adhere to their 1961 resolutions, Old Indian Bottom would be forced to realign with the Pratt side as a condition of correspondence with New Salem, Union, Philadelphia, Northern New Salem, and the other Old Regular clusters in fellowship with these four.[44] This would be a bitter pill for Old Indian Bottom members, given that they view themselves as the true trunk of the Indian Bottom branch of Old Regularism.[45]

All of the above serves to show how complicated these individual questions of correspondence can become, depending not only upon the wishes of any present slate of association delegates, but also upon multiple layers of precedents and a network of other associations, all prepared to object to irregularities in procedure. In addition, there are the numerous difficulties arising out of the personalities involved in these disputes — strong-willed local church moderators and also association moderators trying to maintain delicate coalitions of power. In summary, the case of Old Indian Bottom would be much simpler were it to involve only two associations, were it to be free of entanglements with precedents, and were the various associations to be able to accept as an accomplished fact the permanent separation of the two sides of Indian Bottom. At the time of this writing there appears to be little likelihood of that acceptance or of changes in the other two factors. Therefore, Old Indian Bottom may forever remain in a loner state.

For the purpose of complete factuality in this discussion, there is one other topic that needs to be mentioned in reference to Old Indian Bottom: it is sometimes referred to as the "colored side" of Indian Bottom, because its fellowships contain the heaviest concentration of Old Regular blacks.[46] For example, the Little Home church, mentioned earlier as having such a perfectly integrated congregation, is a member of this association.

I have no evidence that this factor either formally or informally influenced the actions of 1959–60, but because of the occasional employment of the term given above, "colored side," and because of the era in which this split occurred, it seems wise to at least mention this race factor. Frankly, I would be disappointed were I to discover substantial evidence of racial motivations in this series of actions, since I was so impressed by the apparent racial harmony present in the Little Home fellowship (discussed in chapter 5), and since such evidence would challenge the thesis advanced by Ron Short in his essay "We Believed in the Family and the Old Regular Baptist Church."[47]

In response to an earlier version of this chapter, Elder Atlas Hall of Kite, Kentucky, wrote me a letter in which he addressed this "colored side" issue at some length. Because Hall's thoughts are clearly expressed and represent a point of view that appears to be in full support of Short's thesis, I want to quote a significant portion of that letter. Furthermore, I want to quote this letter without any omissions.

> In reference to the term "colored side," as it is applied to the Fugate faction, I would like to address my observations and opinions as it relates to that topic, having resided in Knott County for over 29 years, acquainted with the opposing factions (with relatives in both), having attended Old Regular fellowships since I was about 4 years of age, and my interest in etymology.

Permit me to first say that "colored side" is only one term used to describe the Fugate faction of Indian Bottom. Others include: "off side," "disorderly side," "unorthodox side," "Fugate side," "Hillie Reedy side," "black side," and *yes*, "nigger side."

Except for those who employ the term "nigger side" (and the number who use this term is very small), there are no racial overtones in the use of the term "colored side." A majority of our Black citizens would define themselves as "colored." Even that venerable organization, NAACP, doesn't call itself "black."

In Appalachian vernacular the term "colored" is considered a respectful way to identify a Negro individual. Very few of the elderly citizens of this area refer to a Negro individual as "black," simply as that term is of very recent use and origin. The youthful individuals will refer to a Negro individual as a "black." Employment of the term "Negro" is used as contrasted with the term "Caucasian."

There certainly was no formal or informal influence by the Old Regular fellowships in the occasional employment of the term "colored," and the citizens of this area (both races) were only concerned with individual relationships in the late 1950's and through the late 1960's when racial strife was being experienced in other areas of our nation. Of course, there were (and are) exceptions, however the citizens (of both races) take pride in the racial harmony that is experienced in our area, and I rest assured that the racial harmony that you observed at the Little Home fellowship extends to the geographical area as well. Having taught in the public schools of Knott County, I can assure you that we have racial harmony in that area as well.[48]

Since I know Elder Hall quite well, I have no trouble accepting in full the sentiments of this statement.

The Union Association Split, 1961–62

The Indian Bottom-Thornton Union controversies discussed above were generated by differences on the "order" side of the "adherence to faith and order" dictum, in the sense that the alleged violations of the bobbed hair rule, augmented by charges and countercharges about association procedures, touched on issues of practice as opposed to doctrine. The controversy to be discussed now, however, was essentially doctrinal in nature, although it also involved one major procedural argument, the question of whether Union Association's constitution permitted the expulsion of a member fellowship by only a majority vote. Like the previously examined controversy, this Old Regular dispute resulted in the formation of a new association, this time the Bethel alliance.

Bethel is one of the smaller clusters of Old Regular churches, containing only eight fellowships and a total membership of 274 (1986 statistics).[49] Like Old Indian Bottom, it maintains correspondence with no other association, existing only as an adrift and loner group, unrecognized by a single Old Regular fellowship outside the Bethel alliance. Indeed, the isolation of this group of Old Regular congregations seems more complete than that of Old Indian Bottom, in part perhaps because Bethel Association had been declared (rightly or wrongly) to be in doctrinal errancy. In contrast, it appears that the mainline alliances within Old Regularism (Union, New Salem, Sardis, Northern New Salem, etc.) give Old Indian Bottom a kind of unofficial recognition, acknowledging in this manner that this highly traditional association has been unhappily caught in a regrettable logjam of precedents. This appearance of quasi-recognition develops, in large part, from the fact that the Old Indian Bottom congregations receive a significant number of friendly but unofficial visitations by individuals in churches of these mainline clusters. The sequestering of the Bethel fellowships, however, seems more complete, a circumstance that may be due to the fact that this association was born out of controversy over doctrine rather than over practice.

The origin of the Bethel alliance dates from 1961, when Union Association voted 127 to 25 to drop Bold Camp Church of Pound, Virginia, from the association's role of fellowships. This action culminated a doctrinal dispute that had first erupted nine years earlier, when Union's 1952 session delegates adopted, by majority vote, the following statement:

In answer to the queries from the Old Elkhorn Church
we as advisory council say to the Bold Camp Church and to
all our churches in this association, if you have any one
preaching when the Light of Christ appears to a sinner that
it gives him Eternal life or preaching that they are a child of
God before they are born again or anything that would
cause a sinner to settle down on anything short of Eternal
Salvation by grace to ask them to stop preaching it or exclude them from the fellowship of the church.[50]

This statement was later ordered to be reprinted in the 1961
Union Association minutes and then was used in 1962 as the
basis for excluding the Bold Camp Church, later to be re-
named Fairview when part of the membership formed a second Bold Camp church and returned to their affiliation with
Union.

Union's expulsion of Bold Camp (Fairview) precipitated additional actions that resulted in six other fellowships' (Bethel,
Mt. Olive, Long's Fork, Turner, Rose Hill, and Hylton) with-
drawing from Union Association, the largest split that this
giant of Old Regularism had ever experienced. Although parts
of Bethel and Hylton also later returned to the Union fold,
the split temporarily wounded the giant, not only in numbers but in general association harmony. Indeed, feelings
still run deep, particularly in Bethel Association, relative to
the several issues that were involved.

The second part of the doctrinal advisement quoted above,
that the accused elders stop "preaching that they [redeemed
sinners] are a child of God before they are born again," al-
ludes to the Primitive Baptist belief in particular election, a
theology that Old Regularism specifically rejected in the early
1890s (discussed in chapter 1). The first segment of the doctrinal advisement, however, treated an Old Regular dispute
that may never have been clearly resolved — at least in the
Union Association — until this more contemporary controversy erupted.

At the core of the dispute was the question of exactly when
salvation comes to the sinner. Does it come when that sinner
first hears his or her "call" and views the "Light of Christ,"

thus experiencing an immediate transformation from "out of darkness and into his marvelous light" (I Pet. 2:9); or does that call simply make the sinner aware of his or her "blackened" state, precipitating a period of "travail" during which he or she strives (through prayer, supplication, and "works") for forgiveness, with salvation coming only at that point at which a "conviction" of forgiveness occurs?

A contemporary expression of this second position has been provided by Elder Bill Campbell, moderator of Bull Creek Church (Union Association). Campbell argues that a person's call is little more than his or her God-revealed awareness of personal sin, that "hearing and responding" to this call "initiates the process of repentance," that "works are required before salvation is applied," that these works are not those such as "doing good to others or paying of tithes," but that they are works such as "taking heed to the call to repentance and [manifesting a] belief in God."[51] For Campbell, a person's call is the beginning of the redemption process rather than the end, with the above-mentioned "prayer, supplication, and works" being required to complete the progress toward salvation. This is sometimes called the "travel [or travail] from Nature to Grace" doctrine, since it involves a struggling movement toward redemption. Any process less complete than this, Campbell argues, might (in the words of the 1961 Union Association statement) "cause a sinner to settle down on" some state "short of Eternal Salvation by grace."[52]

It appears safe to assert that at the time of this writing the salvation doctrine expressed by Campbell is the generally accepted — though perhaps not universally accepted — position within Union Association and mainline Old Regularism. In addition, it seems correct to state that the "Light of Christ" doctrine, as developed above, was the main heresy with which the 1961 Bold Camp leadership was charged.[53]

What is not clear is whether the leadership of the congregations that were initially to constitute the Bethel Association (Bold Camp, Bethel, Mt. Olive, Long's Fork, Turner, Rose Hill, and Hylton) were actually advocating this "Light of Christ" doctrine, at least as understood by their opponents. A flood of circular letters and other statements in Bethel Association minutes argued that this body of elders had never been adequately heard and that their doctrinal positions consequently were distorted.[54] But what angered the Bethel camp the most was the fact that Union Association appeared to violate its own constitution when expelling Bold Camp.

In 1962 the sixteenth article of the Union Association constitution read exactly as it does today: "All matters coming before the Association shall be decided by a majority of the members present, except receiving and dismissing Churches and Associations, which shall be by unanimous voice."[55] The vote to exclude Bold Camp, however, was recorded as 127 for and 25 against, a solid majority but not unanimous.[56]

That action was taken on September 15, 1962, and exactly one week later this alleged procedural irregularity became the first matter to be mentioned in the resolution instituting the establishment of Bethel Association.[57] The procedural irregularity charge noticeably disturbed some elements of Union Association, as evidenced by item 12 in Union's 1963 minutes:

> The Pilgrim Rest, Little Jocie, Caney Fork Churches requested Item 16 of the Constitution be changed to conform to the 1925 minutes. We the Union Association as advisory council upon motion and second advise that we leave the item as it now is for another year to give the brethren time to meditate and pray over the matter. No further action will be taken until a church requests it.[58]

The concerns behind this Pilgrim's Rest, Little Jocie, and Caney Fork request were that prior to 1925 this article 16 of the Union constitution had read exactly as it read in 1962, demanding a unanimous vote for dismissions.[59] An amendment passed in 1925, however, changed that article to read as follows: "All matters, coming before the Association, shall be decided by a majority of the members present."[60] There the wording of this article remained until the 1950s, when it was changed back to the pre–1925 form: " . . . except in receiving and dismissing churches and associations, which shall be by a unanimous voice." Given the action that had been taken against Bold Camp—approved by only a majority vote—it seems obvious why the Pilgrim's Rest, Little Jocie, and Caney Fork fellowships preferred the 1925 wording.

In 1964 Union Association found a more satisfying resolution for this entire issue. At that year's association meeting a request again was made that an explanation of article 16 be provided. This time the Union Association leadership apparently was prepared for the query, with the result that the following statement was issued:

> It was moved, seconded and passed that the same explanation concerning churches dealing with members should apply to associations dealing with churches. The old brethren gave the following explanation, to this Item 16, in item 11 of our 1911 minutes: "We understand, according to our constitution, all matters coming before any church should be decided by a majority of the members present, except receiving and dismissing members. We understand . . . the term, 'receiving members,' to mean receiving members into the fellowship by experience and baptism, by letter, and by recommendation, and 'dismissing members,' to mean dismissing from the church by letter, and excluding members may be done by a majority of the members present and that a majority may rescind an act of excluding a member and restore such excluded member back to fellowship."[61]

What must be understood here is that this statement carefully defined "dismissing" to apply only to the act of releasing (by letter) a member to another church or, by extension of this reasoning, to the releasing of a church to another association. Exclusion, therefore, fell outside the purview of the "which shall be by unanimous voice" phrase, thus providing sanction for the procedure by which Bold Camp was excluded.

This discussion of the procedural irregularity charge, and of the rationale ultimately employed to meet the allegation, is important because it demonstrates the legalistic nature of Old Regular operations. Union Association might have lived with the unrebutted assertion that it had violated its own constitution in doing something that a large majority of its delegates wanted to do, but such a judgment would not have been a comfortable one. Thus the discovery of a sanctifying precedent or constitutional interpretation was necessary, even if the association had to reach back to 1911 to find such a justification. Perhaps what went unnoticed, however, was one word in the troublesome constitutional phrase: " . . . and dismissing Churches and *Associations* which shall be by unanimous voice [emphasis mine]." Members may be "dismissed" by letter to another church, and churches may be "dismissed" by resolution to another association, but what then would "dismissing" an association mean? Surely this part of the phrase must refer to the breaking of fellowship. There appears to be no other way an association can be "dismissed."

Some Concluding Thoughts

These two extensive discussions of Old Regular disputes have been employed not only to demonstrate the occasional contentiousness of this Baptist tradition, but also to illustrate the faith's heavy dependence upon a rule of law and precedents. The staunch traditionalism that characterizes this subdenomination has been maintained largely through this legalistic approach to doctrine and practice, an approach that provides a creedal, structural, and procedural stability not always enjoyed by other Appalachian religious factions. Articles of faith, rules of decorum, constitutional codes, and decades of precedents combine to form the relatively unchanging essentials of Old Regular faith and order. The Regular side of this subdenomination's Regular Baptist and Separate Baptist origins has tended to dominate, thus maintaining the rigid forms so necessary for long-term stability; and even though there have been numerous Old Regular splits over the last century and a half, the resultant sides have never been all that far apart in either doctrine or practice. Although Old Indian Bottom, New Salem, Thornton Union, and Bethel may not correspond with each other, it is not difficult to see that they are all of the same Old Regular Baptist tradition.

7. "What Will I Leave Behind?": The Future of Old Regularism

Elder Ivan Amburgey of Pinetop, Kentucky, one of the most popular preachers in the larger Indian Bottom Association and throughout Old Regularism, enjoyed a career as a country music performer before he abandoned that life style for the unpaid ministry of an Old Regular exhorter. Furthermore, he continues to use his musical talent, having become a favorite liner and singer (as well as preacher) at association meetings and special services. Amburgey has also written some Old Regular hymns that have found their way into the little songbooks employed in this subdenomination's services. The title of one hymn attributed to him, "What Will I Leave Behind?," seems fitting as the heading for this chapter, intended as a speculative look at the present and future of Old Regularism.[1]

A number of times in the last six years, especially after I became broadly recognized by Old Regulars as a student of their faith and practice, I have been asked, "Well, what do you think? Do you guess we'll last?" Indeed, I have received the question, or some version of it, so many times that I began to sense this to be a significant concern of the subdenomination. One elderly woman at the 1987 Union Association meeting expressed her version of the concern this way: "I have nine great–grandchildren. Do you think they will sit under a tent and hear preaching and singing like this?"

I don't intend this chapter as any definitive answer to that question. Obviously there are too many variables to be considered. Nevertheless, I will advance some speculative queries, the first being, what do the numbers say?

Do the Numbers Suggest a Dying Faith?

I have already indicated that the Old Regulars are not a large body of people — approximately 15,000 actual members, with perhaps another 15,000 or 20,000 nonmember regular church attendees. Those are totals at which proponents of the televangelism megaministries of the late 1980s might scoff. Certainly there is not in these numbers any suggestion of national impact.

The small numbers, however, would not significantly disturb the typical Old Regular Baptist, inbued as that individual is with that idea of a "peculiar people." Indeed, I am convinced that this typical Old Regular would accept, without great disturbance of mind, the inevitability of the subdenomination's relative smallness; but I am equally convinced that this individual would be comforted by an assurance that the faith would be around until some end of earthly things. After that, what would matter?

> Let thy kingdom, blessed Savior,
> Come and bid our going cease.
> Come O come and reign forever,
> God of love and Prince of peace.[2]

With that Old Regular's concern in mind, let's look at some association membership statistics to see if there are any trends at work. Table 2 provides a fifty-year picture, at ten-year intervals, of the memberships of New Salem and Union associations, with Thornton Union added after that alliance was organized in 1945. Table 3 focuses strictly on Union Association and reports more complete statistics for the years 1980 through 1987. Finally, Table 4 records data that give us a contemporary membership gain-loss perspective for twelve of the associations.

A few terms in Tables 3 and 4 may need explanations. "Restored" refers to members who have been excluded and then returned to fellowship. The "Received by Letter" category includes individuals who have transferred to a church from some

Table 2   Membership Totals, 1930–1980
          New Salem, Union, and Thornton Union Associations

1930	New Salem	1,848
	Union	1,839
1940	New Salem	2,155
	Union	3,685
1950	New Salem	2,681
	Union	3,356
	Thornton Union	1,310
1960	New Salem	3,027
	Union	3,854
	Thornton Union	1,587
1970	New Salem	3,093
	Union	3,516
	Thornton Union	1,457
1980	New Salem	3,165
	Union	3,574
	Thornton Union	1,852

other fellowship in the association or in a corresponding association. "Received by Recommendation" refers to individuals "rescued" from fellowships considered to be in disorder. Individuals involved in this procedure are not rebaptized, but are simply accepted into membership upon "recommendation." The "Dismissed by Letter" group are persons who have been released to join another fellowship in the same or a corresponding association.

New Salem and Union are included in Table 2 simply because they are the largest of the various Old Regular fellowship clusters. Thornton Union is added because it is generally viewed as being more "modern" than the New Salem correspondence group (Union, Sardis, Mud River, Old Friendship, Philadelphia, Northern New Salem, and Indian Bottom), giving us opportunity to see if numbers are increasing in that type of an orientation.

Membership totals in Table 2 suggest that both New Salem and Union experienced growth during the 1930s, 1940s,

Table 3 Union Association Statistics, 1980–1987

	1980	1981	1982	1983	1984	1985	1986	1987	Totals
1. Received by Experience and Baptism	219	175	142	127	122	110	105	96	1,096
2. Restored	10	6	9	5	7	12	4	18	71
3. Received by Letter	99	61	59	62	65	100	64	90	600
4. Received by Recommendation	8	0	3	0	0	1	5	3	20
5. Excluded	34	51	34	41	59	68	64	69	420
6. Dismissed by Letter	67	63	69	42	98	74	69	67	549
7. Deceased	80	104	87	83	85	89	102	104	734
8. Yearly Total Memberships	3,574	3,548	3,571	3,599	3,505	3,326	3,255	3,225	

Note: The 1986 statistics are incomplete because that was the year one church's letter remained in controversy.

and 1950s; but that the 1960s and 1970s became periods of leveling off, with even a slight downturn for Union. Were we to examine more recent statistics we would discover that by the mid-1980s that downturn had also developed for New Salem, with that association's total membership sliding to 3,090 in 1984 and then to 2,951 in 1986.[3] Then, as Table 3 indicates, Union's membership continued to drop slightly during the '80s, even though their total number of churches rose from 67 in 1980 to 73 in 1987.[4]

If Union Association's statistics are representative, Table 3 gives us some additional information concerning how these drops may be occurring. By seven years into the decade of the 1980s, Union Association fellowships had baptized 1,095 new Old Regulars, but they had lost 734 members by death. Add these 734 deceased members to the 420 who were excluded (giving a total of 1,154) and we may see where the shortfall is occurring, especially since the "Received by Letter" and "Dismissed by Letter" totals show a credit in Union's favor. This credit from the "Letter" columns becomes meaningful when we realize that we do not know how many of the 420 excluded individuals were later restored.

Has Thornton Union fared any better than New Salem and Union in membership gains or losses? This group of churches did experience a moderate but steady growth from 1950 to 1980 (Table 2), but like their more traditional cousins they have lost some of that gain — in fact most of it — in the 1980s, dropping to 1,715 in 1982, 1,563 in 1986, and 1,413 in 1987.[5] The fact that Thornton Union is somewhat more "modern" than New Salem and Union may not be making any difference in membership gain or loss.

Table 4 provides a picture of recent gains or losses for twelve associations. By using statistics from the most recent minutes I possess for each of these fellowship clusters, I have arranged data columns for "Baptized," "Restored," "Excluded," and "Deceased." For the year in question, the "Baptized" and "Restored" figures may be considered gains for an association; while the "Excluded" and "Deceased" figures may be considered losses, thus producing the final column, the actual membership gain or loss for the year.

Table 4 includes data from four years (1984 through 1987), but if these numbers can be viewed as representing one year in the mid–1980s, then we have a clear picture of how the slow attrition in Old Regular memberships is developing. The figurative year would have registered a total depletion of 152 members from within these twelve associations, not a huge drain, but one which might cause some deep concern if repeated year after year.

Nevertheless, I don't want to belabor these statistics, because there is a possibility that they do not signal any long-term trend. Still, the numbers might warrant Old Regular consideration, if for no other reason than to ask why the sub-denomination's momentum of the 1930s, 1940s, and 1950s has been slowed so in the 1970s and 1980s.

On two occasions Elder Bill Campbell has told me that, in his opinion, Old Regulars have "turned the corner" on the youth problem, that there are more young people attending these churches than there were ten or fifteen years ago.[6] Unfortunately, there are no statistics that can either confirm or deny that conclusion, since no Old Regular association keeps records on age distributions within its membership, much less within the body of nonmember visitors. In addition, my own observations date back only six years, thus failing to provide a perspective from which I could make more than an educated guess about the question. The only observation that I feel rather comfortable in making is that compared to certain other small Baptist subdenominations of the region — in particular the Missionary and Free Will Baptists — Old Regulars give many indications of becoming above average in age. After having made that statement, however, I feel that I must again call the readers' attention to Tables 3 and 4 and to the fact that baptisms are keeping up with membership mortality, even if just barely.

This discussion of gains and losses in memberships, however, must ultimately be given another perspective, that of

Table 4 Contemporary Gain/Loss Statistics for Twelve Associations

Association	Year of Minutes	Baptized	Restored to Membership	Excluded	Deceased	Gain/Loss
Bethel	1986	2	1	4	8	−8
Indian Bottom	1985	68	4	26	29	+17
Mountain #1	1984	15	0	0	12	+3
New Salem	1986	90	2	23	106	−37
Northern New Salem	1987	26	4	15	15	0
Old Friendship	1986	17	0	13	14	−15
Original Mountain Liberty	1987	9	4	2	4	+7
Philadelphia	1986	6	0	13	9	−16
Sardis	1985	32	1	16	36	−19
Thornton Union	1987	25	0	3	37	−15
Union	1987	96	18	69	104	−59
Totals		389	34	187	388	−152

Note: Contemporary statistics not available for Cumberland, Friendship, Kyova, Mountain #2, or Mud River.

the more traditional of the Old Regulars. Redemptions and subsequent church memberships, reason the proponents of this perspective, are not really the consequences of something the church does. The call, the taking heed of that call, and the travel from nature to grace are steps in the redemption process controlled solely by God and the sinner in question. True, the church can establish an environment of piety, love, joy, and caring fellowship, and the preacher can urge all the unredeemed to take note of their calls; but the final magic that becomes "election by grace" involves God and one individual sinner. During periods of membership decline perhaps what is being manifested is either something in the will of the Deity or something in the nature of the men and women of the moment.

Therefore, should the faithful get all upset over a decade of sagging memberships and decide to organize Sunday schools and discontinue lined singing, perhaps in the process joining themselves to the weakened nature of the moment; or should they just go on with practices believed to be right, letting God call and redeem in His own good way?

If Old Regulars were just to join the parades of popularity, argues Elder Wardie Craft (of Thornton Union, and not the most traditional of association moderators, as we will see shortly), they would simply be taking on "the garments of Babylonia." "Little by little, it seems to me," he said in a 1982 circular letter to his association, "that the old gospel church today is following the footsteps of old Israel under the law. Our love today is growing cold. Our shouting has almost stopped in many churches. Our old time songs are being replaced by worldly and radio songs. The prayers of our fathers and mothers have almost ceased. The promise of many of our preachers does not stand dependable. In many of our churches we can hear beautiful words but can't feel much power; and many are failing to take God's word for their guide. I fear that we are borrowing too many things from Babylon that will not work in God's house."[7]

So the solution to dropping memberships, most Old Regular voices proclaim, is not to change to bring the numbers up, but to hold fast until wanderers return to the fold. "Do you want me to get on the radio and TV and urge them in?" asked Elder Raymond Smith, suggesting by the question that cosmetic changes in the Old Regular method of worship would be just as improper as an Old Regular electronic ministry would be, both employed to evangelize, to attract greater numbers. "That's man trying to call," he said, "not God."[8]

What Institutions
Will Old Regulars Leave Behind?

Small Baptist subdenominations of Appalachia have occasionally been criticized because they have established no lofty and lasting institutions—schools, orphanages, hospitals, seminaries, and the like.[9] By these standards Old Regulars certainly would look weak and unproductive. Not a single institution like those just mentioned exists today as a tribute to Old Regular organizational skills and motivations toward social outreach. There was one attempt at such an accomplishment, shortly to be examined, but otherwise the slate is remarkably clean.

Indeed, Old Regular meetinghouses themselves seldom appear to be the monuments to congregational sacrifice—or to power, wealth, and vanity—that the mainline and high-church denominations frequently build. With some marked exceptions, these meetinghouses usually seem so temporary, so tentative, giving the appearance of being serviceable structures built to meet the needs of a moment, but not as facilities intended to last extended periods of time. My discussion in chapter 3 of the place of "place" in Old Regular worship serves to explain in part the subdenomination's attitude toward buildings, but there is another level of thought that needs to be added, one that I feel more completely expresses Old Regular values relative to church edifices.

A building, declares orthodox Old Regular thought, is a

thing of nature, not spirit — a temporal entity that ultimately will have little or no bearing on salvation and the afterlife. Why then, it is asked, do other religious groups place so much emphasis upon buildings, upon raising more and more money to construct their monuments ever wider and ever higher? The impression is given, the Old Regular tends to say, that spirit is in the structure, rather than in actions taken within the structure. This, in turn, cheapens the really important factors of spirituality.

On two occasions I have attended Saturday business meetings (at Tivis Chapel and Ash Camp) when consideration was given to the needs of the physical church. These discussions included a proposal to purchase ceiling fans, some announcements relative to the repair of a roof, and a plan to construct an outside shed to shelter the serving area during dinners-on-the-ground. In both instances I was struck by the informal and low-pressure nature of the process: generally just an announcement that said such and such needs to be done, and if anyone cares to contribute he or she is invited to do so. What would then take place was that individuals would move forward and place cash contributions on the stand. Visitors to Old Regular churches will never see offering plates passed among the congregation, either for special needs or for regular monthly offerings; they will hear few, if any, discussions of money; and they will find themselves totally removed from that more mainline ecclesiastical value construct that equates mission with monuments, piety with possessions.

That is the positive side of the picture. Perhaps the negative side is that Old Regulars seldom think about institutions that have a larger social outreach. Thus they are not involved in money-raising schemes necessary for such purposes.

The one significant exception to this statement was the establishment, in the late 1940s, of the Old Regular Baptist Orphanage. Conceived initially by Elder Wardie Craft and his wife, Sister Hazel, this orphanage existed for only eleven years before it fell a victim to disunity within the management structure, eventually closing completely in 1959.[10]

Because Elder Wardie and Sister Hazel Craft figured so prominently in this Old Regular experiment in the establishment of a charitable institution supported by a number of the associations, I want to take a momentary sidestep in this discussion and introduce their story. I will return to the orphanage shortly.

Brother Wardie and Sister Hazel Craft:

In August 1987, Elder Wardie Craft moderated his ninth annual session of the Thornton Union Association, having been elected to this position at the beginning of the 1979 association meeting. There is perhaps more diversity in doctrine and worship practices in Thornton Union Association than there is in any of the other Old Regular clusters of fellowships, and Elder Craft must assume a tolerant leadership style as he governs this group of individualistic churches, some even fellowshipping with congregations of the Eastern District Association of Primitive Baptists.[11] Indeed, at the present moment Thornton Union is in formal correspondence with the Mt. Zion Association of United Baptist.[12]

Elder Craft's acceptance remarks in 1979, when he assumed his association moderator position, stressed this policy of tolerance. According to the minutes of that Thornton Union annual session, Elder Craft "expressed his desire for peace and love among the brethren of the association and to all *old time Baptist in all Associations* [emphasis mine]. He said," continued the Thornton Union clerk's report, "his philosophy was to 'build and to gather' not to separate or to tear down God's people. He stated he wanted and would work for correspondence among all old time Baptists on the basis that each Church hold its own key and that each Association run its own business and affairs."[13]

This open attitude toward "all old time Baptist" has even resulted in some contact between Thornton Union and the Little River Regular Baptist Association in North Carolina (mentioned in chapter 1) and in some stand-sharing activity between Thornton Union elders and at least one elder of the Paint Union United Baptist Association.[14] All of this has motivated some of the other, more traditional, Old Regular associations to charge that Thornton Union corresponds or fellowships with just about anybody.

When he hears these charges Elder Craft is hurt, because he argues that a basic principle in the constitutions of all these "old Baptist" associations is that clause about the individual church holding "its own key." By Brother Wardie's interpretation this means that each individual church is an autonomous unit and should not be interfered with unless the fellowship goes completely astray in doctrine.

When I talk to Elder Craft I hear him promoting a vision of Old Regular Baptist unity, through all the associations either coming back together or through their reestablishing correspondence. But my impresssion is that this will never happen, that, in fact, the movement is more likely to be toward additional splits. Still, Elder Craft has his vision, and it seems to be one that includes some Regular and United associations as well.

After graduation from Morehead College, sometime back in the late 1930s or early 1940s, Craft became a history teacher and then the principal of a high school in Cannel City, Morgan County, Kentucky. His wife, Sister Hazel, also taught school but in the elementary grades. Their college training and teaching experiences have given the Crafts a degree of learning and judgment not always possessed by Old Regulars.

Wardie Craft's interest in history has also fed his love for preserving things, and he and Sister Hazel have turned their home in Caney, Kentucky, into a museum of sorts. The two-story house has been tastefully redecorated and then crammed with antiques—wonderful four-poster beds, wardrobes, highboys, sideboards, hutches, nineteenth-century hearth accessories, Sister Craft's antique doll collection, Appalachian needlework, and a host of other collectibles, including items from a lifetime of working in mountain schools.

Outside, Elder Craft has begun, with some help from a local historical society, to turn the four or five sloping acres surrounding his house into a park, dedicated both to the early mountain culture in general and to elements of nineteenth-century Kentucky Baptist history, especially the contributions of Elder Daniel Williams, one of the earliest Baptist patriarchs of Kentucky. A number of old log cabins have been moved from other locations and rebuilt on this land, one to represent a school, another to represent a church, one as a blacksmith shop, and several others to represent homes or other structures in a frontier community. Nearby the old hearth and fireplace stones of the Daniel Williams cabin have also been reassembled, and a large granite monument to this pioneer Baptist minister has been erected.

These sites, along with others, constitute what the Crafts have named Memory Hill, and the entire complex — including the house and antiques — has been conceived by these former school teachers as a park to be visited by school children and anyone else who might want to learn about pioneer traditions in the mountain areas of Kentucky. Indeed, Memory Hill is frequently experienced by bus loads of school children from Morgan and surrounding counties, much to the delight of Elder and Sister Craft.[15]

Caney, Kentucky, can be reached by taking Highway 460 west from West Liberty and then turning south on Route 191. Elder Craft's church, Redeemed Church, is visible on the right as the traveler enters the small community of Caney, and the Crafts' home is directly across the road on the side of a hill.

Old Regular Baptist Orphanage

Wardie and Hazel Craft had no children of their own, but they formally adopted five, and have been informally adopted themselves by numerous young people who have considered the couple their foster parents, some coming from the orphanage about to be discussed. Sometime in the 1940s Brother Wardie and Sister Hazel conceived their idea for an Old Regular Baptist orphanage, first proposing that it be established on their property in Caney, Kentucky, and also proposing that they be appointed the home's directors. Brother Wardie eventually wrote two letters promoting his idea, one to Elder G. Bennett Adams of Mayking, Kentucky, then moderator of Thornton Union, and one to Elder Charles Cornett of Hazard, Kentucky.

Adams was a particularly dynamic Old Regular leader, and he and Cornett took Brother Wardie's idea and promoted it, but they changed the location for the orphanage to an old farm on Smoot Creek in Letcher County. In addition, much to the Crafts' disappointment, Brother Wardie and Sister Hazel were not installed as the first directors of the institution.

This orphanage would become, to my knowledge, the first and only cooperative venture between several Old Regular associations in the establishment of a charitable institution.[16] A governing board was formed, with representation from Thornton Union, Sardis, Union, and New Salem associations, and a plan for raising support money was developed.[17] The main source of funds would become the contributions made by member fellowships of the various associations, and these contributions would be generated by taking the children to the respective churches for singing performances. Indeed, one favorite hymn — requested by most of the fellowships — was "The Orphaned Girl":

> "No home, no home," cried a little girl,
> As she stood in the prince's hall.
> Trembling she stood on the Marble steps
> And leaned on the polished wall.
>
> Her clothes were thin and her feet were bare,
> And the snow had covered her head.
> "Give me a home," she feebly cried,
> "A home and a bite of bread."
>
> "A father's love I never knew."
> And tears dropped from her eyes,

"My mother sleeps in a new-made grave."
'Tis an orphan here tonight.

The night was dark and the snow fell fast,
As the rich man closed his door,
His proud lips curled as he scornfully said;
"No home nor bread for the poor."

"I must freeze, I must freeze." The trembling child cried,
And sank to the steps of the door,
To wrap her feet in her tattered dress,
All covered with sleet and snow.

The hours rolled on and the midnight storm
Rolled on like a funeral knell,
The earth seemed wrapped in a winding sheet,
And the chilly snow still fell.

The rich man slept on his velvet couch
And dreamed of his silver and gold,
While the orphan lay on a bed of snow,
And murmured, "So cold, so cold!"

When the morning dawned the little girl
Still lay at the rich man's door,
But her soul had fled to its home above
Where there's room and bread for the poor.

No more she stood at the rich man's door,
And cried, "So cold, so cold!"
With a crown on her head and a harp in her hand
She sang in a house of gold.[18]

The message of these melodramatic verses was not lost on Old Regular congregations, and contributions apparently were generous as the children were transported from church to church, traveling as far north as Michigan. The only quarrel that Elder Wardie Craft had with the system, after he and Sister Hazel were later appointed directors of the home (1954–56), was that some members of the governing board wanted them to dress the children in nothing but patches to add to the pathos of these performances. Much to their credit, Brother Wardie and Sister Hazel resisted this advice.

The Old Regular orphanage home lasted only until 1959,

at which time it became entangled, along with its other problems, in the discord that was developing between Indian Bottom, Thornton Union, and all of the associations corresponding with New Salem and Union. It seems fair to say that the Old Regular associations proved incapable—at least in this instance—of making such a joint venture work. Elder G. Bennett Adams, apparently one of the most energetic and talented leaders Old Regularism has produced, died in 1950, two years after the orphanage home idea was brought to fruition, and the project suffered from the loss of his guiding hand.[19] It was a "noble experiment"—my promise to Sister Hazel Craft was that I would use this term—that ultimately did not work.

Associations as Lasting Institutions

Perhaps the strongest and most lasting Old Regular institution is the association itself. This is the organization—with all of its rules, regulations, and doctrines—that receives the most respect and honor, directed at its leaders, traditions, history, and precedents. It is the structure that ultimately holds the larger brotherhood-sisterhood together, that maintains, channels, or directs the powers, vicissitudes, and foundational undergirdings of faith and order.

It is a remarkably democratic institution, and thus is formed from the entire base of the particular Old Regular population in question; and yet it is a body of law, precedents, and tradition that should not be altered in any precipitant and reckless sort of way. It may be tied to specific real estate for its annual sessions, as in the the case of New Salem and Indian Bottom, but it is not a thing of land and buildings; instead, it is a thing of spirit, commitment, love, and obligation—a contract, a covenant, that helps unify, stabilize, and preserve.

Ironically, perhaps, the association can also be that agent of cultural tyranny discussed in chapter 6, with policy enforcement ramifications that divide, isolate, and insulate. That may be a price one has to pay for any form of social, cultural, or religious cohesion (the "peculiar people" concept), but at times it certainly has its negative consequences. Perhaps more than anything else, the association, with its annual sessions of great debate and equally great praising and fellowshipping, is a thing of considerable vitality and excitement, especially in the case of the larger Old Regular clusters. The events seem to be the stimuli that keep small congregations going through those long winter months when there are no union meetings, memorial meetings, and sacrament meetings to stir the passions and intensify the spirit. Certainly to this outside observer, these happenings have become one of the most interesting factors of Old Regularism.

What Traditional Customs Will Remain?

Older, more traditional Old Regulars frequently express their concerns about the preservation of the faith's old-time ways. Remember the hymn "In the Good Old Fashioned Way," which has become very much of an ideological anthem for many of these individuals:

> I am on the gospel highway
> Pressing onward to the goal,
> Where a rest for me remaineth
> In the homeland of the soul.
>
> Every hour I'm moving forward;
> Not a moment to delay;
> I am going home to glory,
> In the good old fashioned way.[20]

In speculating about the future of Old Regularism, therefore, it seems that one must ask how many of these old fashioned ways will stay in vogue, and for how long. How long, if not forever, will Old Regular women tolerate their restricted involvement in church governance and formal worship operations? How long, if not forever, will they live with the "no bobbed hair" rule, even though it is not rigidly enforced in all fellowships? How long, if not forever, will the lined singing method remain? How long, if not forever, will the distinctive Old Regular preaching styles be preserved? How long, if not forever, will the emotional shouting and praising be practiced? Will future young generations of Old Regulars insist, as a prerequisite to remaining in the faith, that these traditions be dropped, or severely modified? If these traditions are dropped, or severely modified, will the world still have Old Regularism?

First, let me report that I don't currently see or hear any great revolution occurring within the ranks of Old Regularism. Those who have found their spiritual home within this subdenomination appear to have accepted, at least in a general sense, the disciplines of the faith. Those who have not are no longer — or never were — a part of the picture I see during my Saturday or Sunday visitations. The only way in which they might be represented in the observations I have made is that they constitute the diminishments in numbers examined at the beginning of this chapter.

All of the above, however, does not mean that there are no pressures operating within Old Regularism for a change. For example, women apparently are slowly pushing for greater influence, and Old Regular men feel this push. As support for this statement let me quote a rather lengthy segment of one of the letters Elder Atlas Hall wrote in response to an earlier version of this work I asked him to read and critique. Elder Hall was responding to the discussion, included in chapter 5, of the occasional involvement of women as clerks and treasurers.

> I believe that the shortage of males will result in the elimination of "assistants" in the churches, with females serving as clerks in the associations which now permit it, however, I very seriously doubt that sisters will remain under this status without any objections about a male dominated leadership. I feel confident that no Old Regular association will ever permit female clergy, as it would violate both custom and or-

thodoxy of doctrine. Many of the sisters have been dissastis-
fied with the "male only" leadership for several years, with
the younger sisters being the most dissatisfied, but there has
been no expression of this in church council minutes, however, I am sufficiently convinced that this dissatisfaction will
be expressed before too long. Not too many years ago a sister
was required to have a male spokesman in the church council if she wanted to speak, or to defend herself. That restriction has now ceased. I cannot visualize the sisters ever desir-
ing more than the privilege of speech, the privilege of being
a deaconess, treasurer or clerk, nor do I believe that they
will desire the privilege of debate, except in a limited capacity, or the privilege of submitting motions and/or seconds
in the church council. Even among those churches which
have female clerks, the female clerk will refrain from debate
or deliberation. The clergy will continue to remain in the
domain of the males. Even among those females who believe
in equality, there is no desire or belief that the clergy should
be available to the female members.

Among those churches which permit female members to
be a clerk or treasurer, and even in the Mountian Association
which permits female delegates, the sisters still refrain from
taking part in the actual discussion or debate of items of
business. The sisters will generally reserve their comments or
opinions for discussion after the council meeting. At that
time, they will often give their opinions or views, and if they
can convince (and generally they can), the males will ratify
an action at a future church council which the females are
not in agreement with, thus being assured that their participation is acceptable and appreciated. Please recall the Pauline directive in regard to participation by females in the
church council: "Let the woman learn in silence with all
subjection. But I suffer (permit) not a woman to teach, nor to
usurp authority over the man, but to be in silence." I Timothy 2:11-12. "Let your women keep silence in the churches;
for it is not permitted unto them to speak, but they are commanded to be under obedience, as also saith the law. And if
they will learn anything, let them ask their husbands at
home; for it is a shame for women to speak in the church."
(I Corinthians 14:34-35)[21]

One reason I have quoted such a lengthy segment of Elder
Atlas Hall's letter is that I do not want him to be misunder-

stood by his Old Regular brethren as a result of an omission from the statement that I had made. What I hear in Elder Hall's explanations, nevertheless, is a recognition that Old Regular women have been exerting some pressure for change and will continue to do so, but that there are boundaries beyond which, it is perceived, changes will not be allowed to go. More traditional voices than that of Elder Hall would say at this point, however, that the women — in some churches and associations — have been allowed to go too far already.

What about the continuous debate over hair and dress styles? Will there be marked changes made in these areas? First, it seems fair to say that in regard to these particular regulations there is already a rather sharp variance between pronouncements and practices. Many Old Regular women are cutting their hair, although not radically, and these same women are not particularly fearful of wearing slacks when working around their homes, at least so I am told. Nevertheless, I know of no Old Regular church where women are permitted to wear slacks, pantsuits, jeans, short dresses, or just generally tight and/or revealing attire to services; and most of these women would still feel hesitant to be seen in public in anything other than the most modest of clothing. Finally, I still hear stories of women being asked to leave churches because of dress considered too improper.

Some of the older, more traditional elders do, however, occasionally become extreme in their attacks upon modern female clothing, and such attacks have been known to anger the younger women. I have one example to relate that has been told me by two sources, but because the accounts were somewhat different in detail I will give the narrative a rather general retelling. Apparently at one association meeting an elder took the stand and delivered a bit of a diatribe against some items of contemporary female clothing, including shorts, tight blue jeans, and panty hose, with the result that when he returned to his car later that day he found a pair of panty hose stretched across his windshield, perhaps as a not so subtle protest statement.

What are some old time practices that this subdenomination could not give up and still remain Old Regular? Any answer to that question would necessarily be subjective, since there are no set requirements — agreed to by all concerned — for being labeled Old Regular, excluding perhaps the holding of a limited number of doctrinal positions. Still, were I to respond to that question the way I think most traditional Old Regulars might respond, I would include such things as lined singing, footwashing, certain minimals in gender separation and gender role delineation, the basics of impromptu preaching, a generally recognized preaching style, the standard pattern of worship described in Chapter 2, congregational shouting and praising, the tradition of an unpaid ministry, the practice of relatively late baptisms, many of the customs pertaining to association sessions, and perhaps a host of other behaviors if faced with the option to say they could go or not.

My point here is that Old Regularism is more than just doctrine. It is a life style and a multitude of distinctive worship practices and traditional attitudes. Some of these styles, practices, and attitudes are perhaps more important than others in defining the essence of the faith and order; and change obviously will become more threatening as it affects these essentials.

A Concluding Thought

I don't expect to see Old Regularism disappear from the central Appalachian scene any time soon. There is too much passion and dedication within the faith, and I find it difficult to imagine that these intensely committed people will allow their religion to fade into history with any degree of suddenness. In addition, at the immediate moment there may be some people who are returning to these "old-time ways" as much out of a sense-of-roots nostalgia as out of fervent commitment to the codes.

Some change, however, seems inevitable, but how much will be tolerated is hard to predict. Already some associations, as indicated much earlier, declare other fellowship clusters not to be Old Regular, arguing that a defining line has already been crossed. Because individual Old Regulars place this defining line at different points in the range of doctrine and practice, the natural course of events in the near future might be toward more splits—one group accepting more female involvement, another less; one group advocating more evangelism, another less; one group insisting on singing only by the old lined method, another group making no such demand.

As Old Regulars face this peril of more splits, obviously much will depend upon leadership. Traditionally, members of the subdenomination have placed much faith in their association moderators, and the respective fellowship clusters have produced at times men of particular strength and judiciousness. The associations may need to do so again to avoid a slow disintegration into ever smaller and weaker units.

Epilogue

Old Regularism is more than just a religion. It is also a cultural orientation, a faith, and a life style strongly tied to a total regional experience from which individuals like Sister Rena Caudill have difficulty being separated. I cannot explain why this variation of the Baptist denomination developed in central Appalachia, except by pointing to the obvious historical influences — the convergence of the Regular and Separate traditions, the waves of change wrought by other forces, such as the antimission and Campbellite movements, and the general isolation that for decades protected all Appalachian cultural elements — but I feel confident in arguing that religion and region, practice and place, merged to create a spiritual expression originally not heard outside the Cumberland scene. Remember this verse from Sister Beulah Jones Patrick's poem:

> If you wonder who I am,
> Why this way I do feel,
> I'm an Old Regular Baptist
> Who's been raised in these old hills.

The "old hills" line makes my point. Indeed, I have some difficulty thinking of Old Regularism in Washington state, or Michigan, or Florida, or Phoenix, Arizona (where one New Salem fellowship has been established), or even in North Carolina, especially on the coast. There is in my imagination an "Old Regular country," as I argued at the beginning of this work; and were the particular part of that country (that I would be envisioning) to be in Letcher, Knott, Floyd, or Pike County, Kentucky, or Wise, Dickenson, or Buchanan County, Virginia (among other possible sites), there would be mountains, and coal mines, and roads winding over ridges, and narrow streams providing the Baptismal waters, and the inconspicuous meetinghouses with their inconspicuous signs, and cars and pickups jammed together around the churches and along the roads, and that distinctive mixture of sounds that characterizes the Old Regular expression.

The images of Old Regularism that I will hold most clearly, long after I have moved on to other projects, are those associated with visits to such churches as Mary Lou, Tivis Chapel, and Little Sarah, where environmental surroundings added appreciably to the experience; while the sounds of Old Regularism that will remain will be the lined singing of "the old songs of Zion," the spirited preaching, and the exuberant shouting and praising. Such sights and sounds have already blended in my consciousness to create a composite Old Regular image, one that will share a place with the many positive memories of open, helpful people I have encountered during the last six years.

I am always flattered when people allow me to witness some of the most intense scenes of their spiritual lives. In doing so they make themselves vulnerable, trusting that I will not abuse the privilege and misuse the knowledge I gain. Indeed, such trust at times becomes a heavy and confining burden, as I measure the intent of my every retelling of a story, my every description of a scene.

After I witness an episode of deeply felt religious expression I try to find a way to color with full respect my subsequent recounting of the event. That usually makes harsh criticisms, were I to feel them justified, very difficult. So my Old Regular friends must realize that everything that I have seen in the last six years has not completely pleased me. I have simply tried to "accentuate the positive" as I present your story to an outside audience.

There is, in truth, much good in Old Regularism: the warm fellowshipping during the services, the live-and-let-live tolerance of the faith (no constant attacking of other denominations), the strong commitment to church community, the fervent dedication to ideals of brotherhood and sisterhood, the open and joyous expression of a "hope," the constant memorialization of deceased loved ones, the emphasis upon piety rather than property, the general respect for progenitors and ongoing traditions, and the absolute trust in a faith and order. But the practices and politics of Old Regularism can also exhibit all of the human imperfections inherent in the tales of discord related in chapter 6. Because there is much honor and power associated with Old Regular leadership, there are occasionally covert and overt manipulations of doctrinal and procedural disputes to gain recognition and position. That problem is certainly not distinctive to Old Regularism, but since there exists already so much division within this religious family, the subdenomination will need to be particularly wary of the type of would-be-leader who feeds on disunity. Some of the segments of this faith cannot get much smaller and still survive.

At the close of Union Association's "One Hundred Twenty-Eighth Annual Session," while watching the old tent go down, I spoke briefly with an elderly woman who wanted to tell me something about what each association meeting meant to her, but the main concern that seemed to be on her mind was whether she would be in attendance at the next one. I personally hope that she will be there and that this and other Old Regular associations will experience many more such events. There is much in this central Appalachian tradition worthy of preservation.

Notes

Introduction

1. Howard Dorgan, *Giving Glory to God in Appalachia: Worship Practices of Six Baptist Subdenominations* (Knoxville: University of Tennessee Press, 1987); hereafter referred to as *Giving Glory to God in Appalachia.*

2. "Homecoming," *High Country Magazine*, 21 April 1982.

3. *In the Good Old Fashioned Way*, Appalshop Films, Whitesburg, KY, 1973; Ron Short, "We Believed in the Family and in the Old Regular Baptist Church," *Southern Exposure*, 4/3 (1976): 60–65 (hereafter referred to by title); John Wallhausser, "I Can Almost See Heaven From Here," *Katallasete*, (Spring 1983): 2–10; Lynn C. Dickerson, "The Baptists of the Cumberland Mountains," in David N. Mielke, ed., *Teaching Mountain Children* (Boone, NC: Appalachian Consortium Press, 1978), 95–104; reprint from *Appalachian Heritage* (Spring 1975).

4. William Tallmadge, "Baptist Monophonic and Heterophonic Hymnody in Southern Appalachia," *Yearbook for Interamerican Musical Research*, vol. 2 (1975), 106–36.

5. During my presentation on Old Regular gender roles, Women's Studies Sandwich Seminar, Appalachian State University, 1986.

6. Comment made to me during my visit to Bethel Church, Dunham, KY, 15 June 1986.

7. The following are the dates and churches involved in my Old Regular visitations:

10 July 1983	Bethany, Kingsport, TN
24 July 1983	Sandy Ridge, Sandy Ridge, VA
13 May 1984	Bethany (second visit)
10 June 1984	Bull Creek, Maxie, VA
24 June 1984	Sandy Ridge (second visit)
27 July 1984	Sandy Ridge (third visit)
15 May 1986	Ash Camp, Ashcamp, KY
23 May 1986	Tivis Chapel, Haysi, VA
1 June 1986	Bent Branch, Meta, KY

8 June 1986	Little Martha, Leemaster, VA
15 June 1986	Bethel, Dunham, KY
29 June 1986	Hemp Hill, Hemp Hill, KY
6 July 1986	Mary Lou, State Line Ridge Road, VA
27 July 1986	Lebanon, Clintwood, VA
3 August 1986	Little Martha (second visit)
10 August 1986	Lonesome Dove, Canada, KY
16–17 August 1986	Ash Camp (second visit)
23 August 1986	Old Friendship Association Meeting, Mary Lou Church
19–21 September 1986	Union Association Meeting, Wise, VA
27 September 1986	New Salem Association Meeting, Minnie, KY
19 October 1986	Ash Camp (third visit)
15 February 1987	Stone Coal, Garrett, KY
3 May 1987	Little Home, Red Fox, KY
24 May 1987	Holston, Abingdon, VA
30 May 1987	Thornton, Mayking, KY
14 June 1987	Bull Creek (second visit)
21 June 1987	Ash Camp (fourth visit)
28 June 1987	Fairview, Pound, VA
5 July 1987	Hurricane, Wise, VA
19 July 1987	North Springs, Hurley, VA
30 July 1987	New Hope, Winnabow, NC
8–9 August 1987	Lonesome Dove (second visit)
15 August 1987	Thornton Union Association Meeting, Mayking, KY
29 August 1987	Little Freedom (for reinstating of Original Mountain Liberty Association), Vansant, VA
4–5 September 1987	Indian Bottom Association Meeting, Sassafras, KY
18–20 September 1987	Union Association Meeting, Wise, VA
26 September 1987	New Salem Association Meeting, Minnie, KY
31 January 1988	Little Sarah, Haysi, VA
14 February 1988	Bethlehem (for funeral of Elder John Layne) Grundy, VA
5 June 1988	Ramsey Ridge, Ramsey Ridge, VA
26 June 1988	Samaria, Wolfpit, KY
17 July 1988	Ash Camp (fifth visit)
20 August 1988	Thornton Union Association Meeting, Mayking, KY

3 September 1988   Indian Bottom Association Meeting,
                        Sassafras, KY
16 September 1988 Union Association Meeting, Wise, VA
24 September 1988 New Salem Association Meeting,
                        Minnie, KY

Chapter 1

1. Mt. Zion Old Regular Baptist, Morton, Washington, member of New Salem Association for over thirty years, failed to "letter up" to that organization in 1986: 1986 *Minutes*, New Salem Association, 104. Minutes cited in this volume have been housed in the Appalachian Collection, Appalachian State University, Boone, NC.

2. Associations and individual fellowships vary in their application of this rule to home and work settings, but they are consistent in disallowing such attire for church services.

3. 1957 *Minutes*, New Salem Association, vol. 2, 781; in mimeographed collection compiled by Dexter Dixon and Walter Akers, *Minutes of the Burning Spring Association of Baptist, 1813–1824* and *Minutes of the New Salem Association of Old Regular Baptists, 1825–1983*, 2 vols. (Published by the compilers, 1984); housed in the Appalachian Collection, Appalachian State University; hereafter cited as Dixon and Akers.

4. George Hood, *A History of Music in New England* (1846; reprint, New York: Johnson Reprint, 1970), 47; William Tallmadge, "Baptist Monophonic and Heterophonic Hymnody in Southern Appalachia," *Yearbook for Interamerican Musical Research*, vol. 2 (1975), 106–36.

5. Dixon and Akers, vol. 2, 781.

6. See the "Articles of Faith" of any of the associations; for example, Article 7, 1986 *Minutes* of the Union Association, 28.

7. 1987 *Minutes*, Union Association, 26–27.

8. 1986 *Minutes*, New Salem Association, 103–05.

9. 1986 *Minutes*, Thornton Union Association, 3 and 101–09.

10. 1985 *Minutes*, Indian Bottom Association, 49.

11. 1986 *Minutes*, Indian Bottom Association, 61.

12. 1976 *Minutes*, Friendship Association, 34.

13. Elder Atlas Hall, letter to author, 28 January 1988, in response to an early manuscript of this work.

14. 1985 *Minutes*, Sardis Association, 66–67.

15. 1986 *Minutes*, Old Friendship Association, 64; 1986 *Minutes*, Bethel Association, 28; 1986 *Minutes*, Philadelphia Association, 47; 1986 *Minutes*, Mud River Association, 22.

16. 1987 *Minutes*, Northern New Salem Association, 23; 1987 *Minutes*, Original Mountain Liberty Association, 30.

17. *Organization and Proceedings of the Mountain Liberty Association* (1973), 27.

18. 1984 *Minutes*, Mountain Association, 21.

19. Elder Atlas Hall reports that Kyova Association has adopted "open communion," a practice no other Old Regular associations would accept; letter to the author, 28 January 1988.

20. 1974 *Minutes*, Cumberland Association, 29.

21. There are, however, two early hymnals that appear to have been sources for many songs included in the more contemporary Old Regular collections: *The Sweet Songster*, Edward W. Billups, compiler (Wayne, WV: Arrowood Brothers, 1854); *Thomas Hymnal*, Elder E. D. Thomas, compiler (Wayne, WV: Arrowood Brothers, 1877). Elder Atlas Hall reports that, at the time of this writing, these works are still in print; letter to the author, 28 January 1988.

22. Three such publications have been placed in the Appalachian Collection, Appalachian State University: *Old Regular Baptist Song Book*, 1982–83 edition, Elders Baxter Osborne and Roy B. Akers, compilers (Ashland, KY: Pippa Valley Printing and Publishing, 1982); *Some of Our Favorite Songs*, Brother C. B. Smith, compiler (Dwale, KY: Arrow Printing Co., 1987); *Old Regular Baptist Songs of Zion* (Swords Creek, VA: n.n., 1987).

23. Elder Bill Campbell suggested I qualify this statement by noting that in one sense Old Regular preachers do "evangelize": they urge the unredeemed to accept their calls. Response notes to an early manuscript of this work, 31 January 1988; hereafter identified as Campbell manuscript notes.

24. Elder Campbell again urged I make the same qualification mentioned in note 23; Campbell manuscript notes.

25. Visitation notes, 29 June 1986. Visitation notes cited in this work are housed in two locations, The Appalachian Center, Berea College, Berea, KY, and the Appalachian Collection, Appalachian State University.

26. Interview of Elders Bill Campbell and Toby Bailey, 31 January 1988, at Bailey's home in Birchleaf, VA.

27. Campbell manuscript notes.

28. Visitation notes, 27 July 1986.

29. Ibid.

30. 1987 *Minutes*, Union Association, 37.

31. Visitation notes, 1 June 1986.

32. Visitation notes, 14 June 1987.

33. Concluded from discussion with two relatively young Old

Regular leaders, Elder Bill Campbell, Vansant, VA, and Deacon Ted DePriest, Castlewood, VA; interview conducted 23 May 1986, Tivis Chapel, Haysi, VA.

34. In addition to omitting the final stanza of this peom, I have taken liberty with the original punctuation.

35. J. H. Spencer, *A History of Kentucky Baptists*, vol. 1 (1886; reprint, Lafayette, TN: Church History Research & Archives, 1976), 11–13, 482–83; hereafter referred to as Spencer.

36. William Warren Sweet, *Religion on the American Frontier: The Baptists* (New York: Cooper Square Publishers, 1964), 3–17; hereafter referred to as Sweet. For the Philadelphia Confession see *Baptist Confession* (Portland, MA: Thomas Baker Wait, 1794) [*Early American Imprints, 1639–1800*, Evans Numbers, 26614]; hereafter referred to as *Baptist Confession*.

37. Spencer, vol. 1, 102–11.

38. Ibid., 543–47.

39. Robert Taylor Semple, *History of the Baptists in Virginia* (1810; reprint, Cottonport, LA: Polyanthos, 1972), 99–101.

40. Spencer, vol. 1, 482–83. Associations of Separate Baptists still exist in Kentucky, Indiana, Illinois, Florida, and perhaps elsewhere, with articles of faith that proclaim an Arminian atonement doctrine. See 1987 *Minutes*, South Kentucky Association of Separate Baptists in Christ, 16–18, 20.

41. Spencer, vol. 1, 546.

42. Dixon and Akers, vol. 1, A: 1–2. In vol. 1 of the Dixon and Akers compilation page numbers start anew at the beginning of the New Salem minutes; therefore, pages of the Burning Spring minutes will be prefixed by A, while pages of the New Salem minutes will be prefixed by B.

43. Ibid., vol. 1, A: 34.

44. Ibid., vol. 1, B: 12 and B: 48; Spencer, vol. 2, 347–49.

45. Dixon and Akers, vol. 1, B: 77.

46. Ibid., B: 86.

47. Ibid., B: 79.

48. Sweet, 58–76; Spencer, vol. 1, 581–643; James E. Tull, *Shapers of Baptist Thought* (Valley Forge, PA: Judson Press, 1972), 101–27.

49. Dixon and Akers, vol. 1, B: 90.

50. Ibid., vol. 1, B: 146.

51. Rufus Perrigan, compiler, *History of Regular Baptist and Their Ancestors and Accessors* (Haysi, VA: Published by Perrigan, 1961), 35; hereafter referred to as Perrigan.

52. Dixon and Akers, vol. 1, B: 115 and B: 117.

53. Perrigan, 276.

54. 1980 *Minutes*, Original Mates Creek Regular Primitive Baptist Association, 42 [underlining mine].
55. Dixon and Akers, vol. 1, B: 121.
56. Ibid., B: 224.
57. " . . . some men and angels are predestined, or foreordained to eternal life. . . . "; *Baptist Confession*, 11.
58. Dixon and Akers, vol. 1, B: 189, 197, and 217 [emphasis mine].
59. 1867 *Minutes*, Burning Spring Association (1867; reprint, Catlettsburg, KY; Big Sandy Herald, n.d.), 6; Appalachian Collection, Appalachian State University.
60. Dixon and Akers, vol. 1, B: 221.
61. Ibid., B: 225.
62. For a current expression of Free Will atonement doctrine see articles 4–7 of the Articles of Faith of the John-Thomas Association of Freewill Baptists (churches in Virginia, Kentucky, Ohio, and Indiana): 1981 *Minutes*, John-Thomas Freewill Baptists, 35. Some Free Will fellowships spell their name as one word, and some spell it as two. I have chosen the latter option.
63. Campbell manuscript notes.
64. Dixon and Akers, vol. 1, B: 276.
65. *Baptist Confession*, 11–12.
66. New Salem, Northern New Salem, Sardis, Old Friendship, Indian Bottom, Old Indian Bottom, Philadelphia, and Mud River.
67. Dixon and Akers, vol. 1, B: 350.
68. 1982 *Minutes*, Little River Regular Baptist Association; 1983 *Minutes*, Original Mountain Union Baptist Association.
69. 1982 *Minutes*, Little River Regular Baptist Association, 12.
70. 1983 *Minutes*, Original Mountain Union Association, 1.
71. Dixon and Akers, vol. 1, B: 146.
72. 1982 *Minutes*, Little River Regular Baptist Association, 5.
73. 1983 *Minutes*, Original Mountain Union Baptist Association, 10.
74. Dixon and Akers, vol. 2, B: 781.
75. Previously discussed in *Giving Glory to God in Appalachia*, 28–29.
76. Ibid., 34.
77. Dixon and Akers, vol. 2, B: 842 and B: 991.
78. 1986 *Minutes*, Thornton Union Association, 8.
79. Visitation notes, 24 May 1987.
80. Dixon and Akers, vol. 2, B: 45.
81. Ibid., B: 212.
82. 1927 *Minutes*, Union Association, 7.
83. Dixon and Akers, vol. 1, B: 570.

84. 1948 *Minutes*, Union Association, 4.
85. 1964 *Minutes*, Sardis Association, 6.
86. 1985 *Minutes*, Sardis Association, 9.
87. 1979 *Minutes*, Union Association, 6.

Chapter 2

1. *Old Regular Baptist Song Book*, 1982–83 Edition (Pippa Passes, KY: published by Baxter Osborne and Roy B. Akers, 1982), 13; hereafter referred to as *Old Regular Baptist Song Book*.
2. The 1986 Union Association statistics showed only six of its seventy-two churches to have memberships of over one hundred, while fourteen memberships were reported at less than twenty; 1986 *Minutes*, Union Association, 26–27.
3. Visitation notes, 27 July 1985.
4. *Old Regular Baptist Song Book*, 157.
5. 1986 *Minutes*, Thornton Union Association, 105.
6. 1985 *Minutes*, Sardis Association, 64.
7. Elder Atlas Hall, letter to author, 28 January 1988.
8. Elder Bill Campbell interview, Vansant, VA, 23 May 1986.
9. Visitation notes, 7 July 1986; 1987 *Minutes*, Union Association, 23.
10. 1987 *Minutes*, Union Association, 9–17.
11. Ibid.
12. Elder Raymond Smith interview, Canada, KY, 8 August 1987.
13. I have discussed this basic Appalachian preaching style in greater detail elsewhere: "Hanging Their Toes in the Heavens," *Giving Glory to God in Appalachia*.
14. Visitation notes, 18 May 1986; visitation notes, 29 June 1986.
15. Elder Raymond Smith interview, Canada, KY, 8 August 1987.
16. 1985 *Minutes*, Sardis Association, 67.
17. Elder Atlas Hall, letter to author, 28 January 1988.
18. Visitation notes, 19 July 1987.
19. "We Believed in the Family and the Old Regular Baptist Church," 63.
20. Elder Raymond Smith interview, Canada, KY, 8 August 1987.
21. Visitation notes, 27 July 1986.
22. Visitation notes, 3 August 1986.
23. *Giving Glory to God in Appalachia*, 132.
24. The best example of this phenomenon I have witnessed occurred during a service at the Little Martha Church: visitation notes, 3 August 1986.

25. Campbell manuscript notes.
26. *Giving Glory to God in Appalachia,* 152–57.
27. See 1985 *Minutes,* Washington District Regular Primitive Baptists; housed in Appalachian Collection, Appalachian State University.
28. See Perrigan, 225.
29. Ibid., 225–27.
30. Elder Fred Stiltner interview, Bull Creek Church, 10 June 1984.
31. 1986 *Minutes,* Union Association, 14. Newsome's name is misspelled in the minutes.
32. Elder Bill Campbell interview, Bull Creek Church, 14 June 1987.
33. See description of the closing moments of a preaching service at Bethany Old Regular Church, Kingsport, TN: *Giving Glory to God in Appalachia,* 125–26.
34. 1987 *Minutes,* Union Association, 26.
35. 1986 *Minutes,* Union Association, 26; 1987 *Minutes,* Union Association, 26.
36. Visitation notes, 15 February 1987; visitation notes, 26 June 1988.
37. Elder Raymond Smith interview, Canada, KY, 8 August 1987.
38. Campbell manuscript notes.
39. 1986 *Minutes,* New Salem Association, 15.
40. Campbell manuscript notes.
41. One place where this phrase is frequently found is at the end of obituaries published in association minutes. The obituary writer's closing will often go something like this: "Written by a sister in hope, Naomi Stanley"; 1987 *Minutes,* Union Association, 39.
42. Elder Atlas Hall, letter to author, 23 March 1988.
43. Ibid.
44. *Some of Our Favorite Songs,* Brother C. B. Smith, compiler (Dwale KY: Arrow Printing Co., 1987), 119; hereafter referred to as *Some of Our Favorite Songs.*
45. Visitation notes, 14 June 1987.

Chapter 3

1. *Some of Our Favorite Songs,* 119.
2. *Giving Glory to God in Appalachia.*
3. Howard Dorgan, "Passing Over Yonder," *The Impact of Institutions in Appalachia: Proceedings of the 8th Annual Appalachian Studies Conference,* Jim Lloyd and Anne B. Campbell, eds. (Boone, NC: Appalachian Consortium Press, 1986), 14–23.

4. 1986 *Minutes*, Old Friendship Association, 64.

5. See items, 12, 13, and 14 in 1986 *Minutes*, Old Friendship Association, 7.

6. 1970 *Minutes*, Friendship Association, 45.

7. The most contemporary minutes I have of Friendship Association reports nineteen churches and a total membership of 1,487; 1976 *Minutes*, Friendship Association, 34. The Old Regular associations with which Old Friendship now corresponds consider Friendship to have strayed so far from certain basic traditions that these fellowships no longer warrant being called Old Regular.

8. *Giving Glory to God in Appalachia*, 44–45.

9. *Some of Our Favorite Songs*, 156.

10. Visitation notes, 6 July 1986.

11. 1985 *Minutes*, Union Association, 13 & 16.

12. Ibid., 15.

13. Campbell manuscript notes.

14. Visitation notes, 10 August 1986; visitation notes, 8–9 August 1987.

15. Campbell manuscript notes.

16. 1986 *Minutes*, Union Association, 16.

17. 1987 *Minutes*, Union Association, 28.

18. 1985 *Minutes*, Sardis Association, 18–20.

19. Elder Atlas Hall, letter to the author, 28 January 1988.

20. Ibid.

21. Visitation notes, 8 June 1986.

22. Visitation notes, 27 July 1986.

23. Elder Atlas Hall, letter to the author, 28 January 1988.

24. Ibid.

25. Visitation notes, 27 July 1986.

26. 1793 *Minutes* of the Elkhorn Association, as reprinted in William Warren Sweet's *Religion on the American Frontier: The Baptists* (New York: Henry Holt and Company, 1931), 454.

27. Spencer, vol. 2, 487.

28. Elder Atlas Hall, letter to the author, 28 January 1988; visitation notes, 17 July 1988.

29. Dixon and Akers, vol. 1, B: 61.

30. Ibid., B: 267.

Chapter 4

1. Elder Atlas Hall, letter to the author, 28 January 1988.

2. Interview of Elder Wardie Craft, 10 October 1987. See also 1950 *Minutes*, Union Association, 4.

3. See, as example, language employed in Little Zion Church request, 1980 *Minutes*, Union Association, 5.

4. Elder Edwin May interview, Abingdon, VA, 15 February 1985.

5. 1986 *Minutes*, New Salem Association, 7–8.

6. 1986 *Minutes*, Old Friendship Association, 64; 1986 *Minutes*, Philadelphia Association, 47; 1986 *Minutes*, New Salem Association, 104–05; 1986 *Minutes*, Union Association, 26–27; 1986 *Minutes*, Thornton Union Association, 109; 1986 *Minutes*, Bethel Association, 28; and 1986 *Minutes*, Indian Bottom Association, 61.

7. As examples see 1987 *Minutes*, Mt. Zion Association of United Baptists, 8; 1979 *Minutes*, Senter District Primitive Baptist Association, 1–12; 1976 *Minutes*, Original Mates Creek Regular Primitive Baptist Association, 37–38; and 1977, *Minutes*, Little River Regular Baptist Association, 10–11.

8. 1987 *Minutes*, Union Association, 28.

9. 1987 *Minutes*, Union Association, 26.

10. Elder Atlas Hall, letter to the author, 28 January 1988.

11. Visitation notes, 16–17 August 1986. Other business meetings are reported in Tivis Chapel visitation notes, 23 May 1986, and Lonesome Dove visitation notes, 8–9 August 1987.

12. Elder Atlas Hall, letter to the author, 28 January 1988.

13. See Tivis Chapel visitation notes, 23 May 1986, for description of an Old Regular ordination of a deacon.

14. Elder Atlas Hall, letter to the author, 28 January 1988.

15. *Some of Our Favorite Songs*, 1.

16. Visitation notes, 23 May 1986.

17. Information reported here on the operation of annual association meetings has been drawn largely from these visitations.

18. Dixon and Akers, vol. 2, B: 372.

19. 1986 *Minutes*, Thornton Union Association, 40–41.

20. 1986 *Minutes*, Union Association, 2 & 5. Early Union Association minutes record this church's name as two words, "Bart Lick."

21. See *Organization and Proceedings of the Mountain Liberty Association*, 8–9 September 1973, 8–9. This association fell into disorder for several years and then was reorganized in 1987. See 1987 *Minutes*, Original Mountain Liberty Association, 1–10. Both documents have been placed in the Appalachian Collection, Appalachian State University.

22. Dixon and Akers, vol. 2, 991.

23. 1985, *Minutes*, Northern New Salem Association, 7; 1987 *Minutes*, Northern New Salem Association, 2–3.

24. Darvin Marshall, letter to the author, 30 January 1987.

25. 1987 *Minutes,* Union Association, 7–8; 1986 *Minutes,* Thornton Union Association, 25–27.
26. 1986 *Minutes,* Union Association, 6–7.
27. 1985 *Minutes,* Sardis Association, 10.
28. 1987 *Minutes,* Northern New Salem Association, 7.
29. 1986 *Minutes,* Union Association, 5.
30. 1987 *Minutes,* Union Association, 5.
31. Visitation notes, 15 June 1986.
32. 1986 *Minutes,* Union Association, 6.
33. Information on Brother and Sister Caudill and New Hope Church was gained during two interview sessions with Sister Rena Caudill, one at her home in Winnabow, North Carolina, 30 July 1987, and the second 18 September 1987, at the Union Association meeting in Wise, Virginia. See visitation notes.
34. Perrigan, 333, 414–15.
35. 1987 *Minutes,* Union Association, 27.
36. *Some of Our Favorite Songs,* 92.
37. In Union Association minutes of the late 1960s his last name was spelled "Lane."
38. Perrigan, 195.
39. *Organization and Proceedings of the Mountain Liberty Association,* 8–9 September 1973, 8–9.
40. 1987 *Minutes,* Union Association, 2.
41. *Organization and Proceedings of the Mountain Liberty Association,* 8–9 September 1973, 3.
42. Although I was at this 1986 session I did not personally witness this walkout. I received the information from Darvin Marshall.
43. Telephone interview of Judy Golden, daughter of John Layne, 17 May 1988.

Chapter 5

1. 1985 *Minutes,* Old Friendship Association, 6–7.
2. Elder Atlas Hall, letter to the author, 23 March 1988.
3. 1961 *Minutes,* Union Association, 8–9.
4. Elder Atlas Hall, letter to the author, 23 March 1988.
5. Visitation notes, 15 June 1986.
6. 1987 *Minutes,* Union Association, 20–24.
7. 1982 *Minutes,* Sardis Association, 9.
8. *Giving Glory to God in Appalachia,* 188–209.
9. 1986 *Mintues,* Old Friendship Association, 25–26.
10. 1986 *Minutes,* Union Association, 67.

11. Ibid., 64.
12. Ibid., 52.
13. Ibid., 48.
14. Ibid., 60.
15. Visitation notes, 8–9 August 1987.
16. 1987 *Minutes*, Northern New Salem Association, 15.
17. Elder Atlas Hall, letter to the author, 23 March 1988.
18. One exception is the Mountain Association, which has added to its procedural rules some codes that spell out membership responsibility: 1984 *Minutes*, Mountain Association, 12–14.
19. 1986 *Minutes*, Old Friendship Association, 21–22.
20. 1986 *Minutes*, Union Association, 26.
21. Visitation notes, 8 June 1986.
22. Elder Atlas Hall, letter to the author, 23 March 1988.
23. Dixon and Akers, vol. 2, 1044.
24. Ibid, 1203.
25. See a few of the nonmember obituaries published in the 1987 *Minutes*, Union Association, 56, 60, 62, 65, 67, 70, 78, and elsewhere.
26. Visitation notes, 27 July 1986.
27. 1979 *Minutes*, Union Association, 24; (1980) 22; (1981) 22; (1982) 22; (1983) 24; (1984) 26; (1985) 26; (1986) 26; (1987) 26.
28. Ibid. (1987), 26.
29. Ibid. (1984), 26; *Giving Glory to God in Appalachia*, 152.
30. "We Believed in the Family and the Old Regular Baptist Church," 65.
31. 1958 *Minutes*, Indian Bottom Association, 19–20; Perrigan, 350–51.
32. 1986 *Minutes*, [Old] Indian Bottom Association, 18, 20, 36, and 44.
33. Visitation notes, 3 May 1987.
34. Howard Dorgan, "Response of the Main-line Southern White Protestant Pulpit to *Brown v. Board of Education*, 1954–1965," *A New Diversity in Contemporary Southern Rhetoric*, Calvin M. Logue and Howard Dorgan, eds. (Baton Rouge: Louisiana State University Press, 1987), 15–51.

Chapter 6

1. See list of New Salem orders considered still to be in force: 1986 *Minutes*, New Salem Association, 7–8.
2. Dixon and Akers, vol. 2, 743.

3. Ibid., 722.
4. Ibid., 972.
5. Ibid., 993.
6. Ibid., 1028.
7. Elder Atlas Hall, letter to author, 20 April 1988.
8. Ibid.
9. Dixon and Akers, vol. 2, 1043.
10. Ibid.
11. Ibid., 1061.
12. Elder Atlas Hall, letter to author, 20 April 1988.
13. Dixon and Akers, vol. 2, 1059.
14. Ibid., 1060.
15. 1986 *Minutes*, New Salem Association, 93.
16. Ibid., 94 [underlining mine].
17. 1982 *Minutes*, Sardis Association, 8.
18. Ibid., 9.
19. Dixon and Akers, vol. 2, 742–43.
20. Ibid., 781 & 796.
21. 1956 *Minutes*, Indian Bottom Association, 6; Dixon and Akers, vol. 2, 721–22, 762.
22. Dixon and Akers, vol. 2, 704, 721–22.
23. Ibid., 704.
24. 1956 *Minutes*, Indian Bottom Association, 6.
25. Dixon and Akers, vol. 2, 762.
26. Ibid., 779.
27. Ibid., 829.
28. 1959 *Minutes*, Union Association, 6–7.
29. 1959 *Minutes*, Indian Bottom Association, 4.
30. Ibid.
31. 1959 *Minutes*, Union Association, 6–7.
32. 1960 *Minutes*, Indian Bottom Association, 1.
33. Ibid., 2–3.
34. Ibid., 1–4.
35. Elder Bill Campbell interview, Haysi, VA, 31 January 1988.
36. Dixon and Akers, vol. 2, 829.
37. 1960 *Minutes*, Thornton Union Association, 4–5.
38. 1960 *Minutes*, Indian Bottom Association, 4.
39. 1961 *Minutes*, Union Association, 6–7; Dixon and Akers, vol. 2, 842.
40. Dixon and Akers, vol. 2, 972 and 991.
41. 1986 *Minutes*, [Old] Indian Bottom Association, 5.
42. 1987 *Minutes*, Northern New Salem Association, 8.

43. 1987 *Minutes*, Philadelphia Association, 12–13.
44. 1961 *Minutes*, Union Associatioon, 6–7; Dixon and Akers, vol. 2, 842.
45. 1960 *Minutes*, [Old] Indian Bottom Association, 2–3.
46. Elder Bill Campbell interview, Haysi, VA, 31 January 1988.
47. "We Believed in the Family and the Old Regular Baptist Church," 65.
48. Elder Atlas Hall, letter to the author, 20 April 1988.
49. 1986 *Minutes*, Bethel Association, 28.
50. As republished in 1961 *Minutes*, Union Association, 8.
51. Campbell manuscript notes.
52. 1961 *Minutes*, Union Association, 8.
53. 1962 *Minutes*, Union Association, 9–10.
54. Elder John M. Dotson, "Circular Letter," 1962 *Minutes*, Bethel Association, 11–14; Elder Conrad Stallard, "Circular Letter," 1964 *Minutes*, Bethel Association, 8–11; and Elder J. R. Stanley, "Circular Letter," 1964 *Minutes*, Bethel Association, 12–15. I am indebted to Darvin Marshall for these documents.
55. 1962 *Minutes*, Union Association, 58; 1987 *Minutes*, Union Association, 29.
56. 1962 *Minutes*, Union Association, 10.
57. 1962 *Minutes*, Bethel Association, 3.
58. 1963 *Minutes*, Union Association, 8.
59. 1923 *Minutes*, Union Association, 12.
60. 1927 *Minutes*, Union Association, 17.
61. 1964 *Minutes*, Union Association, 8.

Chapter 7

1. *Some of Our Favorite Songs*, 82.
2. Ibid., 64.
3. 1984 *Minutes*, New Salem Association, 109; 1986 *Minutes*, New Salem Association, 105.
4. 1980 *Minutes*, Union Association, 23; 1987 *Minutes*, Union Association, 27.
5. 1982 *Minutes*, Thornton Union Association, 76; 1986 *Minutes*, Thornton Union Association, 109; 1987 *Minutes*, Thornton Union Association, 85.
6. Interviews, 23 May 1986, at Tivis Chapel, and 31 January 1988, in Haysi, VA.
7. 1982 *Minutes*, Thornton Union Association, 18.
8. Elder Raymond Smith interview, Canada, KY, 8 August 1987.

9. J. F. Fletcher, *A History of the Ashe County, North Carolina and New River, Virginia Baptist Association* (Raleigh, NC: Commercial Printing, 1935), 31–34.

10. All of my information concerning this orphanage has come from two interviews with Brother Wardie and Sister Hazel Craft, 6 June and 19 October 1987, at their home in Caney, Kentucky; from an unpublished manuscript written by Elder Craft in 1982, "The Regular Baptist Orphanage"; from Thornton Union's original action to bless the venture, 1948 *Minutes*, Thornton Union Association, 5; and from one brief mention by Phillip K. Epling, *The Baptist Triumph* (n.p.: n.n., 1953), 11. I am placing a copy of Craft's manuscript in the Appalachian Collection, Appalachian State University.

11. This is one of the more liberal Primitive associations in the Appalachian region, as evidenced by the fact that it has corresponded with both United and Old Regular Baptists. See 1976 *Minutes*, Eastern District Association of Primitive Baptists, 10.

12. 1987 *Minutes*, Thornton Union Association, 7.

13. 1979 *Minutes*, Thornton Union Association, 5.

14. The Paint Union elder in question later brought his fellowship (the Freedom Valley Church of London, KY) into the Thornton Union fold: 1987 *Minutes*, Thornton Union Association, 6.

15. Visitation notes, 6 June 1987; "Memory Hill, Pioneer Park," a pamphlet prepared by the Crafts.

16. 1948 *Minutes*, Thornton Union Association, 5.

17. Elder Craft does not remember if other associations were represented: telephone interview, 24 May 1988.

18. *Some of Our Favorite Songs*, 102–3.

19. 1950 *Minutes*, Thornton Union Association, 16.

20. *Some of Our Favorite Songs*, 119.

21. Elder Atlas Hall, letter to the author, 23 March 1987.

Index

The Old Regular Baptists of Central Appalachia was designed by Dariel Mayer, composed by Lithocraft, Inc., printed by Cushing-Malloy, Inc., and bound by John H. Dekker & Sons, Inc. The book is set in Caledonia and printed on 50-lb. Glatfelter Antique, B-16.

CPSIA information can be obtained at www.ICGtesting.com
Printed in the USA
BVOW072229200312

285684BV00001B/28/A